PERFORMANCE ART IN IRELAND: A HISTORY

EDITED BY ÁINE PHILLIPS

CONTENTS

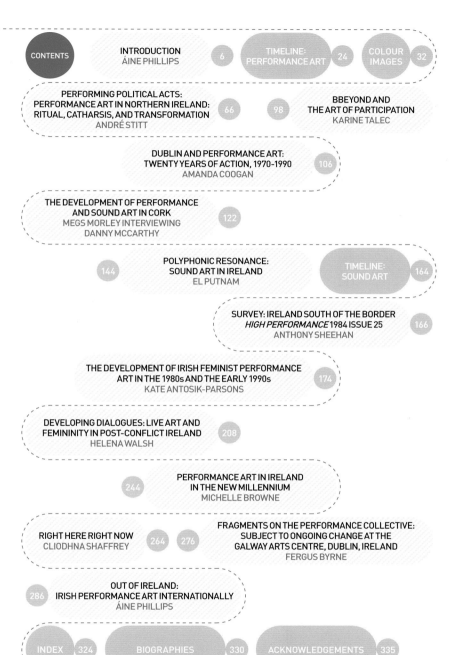

ÁINE PHILLIPS

Introduction

This publication examines Live Art and performance art in Ireland since the 1970s and brings together the writings of artists, critics, and academics who consider different aspects of this history through a series of new commissioned essays and themed articles. A number of older reviews are included that have been previously published but, in the context of this book, shine a fresh light on their subject matter. The purpose of this collection is to create a legacy for performance art in Ireland, to disseminate its histories, and to make it accessible to a wide audience.

The focus of this book is performance art that is made live, in front of an audience. The texts and images represent work where the artist/performer is central and where the body of the artist is crucial to the form and content of the piece or project. We examine work where the artists' body is the site of meaning, the primary material and the aesthetic substance; where there is corporeal presence and a relationship with audience and context, be that site or subject matter. The work surveyed comes from a mainly visual art context.

Writing history is always contingent on the present, as Deirdre Heddon points out in *Histories and Practices of Live Art*,[1] and one of the most important reasons for this book is that performance art has finally reached a point of critical acknowledgement and attention in Irish cultural worlds. However no extensive history of this genre has yet been produced here and this dearth is problematic for students and young artists trying to find their own position and approach for the futures of their practice. Without knowledge of what's gone before, it's difficult to move forward with an assurance of creating original work grounded in precedent. I believe the artists and their works represented in this book will provide references, examples, and stimulus for future projects and the evolution of Live Art in Ireland and elsewhere.

Opposite: Alastair MacLennan and Áine Phillips, *4 Hour Group Performance*, Trouble Festival Les Halles Brussels, 2012. Photo courtesy of the artists.

My intention is to make this book about the performance art history of the island as a whole. By choosing to disregard the political border that divides the north (UK) and south (Republic of Ireland) I want to show how the work of performance operates beyond perimeters, breaks down borders, and expands into new territories of meaning and action, exchange and communication. Performance and Live Art is activist by its very nature and this book seeks to reflect the principles of activism (to promote peaceful efforts to seek beneficial change). A special type of performance art developed out of the Irish context over the past decades and much of it is politically active and deeply socially engaged. As I worked on this publication and in editing each of the contributions – all prismatic narratives – I became aware of the political impetus behind so much work made here: in Belfast responding to the conflict (1970-1990s), by feminist artists in response to gender inequalities (1980-2000s) and by a current generation of performance artists taking on issues of social justice. These works in turn have influenced social and cultural frameworks.

THE EVOLUTION OF IRISH PERFORMANCE ART

As the contributions to this book show, performance art in Ireland began in the early 1970s as Irish political turmoil aroused fervent artistic response and international feminist ideas began to influence Irish society and cultural discourse. At this time a community of strongly focused individual artists began making what they referred to as performed actions and body art both north and south of the border. Artists did not respect the limitations of the political border and many group events took place on the island, especially in the cities of Cork, Dublin, and Belfast, showcasing new performances and supporting practitioners. Feminist artists embraced performance art in the 1980s to speak what was before unspeakable and do what was unthinkable for women in this conservative society where contraception, divorce, and abortion were illegal.[2] Performance became an artistic strategy enacting social change both in terms of sexual politics, social justice, and in response to 'the Troubles', the ethnic nationalist conflict in the north of Ireland. In the

Opposite top: Alanna O'Kelly, *Chant Down Greenham*, 1984. Photo courtesy of the artist.
Opposite bottom: Anne Seagrave, *jamais vu*, 2005. Photo courtesy of the artist.

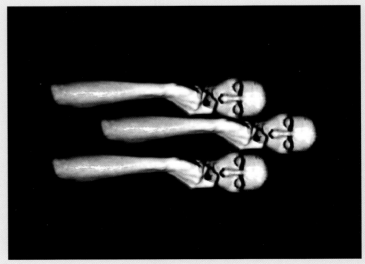

'The turn of the new century saw a resurgence of performance practices under the broader term 'Live Art' gain practical support and theoretical advancement from organisations such as the Live Art Development Agency in London.'

1990s performance often addressed The Body and context (site, history or the present) to question and affirm a changing society and to hold up a mirror to the transforming Irish identities of 'Celtic Tiger' Ireland. The Arts Council, regional Local Authority arts offices and Percent for Art commissioning programmes such as Breaking Ground (Ballymun, Dublin) began to support and appoint Live Art and performance practitioners to execute large scale public art projects.

The turn of the new century saw a resurgence of performance practices under the broader term 'Live Art' gain practical support and theoretical advancement from organisations such as the Live Art Development Agency in London.[3] Funding bodies in Ireland such as the Arts Council and Culture Ireland began to slowly recognise the quality and quantity of work being produced and the compelling impact of live performance on wider audiences for the arts. The designation Live Art allows for diverse performance tactics such as socially engaged interactions with communities, discourse, public talks, and live streamed digital or web based art to fall under its designation. This new naming has opened out the possibility for artists of any discipline to use performance strategies and processes without risking exposure as 'performers' (sometimes a qualitative label) or that they function within a strict parameter of duration, framing or staging and enacted presence normally associated with acts of performance.

The Live Art Development Agency defines Live Art as 'a research engine, driven by artists who are working across forms, contexts and spaces to open up new artistic models, new languages for the representation of ideas and identities, and new strategies for intervening in the public sphere.'[4]

Live performance in Ireland has influenced and subtly transformed contemporary visual art culture and currently many contemporary artists use performance strategies in their object or image based visual art practice; for example, Irish artists such as James Coleman, Jackie Irvine, Orla Barry, and Clodagh Emoe to name but a very few. Much contemporary art practice, such as socially engaged or relational aesthetics, has developed directly out of performance art strategies. Public performance work occurring in Belfast during the 1970s, especially by Alastair MacLennan and André Stitt, provides clear examples of early socially/community engaged, participatory and interactive art. André Stitt provides a lucid account of these works in his text *Performing Political Acts*.

The difficulties of documenting, collecting, and preserving live performance art has caused a lack of significant representation in Irish museums and collections. However, new and more widely accessible documentation processes such as digital recording, video, film and artists' own awareness of making records of work have more effectively enabled the archiving of performance. This should assist in the collecting of this art form by institutions and museums in Ireland. There is an increasing breadth of ephemeral work happening in Ireland and cultural institutions are only beginning to deal with the question of responsibility towards collecting and conservation. This issue uncovers a dialectic between collecting the live moment and/or its documentation, which warrants further debate and resolution. This publication, by reviewing, contextualising and drawing critical attention to the histories and practices of performance art in Ireland attempts to encourage, promote and provoke the professional collecting of this art form in the future.

Performance and Live Art in Ireland is experiencing regeneration now with a profusion of festivals, events, and platforms for artists to show work, to meet and network with peers and programmers. There has been an expansion of funding opportunities and critical writing and publishing. Michelle Browne's text on the current performance art scene in Ireland details these circumstances. These successes rest on the live nature of the exchange between artist, participants, and audience that in performance based work provides a dynamic context for communication, collaboration and social interaction. Live performance often engages with experiences of

risk and intimacy, community and politics. Audiences know that a festival of performance will be dynamic, varied and often unpredictable, original and creative.

Theatre and dance forms in Ireland have been influenced profoundly by performance and Live Art in recent years. Theatre companies such as Pan Pan (directed by Aedín Cosgrove and Gavin Quinn) and Anu Productions (directed by Louise Lowe) have used structural performance processes such as extended durations, the use of improvised script and action, real actions (as opposed to simulated, 'acted' gestures), nudity, expanded reality and identity, site specific performance, real life testimony and audience participation. These companies have also used technical supplements to performance such as video, sound art, and live web streams.[5] All of these strategies were employed by performance artists from the 1970s onwards while theatre in Ireland was still bound to the literary text and to the often rigid historical conventions of drama, acting, and characterisation. In contemporary dance, there has been cross-fertilization in recent decades between performance artists in Ireland with companies and practitioners such as Cindy Cummings and Fitzgerald and Stapleton combining many of the strategies of both disciplines.

In this book, the terms performance and Live Art are used to describe contemporary forms of performance art. In discussing work before the 1990s, as the term Live Art was not in common usage, we refer to performance art exclusively unless making the distinction between performances made to camera or in camera (in a private chamber) as opposed to performance in a live context, as in 'live performance art'.

A BRIEF OUTLINE OF THE CONTRIBUTIONS TO THIS BOOK

The authors of this collection are all practicing performance artists or experienced writers on performance and Live Art. They each contribute a text reflective of their own interests, research, and experience. Although most of the texts have been written for this publication, four shorter pieces are included that have appeared elsewhere or were unpublished. They cover very interesting aspects of the historical or current performance scene and add diversity and richness of texture to the compilation. The sequence of these essays and articles follow a loose chronology and a geography of the country.

Opposite top: Alastair MacLennan, *Lies Isle*, Cyprus International Performance Art Festival, 2013. Photo: Monika Sobczak.
Opposite bottom: Patrick Ireland, *Burial Series #10*, 2008. Photo: Fionn McCann.

We begin with *Performing Political Acts* by André Stitt which covers the early development of performance in Northern Ireland, beginning with the arrival of Joseph Beuys to Belfast in 1974. Stitt looks at how performance artists used ritual and catharsis as a means whereby public artistic testimony, intervention, and memorialising were converted into acts of transformation in the conflicted environment of the Troubles. Karine Talec in her text *Bbeyond and the Art of Participation* writes about current Belfast based performance art collective Bbeyond, in existence since 1998, who have been staging monthly group performance in public places in Northern Ireland for many years. Bbeyond generously promote both their members and artists from across the island while also creating exchanges with international artists and events.

Moving to the south of Ireland, Amanda Coogan in *Dublin and Performance Art, Twenty Years of Action, 1970-1990* examines the performance scene in Dublin from the 1970s to 1990 through narratives of performances remembered or retold. She charts the development of some of the most significant artists who were practicing at the time. One such artist is Anthony Sheehan who has contributed his archival review *Survey Ireland: South of the Border,* published in 1984 in the American magazine *High Performance.*[6] Sheehan's essay is historically dated, making it a unique document reflecting both the performance art scene and Irish political and cultural attitudes of the time.

One of the artists profiled in Sheehan's text is Danny McCarthy who was making his unique brand of performance and sound art from the 1970s in Cork and he talks to Megs Morley in *The Development of Performance and Sound Art in Cork* about much of the work happening in the south of Ireland up to the present day. A survey of sound art in Ireland follows with *Polyphonic Resonance: Sound Art* by EL Putnam who examines the evolution of sound art as a Live Art practice in Ireland.

The Development of Irish Feminist Performance Art in the 1980s and the Early 1990s by Kate Antosic-Parsons shows how radical women performance artists in Ireland used a type of embodied politics to make powerful statements and activist art about gender inequalities and social justice in Ireland form the 1980s onwards. Helena Walsh in *Developing Dialogues: Femininity and Live Art in Post-Conflict Irish Culture* examines how the legacies of these groundbreaking artists influenced the current generation of women performance artists. Her focus is *Labour*, a touring Live Art exhibition featuring 11 Irish women artists in 2012.

Performance Art in Ireland in the New Millennium is written by Michelle Browne and attempts to take stock of the most important events and developments in performance art culture in the south of Ireland. She discusses the work of a number of artists who contribute different approaches to the current practice of performance. Two reviews of significant contemporary group performance events follow. Fergus Byrne's *Fragments on the Performance Collective: Subject to Ongoing Change* is a review written in 2012 of a group performance exhibition that happened over two weeks in Galway Arts Centre. A version of this article appeared in *Visual Arts News Sheet* (*VAN*) in 2012.[7] Cliodhna Shaffrey in *Right Here Right Now* presents an analysis of a major event involving 19 artists performing simultaneously in the historic Kilmainham Gaol, Dublin in 2010.

I have contributed *Out of Ireland*, a text examining the national and international contribution of Irish performance artists who live outside the country. I also discuss the influence and effect some significant international artists have had on the performance art scene in Ireland and the developmental impact of key international organisations, events, and festivals. As a small island on the edge of Europe, external connections are important for the continued evolution and sustainability of our performance and Live Art practices.

The final section *Timeline of Performance Art in Ireland* is a compilation of artists' names, places, dates, and major events linked to performance art on the island since 1972. The purpose of this timeline is to generate a chronology of practice and to create a frame of reference where as many practitioners as possible can be included in the book. In the *Timeline*, artists appear when and where they first made a performance. Significant events are also listed. Some artists' names appear more than once under 'events' but it was my curatorial decision not to repeat the same (famous or very active) artists too often. The *Timeline* is intended as a broad representation of the whole sector.

OTHER HISTORIES OF PERFORMANCE ART:

Previous writing on the history of performance art in Ireland is scarce, although various articles and reviews have been published nationally in *Circa* magazine, *Visual Artists Ireland News Sheet*, and national newspapers by committed writers such as Hilary Pyle, Dorothy Walker and Slavka Sverakova. Internationally, *Performance* magazine, a UK-based European cross-artform journal was published from the late 1970s through to the early 1990s and covered Irish work regularly.[8] *Art Action 1958-1998*, edited by Richard Martel included a paper by Sverakova entitled *Performance Art in Ireland 1975-1998*, which exists as the principal antecedent to this collection.[9]

A written history can only ever offer one version of events and I hope this publication encourages the writing of other histories and critical reviews on the rich and diverse culture of performance and Live Art in Ireland. Categories such as performance to camera, experimental theatre, dance, and relational, community engaged practices are not discussed here. Because of the nature of this collection the essays and texts in this book are selective and subjective. Each author concentrated on one particular aspect of the history according to her or his research interests or focus. Consequently it is inevitable that certain artists whose work did not belong to any of these categories may have fallen between the cracks; future volumes can without doubt cover these unavoidable omissions.

SPECIAL PROFILE : NIGEL ROLFE AND ALASTAIR MACLENNAN

There are repetitions in these texts. Artists are discussed in different ways, each providing various perspectives of analysis and interpretation. Exemplary artists such as Alanna O'Kelly and Anne Seagrave are profiled in many of the texts, as they both contributed such original and powerful work to the oeuvre. Their presence throughout the book forms a comprehensive picture of their contribution. Nigel Rolfe and Alastair MacLennan also appear frequently, and deserve additional elucidation as they have both profoundly influenced how performance art unfolded in Ireland and how its reputation expanded internationally.

Both artists came from the UK to live and work in the south and north of Ireland respectively in the mid 1970s. In different ways each brought a conviction and sufficiency of practice to the vestigial performance scene in Ireland. Each influenced, stimulated, and induced generations of artists here to make live work. Amanda Coogan in *Dublin and Performance Art, Twenty Years of Action, 1970-1990* describes fully the trajectory of Nigel Rolfe's career and prolific contribution. He arrived in 1974 from the Isle of Wight to live in Dublin and has created and performed works nationally and internationally ever since. During the 1980s, he travelled across Ireland to perform his work in regional schools, community halls, and town squares as well as galleries. He brought performance art to a public who had no previous experience of this art form and had no critical framework within which to view it. As a result he revealed new possibilities for the function of performance in society.

A compelling and shamanistic performer, Rolfe uses his body, his actions, and gestures as a conduit to filter and expose issues of social justice and existential being. He has often addressed current affairs in direct ways, sifting the topic or subject through his body. In an interview with Linda Burnham in 1984 he observed: 'Life as a source for art is more potent for me than art from art. In a society with such cultural and political contradictions as exist here (in Ireland), sources are strong. I want my work to reflect these sources.'[10] He has stayed faithful to these early aspirations. In his work he has employed a range of materials including flour, dust, and powdered pigment to transform his body into an image of dissolved, dispersed humanity. He has used rope to obliterate his identity, creating a metaphor of strangling violence. Often using sound and experimental music, he infuses his live performances with visceral and emotional resonance.

A respected teacher, Rolfe has lectured at many of the Irish art colleges and internationally at Yale and the Royal College of Art in London. He has been active in curation since 1977 when he was appointed the visual art director at the Project Arts Centre in Dublin. He brought many prominent international performance artists to Ireland during that period, fueling the subject. In recent years his curated projects are often motivated by the intention of supporting the work of younger artists as a producer and mentor. Rolfe also played a vital role in the development of performance art here by presenting and teaching Irish art globally, disseminating our stories and generating the reputational economy of Irish performance internationally.

Alastair MacLennan's enduring body of work represents a sustained, committed and illuminating live practice that communicates directly to his fellow citizens what it means to be human. Arriving in Belfast in 1975 to take the post of senior lecturer in fine art at Ulster Polytechnic, he began to make 'actuations';[11] engaged public works on the streets and in galleries that pushed the limits of conventional definitions of performance, art, and the experience of sharing communal space. The civil war-torn region of Northern Ireland became a powerful context for the development of his performative gestures and 'actuations' that confronted the horrors of every-day violent conflict with images of absurdist and surreal behaviour. This juxtaposition of incongruous performative behaviour with real-life senseless acts of violence and mutilation effectively ridiculed war while valorising the playful and peaceful subversive engagement of the performance. This work offered its viewers an alternative, transcendent reality and a more liberating model of being in the world. His 1977 piece *Target*, described in detail by André Stitt in his text *Performing Political Acts,* encapsulates this approach.

MacLennan retired in 2008 from teaching at the University of Ulster, at which he is now an Emeritus Professor of Fine Art. A colleague, Dr Christa Maria Lerm Hayes writes 'MacLennan's credentials as a highly effective, charismatic teacher... owed to his Zen convictions and was based on his work's focus on failure, duration, and humility: credibility and humanity.'[12]

Opposite top: Nigel Rolfe, *Under Darkening Skys* (Durational Bog Lying), Offaly Boglands, 2011. Photo courtesy of the artist.
Opposite bottom: Nigel Rolfe *The Rope That Binds us Makes Them Free*, 1983. Photo courtesy of the artist.

The work involved 'treading the mill' for a 'working week', sometimes clothed, sometimes half clothed, sometimes naked.

Qualities of peace and equanimity characterise MacLennan's work: his physical and emotional presence in performance is suffused by the meditative attributes of his lifelong Zazen training. He has gained international recognition for the extended durational performances he created since the 1970s, some lasting up to 144 hours such as *Days and Nights* at the A.C.M.E. Gallery London. MacLennan describes this work:

> It was a 144 hour continuous performance/installation or actuation (a term I've coined and prefer) – it was perhaps the first of the really long ones I've done, lasting several days. The Gallery was open 24 hours a day. There was some minimal eating and sleeping (though some later works involve none). The gallery had a shop front, so that passers-by could see what was inside. This proved useful, as over the 6 days and nights a relationship developed between the regular passers-by and the work (as well as with those who came specifically to see it – also with construction workers on the building site opposite). The work involved 'treading the mill' for a 'working week', sometimes clothed, sometimes half clothed, sometimes naked. Some came into the gallery and stood looking. Others sat silently, for long periods… Numerous people kept returning, wanting to communicate.[13]

MacLennan presented many other durational performances at the National Review of Live Art in the UK and he was awarded Honorary Associate of the festival. In 1991 MacLennan performed for 72 hours *Still Tills* a 'catastrophic poetics' according to American reviewer Nancy Reilly.[14] She describes the hooded artist 'strolling a sheep skull through a shopping mall' alongside other performed actions. Another performance of epic duration was *Lie To Lay*, a 120 hour non stop performance and installation for Projects UK, Newcastle, 1986. The work comprised of

Opposite: Alastair MacLennan and Manuel Vason, *Collaboration #5*, Belfast, 2006. Image courtesy of Manuel Vason.

40 hospital beds arranged in rows in a decrepit warehouse with huge quantities of jumble. For five days, MacLennan walked slowly and created arrangements with piles of clothing, bales of hay, and general detritus. In the background the British national anthem played at half speed. In current work he often joins Bbeyond for their monthly meetings (described by Karine Talec in *Bbeyond: The Art of Participation*) performing alongside younger, emerging, and experienced practitioners in long improvised public group performances.

MacLennan has performed his work at festivals, galleries, museums, and in public spaces all over the world. In 2009 I watched him sit resolutely before a fragile table in the freezing Warsaw night, for six hours, with a whole fish on his head, his gaze fixed on a pyramid of unwashed raw potatoes before him. In 2013 we performed together for four hours at Les Halles in Brussels for *Trouble* festival. His body became cruciform. He balanced a shovel across his shoulders, encircled by and slowly encircling an assortment of countless worn shoes, all resonant of their previous owners. Even in a group performance he is always alone and the power of his resonant presence lies in this quality of aloneness and self-completion, even in the midst of crowds. 'MacLennan's solitary male who must, through self-denial and self-determination, bear witness endlessly is echoed in the literature of Samuel Beckett, one of the artist's most seminal influences.'[15] During his extended durational actuations, the viewer senses this sufficiency and the ability of the human spirit to endure. He shows us that the human spirit must endure and he gives the example of how this can be achieved.

The artists MacLennan most admires are '[t]hose who overcome the most, within and without themselves, "take on" the human condition, and who (in effective art) comment on political and social corruption.'[16] I have written elsewhere with a similar intention that I believe performance is embodied critical theory.[17] This is in the spirit of theorist Max Horkheimer who described a theory as critical insofar as it seeks 'to liberate human beings from the circumstances that enslave them.'[18] I believe the artists and art works represented here claim new possibilities for what it is to be human and they liberate us so we may perform our lives and our art in new ways. I hope all the writings in this collection can reveal new understandings and appreciations of performance art in Ireland and what it contributes to world performance and Live Art practice.

1. Deirdre Heddon writes: 'The production of history, taking place in history, is marked by the concerns of its own moment of production.' Deirdre Heddon and Jennie Klein (eds.), *Histories and Practices of Live Art* (Basingstoke and New York: Palgrave Macmillan, 2012), p.10.

2. Divorce was enabled in Ireland in 1997, contraception became freely available in 1993, and abortion is still not legally available in the Republic of Ireland.

3. Many Irish artists, including myself, have been supported by the Live Art Development Agency (LADA) in London in various ways since it was established in 1999. LADA has engaged and commissioned Irish artists on projects which it has initiated and administered. LADA has also advocated for Irish artists internationally, promoting and disseminating our work through publications, exhibitions, conferences, and its Study Room resource.

4. Live Art Development Agency, 'What is Live Art?', *Live Art Development Agency* http://www.thisisliveart.co.uk/about/what-is-live-art/ [accessed 8 April 2014].

5. For more information on contemporary theatre and dance theatre in Ireland see: Fintan Walsh (ed.), *That Was Us* (London: Oberon Books 2013).

6. *High Performance* magazine was published in Los Angeles quarterly from 1978 to 1997, and edited by Linda Frye Burnham and Steven Durland.

7. Fergus Byrne, 'Subject to Ongoing Change: Fergus Byrne on The Performance Collective Events', *Visual Artists Ireland News Sheet*, (November/December 2012) , <http://visualartists.ie/articles/van-novemberdecember-2012-subject-to-ongoing-change/> [accessed 16 December 2014].

8. The *Performance* magazine archive is located at the University of Bristol, see: 'Performance Magazine Archive', *University of Bristol*: <http://www.bris.ac.uk/theatrecollection/liveart/liveart_PMAG.html> [accessed 10 December 2014].

9. Richard Martel, (ed.), *Art Action 1958-1998* (Canada: Éditions Intervention, 2001).

10. Linda Burnham interview with Nigel Rolfe in 'An Englishman Searches Ireland's Landscape, Inventing an Archaeology', *High Performance*, 7.2 (1984), 62-65, (p. 62).

11. Alastair MacLennan's own preferred term for his performance/installations.

12. Christa Maria Lerm Hayes, unpublished email communication with Áine Phillips, 8 April 2014.

13. Cited from Alastair MacLennan 'Archive', *Alastair MacLennan*. <http://www.vads.ac.uk/collections/maclennan/archive.htm> [accessed 10 April 2014].

14. Nancy Reilly, *High Performance*, 16.3, (1991), 20-22.

15. Peter Haining, 'Art Beat: Alastair MacLennan' (2008), *Culture Northern Ireland* website <http://www.culturenorthernireland.org/article/1088/art-beat-alistair-maclennan> [accessed 10 April 2014].

16. Alastair Maclennan 'Statements', *Alastair MacLennan*.<http://www.vads.ac.uk/collections/maclennan/statement.htm> [accessed 31 October 2014].

17. Áine Phillips, 'What is Performance Art', *Live Gallery,* 12 December 2013 <http://www.livinggallery.info/text/philips> [accessed 19 November 2014].

18. Max Horkheimer, *Critical Theory: Selected Essays* (New York: Continuum 1982), p. 244.

A TIMELINE OF PERFORMANCE ART IN IRELAND

1972 — BRIAN O'DOHERTY BEGINS SIGNING HIS NAME PATRICK IRELAND — ADRIAN HALL BELFAST

PHILIP ROYCROFT BELFAST — ALASTAIR MACLENNAN BELFAST — **1975** — JOSEPH BEUYS COMES TO IRELAND — MARGARET GILLEN BELFAST — **1974**

JAMES KING DERRY — **1976** — LYDIA LUNCH PROJECT DUBLIN — NIGEL ROLFE DUBLIN — FRANCES HEGARTY DONEGAL / UK — JOHN CARSON BELFAST

RAINER PAGEL BELFAST — **1978** — EVENT: *PERFORMANCE ART WITH ASK MOTHER* AT QUEENS UNIVERSITY WITH ANDRÉ STITT, GEOFF SHANNON, TREVOR WRAY & ASK MOTHER BELFAST — **1977**

TONY HILL BELFAST — KEVIN ATHERTON BELFAST — KIERON LYONS BELFAST — DECLAN MCGONAGLE BELFAST — DAVE EVANS CORK — ANDRÉ STITT BELFAST

DAVE EVANS DUBLIN — **1979** — EVENT: A.R.E. [ART AND RESEARCH EXCHANGE] IN BELFAST BROUGHT DALE FRANKS (AUSTRALIA), ROLAND MILLER (ENGLAND), ZBIGNEW WARPECHOWSKI (POLAND) WITH STUART BRISLEY (ENGLAND), KEVIN ATHERTON, MARC CHAIMOWICZ, NIGEL ROLFE, KIERAN LYONS, ALASTAIR MACLENNAN AND MARGARET GILLEN

MARK THOMAS BELFAST — LIVE WORK PROJECT DUBLIN — DANNY MCCARTHY TRISKEL CORK — PHILIP ROYCROFT, BRIAN CUNNINGHAM, MARTIN WEDGE, RAINER PAGEL, ANGELA MCCABE, DAMIEN COYLE, VIV CRANE, JAMES KING BELFAST — MARTIN FOLAN DUBLIN

SONIA KNOX MICK MULCAHY NICK STEWART BELFAST — TARA BABEL BELFAST — **1980** — FRANCES LYDON O'REGAN CORK — DAMIEN COYLE BELFAST

MARINA ABRAMOVIĆ AND ULAY PERFORM *REST/ENERGY* AT ROSC DUBLIN — ANGELA MCCABE BELFAST — MARTIN WEDGE BELFAST — JACKIE AHERNE DUBLIN — BRIAN CUNNINGHAM BELFAST

WILLIE DOHERTY NORTHERN IRELAND — NICK STEWART NORTHERN IRELAND — VIV CRANE BELFAST — EVENT: 3 WEE DOLLS / 3 WEE BOYS, PERFORMANCE WEEK AT THE PROJECT DUBLIN — **1981**

EVENT: THE FIRST NATIONAL FESTIVAL OF PERFORMANCE ART (NCAD) DUBLIN — OSCAR MCLENNAN FRANCES HEGARTY DONEGAL — VIRGIN PRUNES DUBLIN — ANNE TALLENTIRE DUBLIN

EVENT: *HIBERNIAN INSCAPE*, IRISH PERFORMANCE ART AT THIRD EYE CENTRE DUBLIN — CATHY OWENS BELFAST — MICHAEL MURPHY DUBLIN — **1982** — ANTHONY SHEEHAN CORK

1989

PHILIP NAPIER
BELFAST

BERNADETTE COTTER
CORK

MAURICE O'CONNELL
DUBLIN

KEIKE TWISSELMANN
BELFAST

BLUE FUNK
DUBLIN

EVENT: *LIVE AT THE PROJECT* – VARIOUS IRISH ARTISTS INCLUDING STEVE DURLAND, EDITOR OF HIGH PERFORMANCE MAGAZINE USA
DUBLIN

TARA BABEL
BELFAST

1987

WOMENS ARTISTS ACTION GROUP (WAAG)
DUBLIN

ANNE TALLENTIRE AND ANNE SEAGRAVE AT ARE (ARTIST RESEARCH EXCHANGE)
BELFAST

PAULINE CUMMINS
DUBLIN

BRIAN CONNOLLY
BELFAST

1988

JACKIE AHERNE
DUBLIN

SEAN O'HUIGIN
CORK

GERARD LESLIE
DUBLIN

FERGUS KELLY
DUBLIN

JULIE KELLIHER
CORK

MAURICE O'CONNELL
DUBLIN

MARY DUFFY
DUBLIN

EVENT: *P.A.N. (PERFORMANCE ART NOW)* THE FIRST SEMINAR HELD ABOUT PERFORMANCE ART IN IRELAND WITH ALANNA O'KELLY, NIGEL ROLFE, ROGER DOYLE, DANNY MCCARTHY AND ANTHONY SHEEHAN AND ITALIAN PEFORMANCE GROUP *MUTUS LIBER* CORK

1986

SEAN TAYLOR
LIMERICK

EVENT: FIRST GROUP PERFORMANCE IN IRELAND *THE DAUGHTERS OF VASECTOMY* CORK ART NOW CRAWFORD GALLERY WITH DANNY MCCARTHY, TADGH CURTIS, RAY LAWTON, CARLA HILL CORK

DENIS BUCKLEY
LIMERICK/UK

EVENT: *IRISH ART NOW* WITH DANNY MCCARTHY & BRIAN KENNEDY
TURIN ITALY

MICHAEL BEIRNE
CORK

JOHN BYRNE
DUBLIN

MICHAEL SHANAHAN
WATERFORD

IRENE MURPHY
CORK

ÁINE O'BRIEN
CORK

MICK O'SHEA

PATRICIA HURL
DUBLIN

GEAROID DOLAN AKA SCREAMACHINE
EVA DUBLIN

ANNE SEAGRAVE AT THE IRISH *EXHIBITION OF LIVING ART*
DUBLIN

1985

MICHAEL SHANAHAN
MALLOW

OLWEN FOUÉRÉ
DUBLIN

PAUL MCCARTHY PERFORMED AT ARTSPACE
CORK

EVENT: *REFERENDUM (LET URX=NO)* PERFORMANCE PROJECT ARTS CENTRE DUBLIN

BRIAN COUNIHAN
CORK

1984

EVENT: LIVE IRISH ART AT FRANKLIN FURNACE WITH ANDRÉ STITT, JOHN CARSON, NICK STEWART, ANGELA MCCABE, DAMIEN COYLE, NIGEL ROLFE, PATRICK IRELAND
NEW YORK

TONY SHEEHAN
CORK

WAAG (WOMEN ARTISTS ACTION GROUP) WITH ALANNA O'KELLY
DUBLIN

PAULINE CUMMINS LOUISE WALSH JACKIE AHEARNE
DUBLIN

PAULINE FLYNN
DUBLIN

OSCAR MCLENNAN
DUBLIN

THREE DAYS OF LIVE ART
BELFAST

DAMIEN COYLE
BELFAST

MICHAEL MURPHY
CORK

MICHAEL BYRNE
WATERFORD

1983

ALANNA O'KELLY
DUBLIN

1990 SANDRA JOHNSTON NORTHERN IRELAND · CINDY CUMMINGS USA/DUBLIN · EVENT IRISH DAYS – CASTLE OF THE IMAGINATION POLAND AMANDA DUNSMORE, NOEL MOLLOY PETER RICHARDS BELFAST · PETER RICHARDS BELFAST

1991 ÁINE PHILLIPS GALWAY · BRIAN CONNOLLY BELFAST · HILARY GILLIGAN SLIGO · AMANDA DUNSMORE LIMERICK/UK · **1993**

PAUL JOHNSON DUBLIN · DESPERATE OPTIMISTS, CHRISTINE MOLLOY & JOE LAWLOR DUBLIN/UK · SANDRA JOHNSTON NORTHERN IRELAND · **1992** · JOYCE DUFFY DUBLIN

EVENT: *IRISH DAYS* BALTIC ART GALLERY POLAND · NOEL MOLLOY ROSCOMMON · **1994** · EVENT (ANNUAL): DUBLIN FRINGE FESTIVAL

EVENT: *SONGS OF THE REAPER* WITH BRIAN CONNOLLY PROJECT ARTS CENTRE DUBLIN · PETER RICHARDS BELFAST · CHRISTOFF GILLEN BELFAST · MICK WILSON DUBLIN · PHILIP NAPIER NORTHERN IRELAND

EVENT: RECURRENT *FIX* CATALYST (EUROPE'S OLDEST PERFORMANCE BIENNALE SINCE 1994) BELFAST · **1995** · MICK WILSON THE PROJECT DUBLIN · AMANDA COOGAN DUBLIN · BRIAN KENNEDY NORTHERN IRELAND

FRANCES MAZZETTI DUBLIN · STEM, SEAN TAYLOR, AMANDA DUNSMORE LIMERICK · DECLAN ROONEY DUBLIN · SINÉAD O'DONNELL DUBLIN/BELFAST · DAN SHIPSIDES BELFAST · **1996**

EVENT: ANNUAL 1996-2000 FIX/INFUSION & THE REAL ART PROJECT WITH ARTISTS EMMA JOHNSON, TOWELL BROTHERS, AILEEN LAMBERT, MICK FORTUNE LIMERICK · FERGUS BYRNE DUBLIN · DECLAN ROONEY CARLOW · EVENT WLADYSLAW KAZMIERCZAK, EWA RYBSKA, PAWEL KWASNIEWSKI *PERFORMAT* ARTHOUSE CURATED BY ANNE SEAGRAVE DUBLIN

INTERMEDIA TRISKEL CORK · KIRA O'REILLY KERRY/UK · DENIS BUCKLEY KERRY · **1997** · BRIAN LOUGHRAN GALWAY · KIRA O'REILLY KERRY/UK

OPERATING THEATRE DUBLIN · **1998** · EVENT: *INNER ART*, CURATED BY TONY SHEEHAN & BRIAN KENNEDY WITH VARIOUS ARTISTS INCLUDING STUART BRISLEY, FIRESTATION DUBLIN · LEAH HILLIARD DUBLIN · NIALL SWEENEY DUBLIN

EVENT: ARTHOUSE *ASPIDISTRA EVENTS* DUBLIN · EVENT: IMMA PERFORMANCE CURATION INCLUDES MARINA ABRAMOVIĆ, JANINE ANTONI, MATTHEW BARNEY DUBLIN · EVENT: *INHALE - EXHALE* WITH BRIAN CONNOLLY, ALASTAIR MACLENNAN & BRIAN KENNEDY TEMPLE BAR GALLERY DUBLIN

SUZANNE GERAGHTY GALWAY · **1999** · ORLA BARRY WEXFORD · AUSTIN MCQUINN TIPPERARY · BLACK MARKET INTERNATIONAL AT GREEN ON RED DUBLIN

EVENT
OFFSIDE LIVE PALLAS
PROJECTS AT HUGH LANE
DUBLIN

MICHELLE
BROWN
DUBLIN

SANDRA
BUNTING
CORK

NOT
ABEL
CORK

LOUISE
MANIFOLD
GALWAY

EVENT: ANNUAL 2005-2009
EXCURSIONS
LIMERICK

TULCA
LIVE
2005-07
GALWAY

EVENT
*BODILY
FUNCTIONS*,
THE GRANARY
CORK

2005

ENSO
LIVE ART
GALWAY

AILBHE
MURPHY
DUBLIN

LEO
DEVLIN
BELFAST

COLM
CLARKE
BELFAST

SINÉAD
MCCANN
DUBLIN

EVENT
*ELECTRIC
RAIN*
CORK

KAIJA
O'KELLY
DUBLIN

VICTORIA
MCCORMACK
GALWAY

AIDEEN
BARRY
GALWAY

DOMINIC
THORPE
DUBLIN

2004

EVENT
*ELECTRIC
RAIN*
CORK

JENNIFER
HANLEY
BELFAST

EVENT
SOUNDIN
SLAVEK KWI

HILARY
GILLIGAN
SLIGO

FRANCES
MEZZETTI
DUBLIN

SIOBHAN
O'KELLY
DUBLIN

PAUL
KING
BELFAST

2003

EVENT: *ELECTRIC RAIN* WITH
AINÉ PHILLIPS, IRENE MURPHY,
ANDREW JOHNSON, COLETTE LEWIS,
ELEANOR RIVERS, NIAMH LAWLOR
CORK

*CLUB
OUTRAGEOUS*
GALWAY

ANITA
PONTON
DUBLIN

EVENT: *BACK UP*, CURATED BY
ANNE SEAGRAVE &
OSCAR MCLENNAN DUBLIN

CIAN
MCCONN
GALWAY

EVENT: *GET UP*,
CURATED BY ANNE SEAGRAVE
& OSCAR MCLENNAN
DUBLIN

ANNE
FFRENCH
CORK

EVENT: CITY FABRIC CURATED
BY BRIAN KENNEDY, FIRESTATION
DUBLIN

HELEN
SHARP
BELFAST

HELENA
WALSH
LIMERICK

SUZANNE
GERAGHTY
LIMERICK

BRIAN
PATTERSON
BELFAST

2002

SASCHA
PERFECT
DUBLIN/NEW
ZEALAND

EVENT: DUBLIN ELECTRONIC
ARTS FESTIVAL

ART TRAIL
CORK

BBEYOND
FORMED
BELFAST

EVENT: *MARKING THE TERRITORY*
IMMA WITH MARINA ABRAMOVIĆ
DUBLIN

EVENT: FIRESTATION ARTISTS
STUDIOS PERFORMANCE WORKSHOP
WITH NIGEL ROLFE
DUBLIN

2001

SALLY
O'DOWD
CAVAN

ANNA & EMMA
MCLOUGHLAN
DONEGAL

TOM
FLANAGAN
GALWAY

EVENT: *THE APPEARANCES PROJECT*
WITH PAULINE CUMMINS, SANDRA
JOHNSON AND FRANCES MAZZETTI
AT ARTHOUSE DUBLIN

HELENA
WALSH
LIMERICK

ANNA &
EMMA
MCLOUGHLAN
DONEGALL

HUGH
O'DONNELL
DUBLIN

SINÉAD
BREATHNACH-
CASHELL
BELFAST

MICK O'SHEA
CORK

IRENE
MURPHY
CORK

JOOLS
GILSEN
ELLIS
CORK

AMANDA
COOGAN
DUBLIN

2000

BERN ROCHE
FARRELLY
DUBLIN

27

NIAMH MCCANN
DUBLIN

ELVIRA SANTAMARIA TORRES
MOVED TO BELFAST

SUZANNE WALSH
DUBLIN

2006

EVENT: 2006-08 *OUT OF SITE*
CURATED BY MICHELLE BROWNE
DUBLIN

EMMA HOULIHAN
CLARE

MATTHEW NEVIN
DUBLIN

CLAIRE-LOUISE BENNET
GALWAY

LISA MARIE JOHNSON
DUBLIN

GARY COYLE
DUBLIN

DYLAN TIGHE
DUBLIN

CIAN DONNELLY
NORTHERN IRELAND

EVENT: *TERMS & CONDITIONS*
BRAY

NAOMI SEX
DUBLIN

TERENCE ERRAUGHT
DUBLIN

2007

VICKY LANGAN
CORK

LINDA CONROY
WATERFORD

AUGUSTINE O'DONOGHUE
DUBLIN

TARA CONSODINE
WATERFORD

LOUISE MANIFOLD
GALWAY

EVENT: *EXCURSIONS*
WITH ALEX CONWAY, AINE O'DWYER
LIMERICK

EVENT: FIRE STATION ARTISTS STUDIOS PERFORMANCE WORKSHOP WITH ALASTAIR MCLENNAN AND BRIAN CONNOLLY

ALEX CONWAY
DUBLIN

EVENT MART MOBILE ART CART
GALWAY

EVENT: *HAVE U MET NOSTI?*
NEW PERFORMANCE FROM NEW EUROPE FESTIVAL
CURATED BY SASCHA PERFECT
DUBLIN

CLODAGH LAVELLE
BELFAST

CARL GIFFNEY
OFFALY

2008

VALERIE JOYCE
GALWAY

EVENT: REGULAR
GRACELANDS
CURATED BY VAARI CLAFFEY
MAYO

DEIRDRE MCPHILLIPS
GALWAY

VUKASIN NEDELJIKOVIC
SLOVENIA/ MAYO

JAMES MCCANN
CORK

NIAMH MURPHY
DUBLIN

EVENT: *VIA NEGATIVA*
CURATED BY BOJAN JABLANOVIC WITH ARTISTS AOIFE HEERY, LISA MARIE JOHNSON, ALEX CONWAY, SASHA PERFECT, AILISH CLAFFEY DUBLIN

EVENT: 2008 – 2013
LIVE@8 CURATED BY ÁINE PHILLIPS, VIVIENNE DICK, AND MAEVE MULRENNAN
GALWAY

CIARA SCANLON
GALWAY

ANN MARIA HEALY
GALWAY

2009

KATHERINE NOLAN
GALWAY

LISA VANDEGRIFT DAVALA
SLIGO

KATE CRADDOCK
DUBLIN

EVENT: REGULAR
LIVESTOCK MARKET STUDIOS
CURATED BY LOUISE WARD AND JOAN HEALY
DUBLIN

MART *CHALLENGING BEHAVIOUR*
GALWAY ARTS FESTIVAL

JOAN HEALY
DUBLIN

PEARL HENNIGAN
GALWAY

KATHERINE ATKINSON
DUBLIN

LYNNETTE MORAN
DUBLIN

EVENT: STRAYLIGHT AT DARKLIGHT
CURATED BY NIAMH MURPHY
DUBLIN

ANNE QUAIL
BELFAST

EVENT P.A. LIVE
DUBLIN

STEVE MAHER
BELFAST

AOIFE CASEY
DUBLIN

ÁINE O'DWYER
LIMERICK

HELENA HAMILTON
BELFAST

CIARAN O'KEFFE
DUBLIN

EVENT: ANNUAL
LIVE COLLISION
CURATED BY LYNNETTE MORAN
DUBLIN

2010

EVENT: REGULAR
UNIT 1
DUBLIN

THE DEVILS SPINE BAND
DUBLIN

OLIVIA HASSET
DUBLIN

TANYA O'KEEFFE
DUBLIN

MARY AHEARNE
GALWAY

JOHN CONWAY
DUBLIN

EVENT: *IMPROMTU*
WITH SEAMUS BRADLEY, PAULA FITZ, ELEANOR LAWLER, KATHERINE NOLAN, AND DONNA MCLOUGHLIN
DUBLIN

EVENT: *SPLIT CHARGE*
AT PROJECT ARTS CENTRE
CURATED BY CIARA MCKEON
DUBLIN

PRE FORM: CIARA MCKEON, TANYA O'KEEFFE, ALAN MAGEE, OLIVIA HASSETT, ALAN DELMAR, AND DEBBIE GUINNANE DUBLIN

EVENT: *4.3.12* AT BLOCK T
PRODUCED BY
PERFORMANCE ART NETWORK
DUBLIN

HILARY WILLIAMS
DUBLIN

EVENT
FIRE STATION ARTISTS STUDIOS
PERFORMANCE WORKSHOP
WITH JURGEN FRITZ
DUBLIN

JOHN FREEMAN
USA/CLARE

CIARA MCKEON
DUBLIN

PAULINE KEENA
DUBLIN

EVENT:
LABOUR 11 IRISH WOMEN ARTISTS
LONDON, DERRY, DUBLIN

DECLAN CASEY
LIMERICK

EL PUTNAM
USA/DUBLIN

KATRINA SHEENA SMYTH
BELFAST

KIERAN HEALY
CORK

NIAMH MCCANN
DUBLIN

EVENT: REGULAR
GRACELANDS
CURATED BY VAARI CLAFFEY
LIMERICK

EVENT:
REMNANT WITH DOMINIC THORPE, AMANDA COOGAN AND AIDEEN BARRY
BALLINA

KARINE TALEC
BELFAST

TRUDI VAN DER ELSEN
CLARE

2012

MAEDHBH FITZGIBBON MOORE
KILDARE

EVENT: ANNUAL
LIVE COLLISION/BITE SIZE CURATED BY LYNNETTE MORAN
WITH ARTISTS BRYONY KIMMINGS, ADAM FEARON, MAURICE JOSEPH KELLIHER DUBLIN

KATHY O'LEARY
LEITRIM

TADA: NIAMH MORONEY
AND DONNA ROSE O'KEENEY
CORK

HELENA HAMILTON
BELFAST

EVENT: REGULAR
DUBLIN LIVE ART FESTIVAL
CURATED BY NIAMH MURPHY

RUTH FLYNN
WATERFORD

EVENT: REGULAR
UNIT 1 CURATED BY CIARA MCKEON
AND DOMINIC THORPE
DUBLIN

TRUDI VAN DER ELSEN
CORK

EVENT: REGULAR
LIVESTOCK WITH DEBBIE GUINNANE, JENNIE GUY, ALAN DELMAR, AND ELEANOR LAWLOR
DUBLIN

NOEL ARRIGAN
GALWAY

EVENT: FIRE STATION ARTISTS
STUDIOS PERFORMANCE WORKSHOP
WITH SANDRA JOHNSTON,
AND ALASTAIR MACLENNON
DUBLIN

EVENT: *THE POTENTIAL OF VACANCY*
CURATED BY SINÉAD MCCANN WITH ARTISTS
BERN ROCHE FARRELY, BRIAN FAY, FRANCIS FAY,
CATHERINE BARRAGRY, CORMAC BROWN, DANIEL MONKS,
DENIS BUCKLEY, AND THE PERFORMANCE COLLECTIVE
DUBLIN

EVENT: REGULAR
TRANSVERSAL
CURATED BY FERGUS BYRNE
AND DEIRDRE MURPHY
DUBLIN

JAYNE CHERRY
BELFAST

2011

ANNA BERNDTSON
AT THE LAB
DUBLIN

MAGDALENA KAROL
WATERFORD

SEAMUS DUNBAR
LEITRIM

ELEANOR LAWLOR
DUBLIN

DARREN CAFFREY
KILKENNY

DYLAN TIGHE
DUBLIN

EVENT: *LIVE SCRATCH*
CURATED BY LYNNETTE MORAN
DUBLIN

EVENT: *RIGHT HERE RIGHT NOW* WITH ÁINE PHILLIPS, AMANDA COOGAN,
BRIAN CONNOLLY, DOMINIC THORPE, FRANCES MEZZETTI, BRIAN PATTERSON,
SINÉAD MCCANN, CATHERINE BARRAGRY, FERGUS BYRNE, MICHELLE BROWNE,
ANN MARIA HEALY, HELENA WALSHE, FRANCIS FAY, PAULINE CUMMINS, VICTORIA
MC CORMACK, ALEX CONWAY, SANDRA JOHNSTON, MEABH REDMOND,
AND NIAMH MURPHY AT KILMAINHAM GAOL DUBLIN

RUBY STAUNTON
DUBLIN

EVE VAUGHAN
GALWAY

EVENT: REGULAR *UNIT 1*
CURATED BY CIARA MCKEON
AND DOMINIC THORPE 2012-14
DUBLIN

DEBBIE
GUINNANE
DUBLIN

CHARLOTTE
BOSANQUET
BELFAST

CIARAN
O'KEEFFE
DUBLIN

REDMOND/
MURPHY
DUBLIN

TERRY
MARKEY
DUBLIN

DEIRDRE
MORRISEY
DUBLIN

EVENT: *REMNANT*
WITH AIDEEN BARRY,
DOMINIC THORPE,
AND AMANDA COOGAN
BALLINA

EVENT:
SUBJECT TO ONGOING CHANGE
THE PERFORMANCE COLLECTIVE
GALWAY

ALAN
JAMES
BURNS
DUBLIN

DUBLIN
LAPTOP
ORCHESTRA

SARAH
HURL
DUBLIN

JENNIE
GUY
DUBLIN

SALLY
O'DOWD
CAVAN

ÁINE
BELTON
DUBLIN

EVENT:
SYMPOSIUM LIVE PERFORMANCE
FROM THE VISUAL ARTS AT THE LAB
DUBLIN

VANESSA
DAWES
DUBLIN

FRANCES
WILLIAMS/
ANNA
SPEARMAN
DUBLIN

FIONA
O'REILLY
DUBLIN

DAVID
NUGENTS
DUBLIN

EVENT:
THE ART OF ENCOUNTER - BBEYOND,
QUEENS UNIVERSITY
BELFAST

2013

EVENT:
GENERATION
CURATED BY FERGUS BYRNE
CARRICK ON SHANNON

SORCHA
KENNY
DUBLIN

EVENT: FIRE STATION ARTISTS
STUDIOS PERFORMANCE WORKSHOP
WITH MARILYN ARSEM
DUBLIN

EVENT: *DESIRE LINES* CURATED
BY CLAIRE BEHAN WITH ARTISTS
CATHERINE BARRAGRY, KATHERINE
NOLAN, KATHERINE ATKINSON,
ELEANOR LAWLER DUBLIN

CEARA
CONWAY
GALWAY

CONOR
FOY
DUBLIN

EVENT:
BETWEEN YOU, ME AND THE FOUR WALLS
CURATED BY MICHELLE BROWNE FOR IETM AT THE PROJECT
ÁINE PHILIPS, FERGUS BYRNE, DOMINIC THORPE,
AND MICHELLE BROWNE DUBLIN

LOUISE
WARD
DUBLIN

PATRICIA
MELO
DUBLIN

JANNA
KEMPERMAN
DUBLIN

EVENT: BELFAST INTERNATIONAL
FESTIVAL OF PERFORMANCE ART
CURATED BY BRIAN CONNOLLY

ÁINE
O'HARA
DUBLIN

EVENT: MART *THE NON ZERO SUM ART GAMES* WITH
ÁINE PHILLIPS, FRANCES FAY, ELEANOR LAWLOR,
VANESSA DAWS, KATHERINE NOLAN
DUBLIN, LISBON, ATHENS

ALAN
MAGEE
DUBLIN

DARREN
CAFFERY
DUBLIN

EVENT:
DEFRAMED INFRACTION
NIGEL ROLFE
VENICE

TANYA
O'KEEFE
DUBLIN

SIOBH
MCGRANE
DUBLIN

2014

EVENT: *THINGS IN TRANSLATION:
THE LEGS FOUNDATION* LFTT LIBRARY
WITH KATHERINE ATKINSON
DROGHEDA

GEAROID
O'DEA
DUBLIN

FATHERS OF
WESTERN
THOUGHT
DUBLIN

EVENT: *NEWTOWN CASTLE
LITTLE PERFORMANCE FESTIVAL*
CURATED BY ÁINE PHILLIPS
CLARE

EVENT: *THE PERFORMANCE CARAVAN*: JENNIFER AHERN,
PETA BEAGAN, RÓISÍN BOHAN, NATASHA BOURKE,
SAMANTHA CONLON, NIAMH COONEY, EILIS COLLINS,
LYNN-MARIE DENNEHY, ALLISON FOGARTY, ÁINE KELLY,
ENYA MAC MAHON, AND LISA WELDON CORK

LIADAIN
HEIRROTT
DUBLIN

EVENT: *HEATRASH WERK* AT IMMA
CURATED BY THIS IS POP BABY
DUBLIN

SINÉAD
CORMACK
DUBLIN

EVENT: *SYMPOSIUM ANTICIPATING PERFORMANCE;
A CURATORIAL QUESTION*, PRODUCED BY UNIT 1
CIARA MCKEON AND DOMINIC THORPE
AT ROYAL HIBERNIAN ACADEMY DUBLIN

EVENT:
PRE FORM AT THE LAB
DUBLIN

EVENT: *SELF-MADE*,
CURATED BY DOMINIC THORPE AND CIARA MCKEON
WITH ARTISTS FERGUS BYRNE, ANNE SEAGRAVE, AND
DEBBIE GUINNANE AT CRAWFORD GALLERY CORK

EVENT: *NEST* FESTIVAL
OF FEMALE PERFORMANCE
KILKENNY

EVENT: *BEL-MAD EXCHANGE*
PROJECT CATALYST
BELFAST

LEONA
CULLY
DUBLIN

DAVID J
MAGEE
DUBLIN

EVENT: *BELFAST INTERNATIONAL
FESTIVAL OF PERFORMANCE ART*
CURATED BY BRIAN CONNOLLY

AINE
O'HARA
DUBLIN

CONOR
O'GRADY
DUBLIN

EVENT: *THESE IMMOVABLE WALLS*,
PERFORMING POWER
AT DUBLIN CASTLE
CURATED BY MICHELLE BROWNE
DUBLIN

Amanda Coogan, *Cutpiece as a Mountain*, 2009. Photo: Colm Hogan.

34

Nigel Rolfe, *Face Drawing*, Dublin, 1979. Photo courtesy of the artist.

Tara Babel, *A Day In The Life...*, Derry, 1988. Photos courtesy of the artist.

John Byrne, *Border Interpretive Centre*, 2000. Photos courtesy of the artist.

Aideen Barry, *Flight Folly*, Mothers Tankstation, Dublin 2011.
Photo courtesy of the artist.

Top: Isabella Oberlander, *Untitled*, Live@8, Galway, 2013. Photo: Áine Phillips.
Bottom: Sean Taylor and Amanda Dunsmore STEM, *Only You live*, 2000. Photo courtesy of the artists.

Austin McQuinn, *Ape Opera House*, 2005. Commissioned by Cork 2005 European Capital of Culture.
Photo courtesy of the artist.

Áine Phillips, *Red Weight*, Krakow, 2013. Photo: Mieszko Stanislawski.

Top: Nigel Rolfe, *Vale of Tears*, Venice, Infraction Deframed, 2013.
Bottom: Nigel Rolfe, *Last Man Standing,* Live Action 8, Gothenburg, Sweden, 2013. Photos courtesy of the artist.

Top: Dominic Thorpe, *untitled performance*, Hui Space, Xiamen, China 2014. Photo: To Yeuk.
Bottom: Dominic Thorpe, *untitled performance*, Galway Arts Centre, 2012. Photo: Joseph Carr.

Anne Seagrave, *Collaboration #1*, London, 2005. Photo: Manuel Vason.

Top: Carl Giffney, *Brodarjev Trg*. 2007. Photo courtesy of the artist.
Bottom: Hilary Williams, *White Form Passing Through*, 2012. Photo: Janet Williams.

Top: Cecily Brennan, *Unstrung,* hd stills, 2007, performer Eimear O'Grady, cinematographer Kate McCullough. Photo courtesy of the artist.
Bottom: Elvira Santamaria Torres and Brian Patterson, *Balance II*, Live@8 Galway, 2013. Photo: Áine Phillips.

Above: Pauline Cummins and Louise Walsh, *Sounding the Depths*, 1992, detail of collaborative
video and photographic installation, collection of the Irish Museum of Modern Art. Photo courtesy of the artists.
Left: Michelle Browne, *The Bearer*, Interakcje Performance Festival, Poland, 2009. Photo: Angelo Pedari.

Top: Niamh Moroney, *X+Y*, 2012.
Photo: Kasia Kaminska.
Bottom: Amanda Coogan, *How to explain the sea to an uneaten potato*, 2009.
Photo: Damien McGlynn.

Top: Lisa Marie Johnson, *Breadbraker Flags and Other Things*, 2014.
Photo: Fatin Al Tami.
Bottom: Olwen Fouéré, *In Here Lies*, Galway, 2005. Photo: Ros Kavanagh.

Helena Hamilton, *NOTETOADISTANTGOD*, 2012. Photo courtesy of the artist.

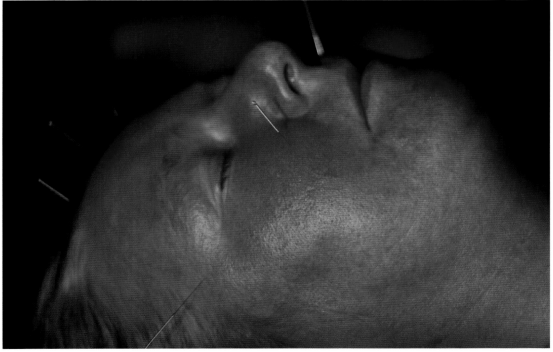

Top: Sandra Johnston, *AN (OTHERWISE) INNOCENT REMARK*, Belfast, 2014. Photo: Jordan Hutchings.
Bottom: Hilary Gilligan, *Healing the Artist*, Sligo, 2012. Photo courtesy of the artist.

André Stitt, *The Institution*, Cardiff, 2005. Photo: Phil Babot.

Debbie Guinnane, *Counterfoil*, 2014. Photo: Joseph Carr.

Catherine Barragry, *Shapeshifter*, durational performance, 2010. Photo: Aoife Giles.

Top: Sandra Minchin, *The Banquet*, 2011. Photo courtesy of the artist.
Bottom: Brian Loughran, 2012, Backloft Gallery, Dublin. Photo: Joseph Carr.

Top: Róisín Bohan, *For the Love of Hirst*, Cork, 2014. Photo: Samantha Conlon.
Bottom: Cian Donnelly, *Strawberry Necklace*, Chapter Arts, Cardiff, Wales, 2013. Photo courtesy of the artist.

Helena Walsh performing at LABOUR, The Lab, Dublin, 2012. Photo: Paddy Cahill

Top: Colm Clarke, *Recourse*, Bristol Arnolfini, Bristol. Photo: Tonya McMullan.
Bottom: Hugh O'Donnell, REMO Plaform Arts Gallery, Belfast 2011. Photo: Catherine Devlin.

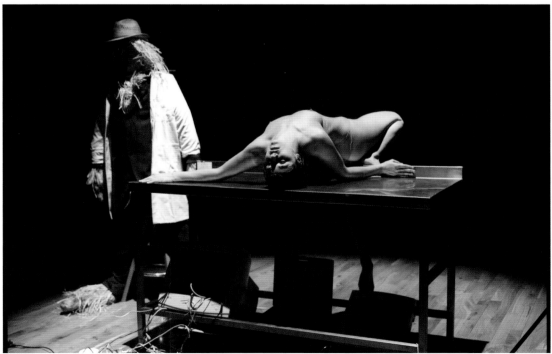

Top: Dylan Tighe, *RECORD*, Cork Midsummer Festival, 2012. Photo: Ros Kavanagh.
Bottom: Sascha Perfect, *Organ City*, 2006. Photo courtesy of the artist.

Ciara McKeon, *Not In Aid*, BelMad,
Catalyst Arts, Belfast, 2014.
Photo: Jordan Hutchings.

ANDRÉ STITT

PERFORMING POLITICAL ACTS:
Performance Art in Northern Ireland: Ritual, Catharsis, and Transformation

I often think about the war in Northern Ireland that made me what I am: holding a gun in my hand when I was 15, seeing a burnt and severed leg in a street in Belfast after a bomb, the smell of excrement mixed with a sweet aroma not unlike lilies, being shot at for going out with a Catholic, random violence and the sound of Jean Jeanie. I also think about making a performance on a frosty morning in 1979 in a derelict church I knew as a child. Naked, my breath caught in the winter light. And, I often think about the sense of freedom, wonder, and dignity making art has afforded me.[1]

Realising the 'bottom line' is never ideological, but human; that art is not in, of, or onto itself. It's for people.[2]

Opposite: John Carson, *Paramilitary*, 1980. Photo courtesy of the artist.

ON YER DOORSTOP

For over 40 years artists have been creating performances, art actions, interventions, and other time-based art in Northern Ireland during a period of traumatic civil conflict. Their work reveals contextual methodologies, issues, and concerns specific to performance art that was happening in a conflict zone on their own doorstep.

In this text, I will explore how and why radical art was made in an environment of political conflict taking place in a developed western society, such as Northern Ireland, and if this art, produced through performance, contributes to personal and/or societal conflict transformation.

I will present examples of my own formative engagement with performance art in Belfast during the 1970s along with examples of simultaneous engagements by other artists in Northern Ireland from this period through to the present. It is not in the scope of this investigation to produce an in-depth 'time-line' of performance art in Northern Ireland during this period. For the purposes of the current text I will focus on examples of artists whose work utilised elements of ritual and catharsis and who, both out of necessity and as a result of 'the Troubles', created an 'experimental exercise of freedom'[3] outside of official institutional art environments.[4]

I will also consider how the transformative possibilities of their work might bear testimony to the specific context of Northern Ireland. As a long-term supporter and advocate of experimental and interventionist art Slavka Sverakova suggests: 'The North… did not release performance from the severe grip of political and moral issues. It felt that the artists trusted performance to do the most difficult and sophisticated jobs in raising awareness to the public.'[5]

Opposite: André Stitt, *Art is Not a Mirror*, Belfast, 1978. Photos courtesy of the artist.

PERFORMING PROTEST

In the early 1970s artistic response to the viscerality of the developing civil conflict in Northern Ireland had tried to find a suitable language for political and social engagement. Protest has a significant and varied history in Northern Ireland. This was reflected by artists' initial responses to the unfolding conflict, euphemistically identified by the media, socially and politically, as 'the Troubles'.

A number of early responses, such as a series of bronze sculptures by F. E. McWilliam, *Women of Belfast* in 1972, tended towards direct protest and a form of illustrative comment made through conventional media such as sculpture or painting, which engaged with the traumatised body at a conventional remove. However, a generation of emerging artists felt an inability to adequately confront daily violence through these traditional means of portrayal and exposition. Robert Ballagh's 1972 *Bloody Sunday Floor Drawings* was an early art-as-performance interface that used the artist's forensic outline to body-map a response to a mass shooting in order to register a resounding act of military transgression: Bloody Sunday, Derry/Londonderry, 30 January 1972. As with McWilliam, Ballagh's work was literal, illustrative and only partially successful. The work being positioned at the Project Arts Centre in Dublin disconnected it not only from its source and location, but also from the aspirations of direct social and political engagement implicit in the artistic actions of recognised performance art activity. The artist did not engage in a 'live' physical interaction witnessed in real-time by a public whereby the artist's body was observed carrying out the action in order to confront or physically challenge the audience in order to seek a reaction. It is, however, in early artistic engagements such as Ballagh's that we see a willingness to emphasise the body relative to a current public event and its subsequent trauma.

Although Ballagh's piece used the body as a template and as a signifier of traumatic public events, the act of drawing around the body was not promoted to the level of public spectacle and confrontation that may be observed or attributed to much of performance art. A public audience was not invited to see the 'live' manifestation of the act itself. The exhibited work constituted a 'trace' or document of the artist's action and was not therefore recognised as a performance artwork at the time.

Both McWilliam's and Ballagh's responses or 'protests' also clearly placed their discourse within a recognised art institutional context: the gallery. However, a significant protest/re-enactment event took place in the summer of 1972 by a group of students lead by Eamon Melaugh on the streets of the Bogside in Derry/Londonderry. The students, wearing paper labels designating their roles, re-enacted procedural searches, arrests, and interrogations concerned with issues of the British state 'internment' of citizens without trial in Northern Ireland. The action presented a powerful visual performance of the procedures used and reaffirmed the reality and quotidian experience in the unfolding warzone. Melaugh, an activist in the Northern Ireland Civil Rights Movement, has described the action as 'role playing.'[6] Here we have a distinction between straightforward street protest as street theatre and what would become an increasingly integrated codification of visual material as an identity for performance art made in Northern Ireland through the 1970s and beyond.

INITIATION

There is no doubt that in terms of a direct action in an 'arts' context Ballagh's work was a significant departure from conventional art making; however, performance art as such did not become a recognised feature of the visual arts in Northern Ireland until at least 1974-75. This recognition was due in part to several visits by the German multi-media artist Joseph Beuys.[7] An artist-run initiative in central Belfast, the Art and Research Exchange (A.R.E.), was founded with a seed grant from Beuys and Nobel prize-winning writer Heinrich Böll in 1977 (with an official opening in 1978) as an art/social interspace.[8] '...'[R]adicalised" by the simultaneous indoctrination and enlightenment from the teachings of the Fine Art course at the College of Art in Belfast, A.R.E. seemed a natural and timely vehicle for driving forward a set of philosophical and theoretical propositions that had been distinctly lacking in the mainstream arts infrastructure.'[9]

As noted above, a conflation of possibilities had emerged during this period with a significant shift in the dynamics of the pedagogical environment at the Ulster College of Art and Design in Belfast (now Belfast School of Art, University of Ulster). This was in part as a result of the recruitment to the lecturing staff of Adrian Hall in 1972 and Alastair MacLennan in 1975. The impact of these artist/teachers alerted, enabled, and encouraged young student/artists to the possibilities of making, thinking, and doing, outside and beyond the confinement of institutional environments and traditions. Implicit in their guidance was the intrinsic relation to real and lived events taking place in the (then) current climate of 'the Troubles' in Northern Ireland. Emphasis was placed on working outside the confines of the institution and 'predictable' art-associated venues. For a student studying art in the early 1970s, the internal and 'hermetic' environment of the college seemed at odds with the reality of the external conflict. While Hall, MacLennan, and other tutors such as David Ledsham and Tony Hill (a Beuys graduate) advocated an experimental inter-disciplinarity, there remained tensions with institutional priorities at the time. As Liam Kelly notes rather dryly in his history of the school 'The Troubles were not only an important political event but also a hugely significant cultural event only too slowly recognised by the college.'[10]

As a result of institutional and political tensions, a creative environment developed whereby students and future artists pragmatically accepted and where transformed by a new DIY role as arts practitioners rooted in an emerging culture of autonomous, self-initiated, self-regulating, alternative spaces on their own doorstep. Isolated instances of performance art meetings and events occurred and were organised for public exposure. These were principally arranged through a committed team at A.R.E. that included Chris Coppock, Anne Carlisle, Belinda Loftus, and Rainer Pagel, which allowed artists to book and organise their own performances. Eventually with the assistance of a burgeoning self-help artists committee, invitations to artists outside Ireland were effected in defiance of the then isolationist political climate. New ideas were transmitted via performances at the A.R.E. by the likes of Dale Franks from Australia, and Roland Miller from England, who also brought Zbigniew Warpechowski from Poland. A host of visiting artists then took part in an Arts Council sponsored event at their 'official' gallery in Belfast in the autumn of 1978, which included Stuart Brisley, Kevin Atherton, Marc Chaimowicz, Nigel Rolfe, Kieran Lyons, and locals Alastair MacLennan and Magaret Gillan. The art college in Belfast also maintained some credible engagement with performance art through a limited programme of visiting artists that included the English performance artist Sonia Knox. During the same period and taking advantage of visiting artists to Belfast, a graduate from the Ulster College of Art, Declan McGonagle, initiated a series of performance art works as part of his new Orchard Gallery programme in Derry/Londonderry.

Meanwhile, through 1979 into the early 1980s, local artists such as Philip Roycroft, Brian Cunningham, Martin Wedge, Rainer Pagel, Willie Doherty, Angela McCabe, Damien Coyle, Viv Crane, James King and others continued with self-organised performances and site interventions. This second phase activity culminated in a major event at a large gymnasium in the Botanic Avenue area in the most 'neutral' part Belfast. In 1982, at the invitation of the independent Neighbourhood Open Workshops, Nick Stewart and Angela McCabe organised 24 performances for audiences over eight weekends by artists from the north and south of Ireland. Thereafter, and increasingly through the 1980s and 1990s, performance art was established as integral to the identity of art made in Northern Ireland through autonomous artists initiatives, independent spaces, and collectives such as Catalyst Arts, Flaxart, Golden Thread Gallery, and Bbeyond; including contemporary work by artists and initiators such as Peter Richards, Brian Connolly, Brian Patterson, Amanda Dunsmore, Colm Clark, Sinéad and Hugh O'Donnell, Christoff Gillen, Sinéad Breathnach-Cashell, and Leo Devlin, to name but a few.

ARRIVAL

The arrival in Belfast of the Scottish artist and teacher Alastair MacLennan in 1975 introduced external performance art influences to an emerging generation of young artists. MacLennan proceeded to create a series of public interventions in Belfast city centre that had a subtle though immediate impact. Crucial to these works was that they occurred in real time, in public space, and outside of institutional visual arts centres. By their very nature they implied direct relationships between contemporary 'lived' experience, present circumstance, and quotidian social and political events. In making works of performance art in Northern Ireland, artists such as Alastair MacLennan has utilised elements of ritual activity based on materials and repetition to consider arts practice as a means for potential transformation, healing, and resolution of inner and outer conflict. As MacLennan has stated: 'Each person is art (and can make what art is). Real art resolves inner and outer conflict. It heals wounds

within and without the self. To HEAL is to make WHOLE.'[11] Indeed for MacLennan art also 'requires a spiritual, ethical basis, free from dogmas. Real art has little to do with refined sensibilities gaining pleasure. Its power is transformative.'[12]

In his life, ritual emerged from a combination of his own Scottish Calvinist background, a theology that he questioned, and the communal discipline and meditation practice of Zen acquired at a monastery in British Columbia in the early 1970's. The importance of ritual deployed in these early developments arose out of (personal) formative social and cultural experiences. These influences have been utilised, converted or subverted by artists such as MacLennan as a strategy for creating relationships between art and life; a blurring of binary distinctions that reflect interior/external, subjective/objective, and ultimately in Northern Ireland: sectarian division.

AIM SEEKING TARGET

In many early performances of street actions ritual repetition played an important part as a means to evoke demonstrative reaction or transformative outcome. Daily throughout August 1977 MacLennan walked to and from work, dressed entirely in black with a plastic sheet over his head reaching to below his waist. Bamboo canes attached to the bottom of the sheet held it in place and also acted as an 'auditory' signal or warning of his approach. Around his neck hung a dart-board. He carried a black hold-all. The journey necessitated negotiating the city centre security barriers where citizens were scrutinised, searched and sometimes singled out for interrogation by soldiers. The work was simply entitled *Target*.

He became aware of anxiety as a shared experience between the searchers, and himself that he could control. As time went on he realised that many of the searchers, especially the younger ones, were more anxious about the situation than he was. This created a type of tension and energy that he was able to manipulate and control and so reverse the status and intimidation of the situation.[13]

Opposite: Alastair MacLennnan, *Target*, 1977. Photos courtesy of the artist.

'What makes MacLennan's simple public action all the more remarkable is the fact that he could have been viewed as a security breech (carrying a bomb in his bag perhaps?) and at its extreme consequence, he could have actually been shot at.'

The ritual of daily business, of going to and from work, is exposed as something territorial and oppressive. The ritual of being searched that became a feature of negotiating Belfast, visualized in the use of a dart board, made the artist a 'target' or marked man; it created a tension in a social situation and disrupted a modified appearance of normality – that of people going about their daily business in a developed western society whilst living in a war zone. This in turn drew attention to a social and political context conditioned by the civil conflict. MacLennan simply but effectively demonstrates that appearances are deceptive. What appears at first normal soon delivers unexpected tensions and poses questions concerning control and authority. What makes MacLennan's simple public action all the more remarkable is the fact that he could have been viewed as a security breech (carrying a bomb in his bag perhaps?) and at its extreme consequence, he could have actually been shot at. By making himself the metaphorical target he could well have become a real target.

This performance, one of MacLennan's earliest in Belfast, also acts as an affirmation of life by creating a cathartic destabilisation of power at the interface between life and death. Catharsis derives from the Greek word for 'purification' or 'cleansing'. The term has been used for centuries as a medical term meaning a 'purging'. The term catharsis has also been adopted by modern psychotherapy to describe the act of expressing deep emotions often associated with events in an individual's past which have never before been adequately expressed.[14] It is also an emotional release associated with exposing and claiming the underlying causes of a problem.

Catharsis in this example, as in much of MacLennan's later work, is derived from a subtle shift in the consciousness of both artist and public. He has noted that the 'purification' or 'cleansing' associated with catharsis '…can be very subtle, subliminal, an alteration in mood or feeling, or a subsiding of tension.'[15]

Through making art as daily ritual activity, and drawing attention to its possible cathartic consequence, MacLennan was reclaiming the physical and social habitat, using himself as a public statement and as an example by creating a work of performance art. In MacLennan's case, we can take his emphasis on '[s]kill in action, where skill is the resolution of conflict' to mean the resolution of conflict by the skill of the artist through the ritual of repetitive tasks activated during the performance.[16]

In psychology, the term 'ritual' may refer to a repetitive, systematic, behavioral process enacted in order to neutralize or prevent anxiety. In the context of Northern Ireland, ritual is used by MacLennan to alleviate a state of anxiety brought about as a consequence of the civil conflict. A ritual is also a patterned action that may be either demonstrative or transformative.[17] The interactive elements here of skill and ritual, indicative of MacLennan's own position, and the way in which he connects statement with intent through the realisation of performance and what he terms an 'actuation' suggests that (his) art aspires to be transformative.[18]

IN TRANSIT

In my own emerging performance art practice throughout 1976-77 I daubed the slogan 'Art Is Not A Mirror It's A Fucking Hammer' on walls and buildings around Belfast. Intentionally crude, the slogans were a provocation that reflected sectarian graffiti prevalent in Belfast at that time. In the autumn of 1978 I finalised these street interventions, or 'akshuns' as I came to call them, with a symbolic ritual immolation that consisted of the burning of my paintings outside the art college in Belfast city centre.[19] The performance was cathartic and transformative; expressed through a purging of traditional formulas and values associated with art making (i.e. painting). The eradication of prior artistic concerns through the use of fire to cleanse and purge enabled me as a young artist to break free of traditional art making and to complete a transformation to a more radical and social/political engagement through performance art. The process of burning with petrol (a direct association with the rioting and petrol bombing in Belfast I had experienced and taken part in before going to art school) accompanied by a sloganeering manifesto converged in an act of purification that drew direct relationships between making art and the physical and psychic environment of Belfast in 1978.

From that point of departure in 1978 I deliberately engaged in art making that was specific to sites in and around Belfast.

Art Is Not A Mirror It's A Fucking Hammer reflected a number of concerns regarding territory, political power, and the potential for ritual as a means of empowerment and for reclaiming or transforming identity. Although concerned with a transitional state – the seeking out of new ways of artistic expression beyond painting – the work also embraced aspects of ritual from the repetition of tasks, and the way the site was laid out, to the almost 'religious' incantation of a manifesto implicit in its title. I personally experienced an overwhelming cathartic release particularly when I let out a primal scream at the start of the 'akshun'. After what was for me a life changing experience, I then spent over a year working in an abandoned and derelict church in my family neighbourhood in Belfast. Neil Jefferies has observed that in my work at the church at this time I had begun '…to experiment with ritualistic actions; [my] interest in utilising them was as part of a holistic process; to heal the psychological damage inflicted upon him by the violent situation [I] was living in.'[20] This series of 'akshuns' at 'the Church' allowed me to formulate a language of materials and strategies for working through site-specific works focused on the use of ritual behaviour and cathartic experience. Thereafter these site-responsive works formed the basis of my performance art activity and identity as an artist for the next 30 years.

I started consciously exploring, inventing and developing 'personal' rituals that would, I hoped, lead me to some form of catharsis, understanding, and realisation, possibly a transcendence of my own conditioned identity. Through making these initial 'ritual akshuns' I identified ritual activity as a means of redressing the limitations of social structure. I identified it as a form of non-conformist art via ritual performance.[21]

Ritual elements have also been used as structural devices and intrinsic references in the work of the artists John Carson and Nick Stewart relative to the social, cultural, and political environment of Northern Ireland. Indeed one can identify codes, signifiers, and materials used in performance art from Northern Ireland as a reflection of the dominant ritual activities carried out within the sectarian divisions: for example violent and repetitive behaviour, the use of meat associated with viscera, petrol, burning, the use of coloured ribbons, clothing, hats, flags, walking sticks, batons, music, paramilitary garments and associated implements. The demographic and environmental influence on performance art of collective, social, communal, and cultural ritual particular to Northern Ireland exerted a central role by means of their political and religious demonstrations and affirmations. John Carson whose performance *Men of Ireland/The Men in Me* most clearly illustrates this in his use of cultural stereotypes. He emphasises this when he says:

> The work directly referred to the religious rituals, and the rituals and symbols employed and paraded by Catholic/Republican and Protestant/Loyalist communities, to preserve and assert their sense of identity. Additionally it referred to codified behaviours and repeated actions, which lead to the formation of stereotypes.[22]

His performance at A.R.E. in Belfast in 1980 consisted of the artist enacting nine different cameos with a total duration (including changeovers) of approximately four hours. Set against a seventies backdrop of civil unrest, economic and industrial decline, and a British government struggling to come to terms with the legacy of its colonial control over Northern Ireland *Men of Ireland/The Men In Me* was a performance that examined Irish male stereotypes. Each time suitably attired as a different Irish character stereotype Carson enacted a 20 minute routine surrounded by a circle of life-size wooden 'cut-outs' of all nine characters with each action accompanied by a recorded sound track of appropriate popular songs.

The first character in the arena was the worker, who set the scene by painting a map of Ireland inside the circle formed by the nine cut-out figures. The four sections of the map corresponded to the four provinces of Ulster, Munster, Leinster, and Connaught. Ulster was painted orange and the other three provinces were painted green.

Next 'The Clergyman' symbolized the religious indoctrination, which determined and defined Northern Ireland's two principal communities. The 'Orangeman' then marched in to assert the Protestant/Loyalist ascendency. 'The Youth' danced violently over the painted map, irreverently messing up and mixing up the orange and the green. 'The Romantic' represented the artist/poet/philosopher trying to rise above the malaise of bigotry, hatred and violence that was prevalent at the time.

The shillelagh wielding, dancing 'Paddy Irishman' happily reinforced the clichéd stereotype of cod Irishness. The masked 'Paramilitary' figure referred to terrorists on both sides of the sectarian divide, who were holding the country to ransom back in the seventies. The businessman was indifferent to the mutual destructiveness of both communities, as long as it did not significantly affect his commercial or economic interests. Last in the arena was 'The Drunk', finding solace along a drink-fuelled road to oblivion. For Carson 'the work was cathartic, in that it helped me recognize and begin to come to terms with conflicting aspects of my own upbringing, and personal and national identity. [...] It was a form of memorializing how extreme and frightening the situation in Northern Ireland was in the seventies.'[23]

Although Carson's performance is more clearly defined, unambiguous and inclusive in terms of Irish cultural references, the use of ritual and repetition has its origins in the Protestant culture that both John Carson and I grew up in. This was exemplified in Loyalist iconography and demonstrations. However, in terms of ritual behaviour in general it would be true to say that a binary identification occurs referring to both sides of the political and religious divide when considering Northern Irish culture and identity as a whole.

There were: religious, quasi-religious, paramilitary orders, and sectarian groupings; the Church, Catholic/Nationalist, Protestant/Loyalist, all developed their own rituals to confer identity. These 'orders' and 'para-groups' integrated religion with politics with social and cultural ideology through ritual to establish dependency. Ritual was ubiquitous, and used to affirm righteous power and control by being a conduit for dominant ideologies.[24]

In Carson's work the cultural cliché reinforces a subjugation of identity to its basic coded denominator. What Rona M. Fields in her banned 1976 study, *Society Under Siege: A Psychology of Northern Ireland*, has termed a form of 'psychological genocide', a control methodology employed by dominant colonial concerns.[25] Fields states that '[psychological genocide] is the mandated destruction of a group with the explicit outcome of eradicating its symbolic power and its capacity for perpetuating its own identity.'[26] The nature of this condition effected both sides and created a position of dependence with a binary whereby both sides become victim. This is also problematic as the nature of ritual in Northern Ireland then becomes a way of asserting communal identity whilst simultaneously victimising the perpetuation of identity through cultural stereotype.

GIVING SPACE TIME

Above all performance, or rather a certain type of performance, satisfies the need for a special kind of space and time, within which events will have a particular weight. The space-time is both framed by the physical boundaries of the performance, and given a sense of ritual through processes such as concentration and repetition. However, this 'ritual' quality is more than merely a formal one. It is not just a matter of a certain ceremonious pace, a certain degree of stylisation, or of a marked distance from everyday life; it is a matter of restoring a specific gravity to actions and objects it is composed of.

Nick Stewart says that, when dealing with Irish identity in a series of performances enacted during 1983-84 entitled *Performance/Ritual for an Urban Environment,* he was attempting to confront the binaries of '[my] cultural upbringing: attempting to create an open space between these, a space not so determined by such binary frames. [I was] trying [to use light] to implicate the audience in the process: to extend the space of the images towards the space of the audience.'[27] In a later performance for the Available Resources project in Derry/Londonderry in 1991 entitled *All Over Walls* a 'shroud' was created from all the pages of the City of Derry/Londonderry telephone directory. The audience followed the artist, who was wearing the 'shroud' and carrying a steel bucket of mud in one hand and an oak branch in the other, on a walk around a portion of the walls. During this walk Stewart periodically beat the walls with the branch, having first dipped it into the bucket of mud. Derry/Londonderry is famous for, amongst other things, its seventeenth century city walls that are amongst the most complete of any city in Europe. The walls have powerful symbolic connotations for both the Unionist and Republican traditions in Ireland.

Arriving at an empty building in the city centre, a former Undertaker's office, the audience was led to the first floor. In a room at the front they found a carefully constructed installation in the wooden floor and an old fire-place with a text of stencilled words added to its mantelpiece saying: CROWDED FULL OF HEAVEN'S ANGELS IS EVERY LEAF OF THE OAKS OF DERRY. This text is credited to the sixth century monk,

The repetition of actions, use of coded materials, their significance in the context of the city, and the way political and religious issues relentlessly weave in and out of the mad woman's consciousness are recognised and correlate with the repetition of codified behaviour, and conditions were taken to extremes in the very environment in which the performance is taking place.

In this performance by Tara Babel, ritual is used as a structural device and as a reference to social conventions across the political and religious divide in Northern Ireland. It allows the artist to inhabit a threshold position between factional territories in order to embody or enact problematic responses to the civil conflict and therefore form a conduit between the private and public. In this and the other works discussed, ritual provided the fulcrum in which to pass from private experience to public engagement through making performed or enacted art in real time in public. In so doing, ritual activity enabled performance art in Northern Ireland to inhabit a liminal space that provided a subversion of social engagement in an environment otherwise dependent on socio-political group affirmation and loyalty. The British cultural anthropologist Victor Turner emphasises this relationship between ritual activity and liminality as enabling a subversion and transition to take place with a view to activating alternatives in socially and culturally constructed space.

By temporarily separating participants from everyday social structure, ritual creates ambiguous social status. Liminality is inherent to ritual, since participants' former identities and obligations to social status must be removed before new identities and obligations can be taken on. Transition from old social identity to a new one necessarily creates ambiguous social status. Most importantly, liminality represents the possibility of standing aside not only from one's own social position but from all social positions and of formulating a potentially unlimited series of alternative social arrangements.[33]

Thus liminality, inherent in ritual activity, is also essentially 'subversive' of everyday social structure, and by association performance art in the context of Northern Ireland with its ritual associations, content, codified signifiers and mannerisms can also be seen as inhabiting a liminal space 'subversive' of everyday social structure. In work, as in other work discussed, repetitive ritual activities create liminal spaces that subvert (and transform) social structure allowing catharsis to take place.

Opposite: André Stitt, *Conviction*, 2000. Photos courtesy of the artist.

TESTIMONY

With the signing of the Good Friday Agreement on 10 April 1998 a major political development in the Northern Ireland peace process was effected. This was followed by a gradual though no less dramatic cessation of paramilitary violence and civil disturbance as Northern Ireland entered a period of conflict transformation.

During the Troubles a form of radical visual art performance had emerged as a response to an environment of political conflict. This was characterised by a fluid and encompassing operating methodology that incorporated elements of ritual and catharsis in order to provide a space in which to draw together and analyse issues of empathy, repression, the transmission of images, cultural and colonial experiences of formation, identity and memory. From the late 1990s to the present there has been a reflection on the previous years of the Troubles by some of the same artists who had been producing performance work since the 1970s and also by new and emerging practitioners. This reflection on the Troubles has at times been a contentious issue. Sandra Johnston an artist who emerged in the 1990s felt that 'artists have a role to play in investigating the cultural, geographic and mediatised residues that continue to inform public opinions, and perhaps subtly interfering into the 'certainty' of entrenched perspectives.'[34] However, reflecting on her own work at that time she suggests that 'in 2004 it was very outmoded to make a 'political' work, there was a prevailing attitude in the Belfast art community to resist making visual representations that involved historical memory and archiving.'[35]

In the last few years this attitude has somewhat changed, there is a greater interest now in the potential of intervening with various residues of the Troubles, and perhaps also some understanding that acts of evidencing could be a valid thing to attempt.[36]

In May 1998, with his work *Naming The Dead*, Alastair MacLennan confronted the legacy of the Troubles up to that point by exposing the public to lists of all those who lost their lives through the Troubles in Northern Ireland from 1969-98. MacLennan spent a day on the Ormeau Bridge in Belfast – a connective artery between Protestant and Catholic territories – tying pieces of paper to the bridge with the names of the dead on them, and placing small flowers along the bridge in an act of both remembrance and memorialising. A highly visible performance 'actuation'

'The akshun took the form of crawling on my hands and knees from my childhood home in Donegall Pass in South Belfast to the Duke of York pub on the other side of the city.'

due to its location, the public engaged with the work by stopping and reading through the lists attached to the bridge. The bridge in effect bore testimony to those who had died and became both a metaphor and potential conduit for confrontation, reflection, and transformation.

In May 2000 I produced a performance 'akshun' in Belfast entitled *Conviction*. The akshun took the form of crawling on my hands and knees from my childhood home in Donegall Pass in South Belfast to the Duke of York pub on the other side of the city. 'A very tough and exhausting akshun. […] My head was covered in tar and feathers. An image from my youth when I saw people tarred and feathered and tied to lampposts as a punishment.'[37]

In *Conviction* I wanted to come to terms with Belfast as an environment that incorporated a personal psycho-geographical history with a symbolic 'ritual' journey that had a correlation to the lives lived and lost in the areas I crawled through. I negotiated divided territory on hands and knees in a ritual act of penance. The work for me became a cathartic act of transformation, redemption, and healing. The performance activity incorporated elements of ritual relative to Catholic culture, acts of penance, and to incidents I witnessed in my own Protestant culture, 'tarring and feathering' as an act of public punishment and humiliation.

The work was also about my father, who drank in the Duke of York pub. In 1968, when I was ten years of age, I was in the pub with my father when some of his friends from the *Belfast Newsletter* showed me photos they had just received from their office across the street. These were photos of Tommy Smith and John Carlos, the two African-American athletes who had given a black power salute at the Mexico Olympic games. It was a profound moment and I suspect the photo had a cathartic effect on me at the time because I was aware that for some inexplicable reason I had been changed. I felt it physically, perceptually, emotionally, and intellectually.

In the moment of receiving the image and by the act of physically holding the photograph I felt a shock of recognition and meaning concerning political and cultural engagement. Thereafter, I became increasingly aware of the nature and possibilities of public protest as performance and spectacle. The moment was transformative and I would identify it as a cathartic experience.

The same year, 1968, was also when I became aware of the Civil Rights Movement in Northern Ireland, and a year I associate with the beginnings of the Troubles. During *Conviction*'s journey across the city I carried photos of the athletes and of my father and his friends, now all dead. The framed photos were hung in the Duke of York pub at the end of the 'akshun'. Sandra Johnston who witnessed the performance in 2000 reflected later that the work was '…a personal testimony to past anguish in his [the artist's] own life, reactivated in the location that makes this action a form of indictment and catharsis.'[38]

Johnston's own site-responsive work also draws from the practical history, formal concerns and methodologies of performance art created in Northern Ireland, albeit in a more subtle form. Central to Johnston's practice is placing herself as an artist in an ethical and moral position of responsibility.

Johnston's *Composure* in 2004 was a performance with a duration of 24 hours. Beginning with a private 'observing' action in the Chapel of Adoration, Falls Road, Belfast, for 12 hours, the work was then completed at Catalyst Arts, where a drawing installation was developed over the remaining hours. The audience was only invited in to experience the final half hour of the action. The work was based on an interrogation of places that are connected to the history of the Troubles, locations for instance, that are stigmatized in public memory by violent events and how this history has impacted upon the current status of such sites.

One of these sites selected was Finaghy Road North, in Belfast, where on 10 August 1976 a sequence of events involving the shooting of a republican paramilitary named Danny Lennon by British Troops resulted in a mother, Anne (nee Corrigan) Maguire, with her four young children Andrew, Joanne, John, and Mark, being hit by the moving vehicle. Three of the children died and Anne took her own life some months later. This incident instigated the forming of the Peace People organisation. As part of her research Johnston interviewed one of its founders, Anne's sister Mairead Maguire:

as part of my research [she] kindly agreed to be interviewed on her thoughts about commemorative acts and what she believed should happen to that location. After this interview I became interested and indeed moved by a text Mairead had written entitled, *An Open Letter To the IRA*, which she had written inside the Chapel of Adoration on the Falls Road. This chapel is open continuously day and night and became a place of refuge for many during the Troubles. I decided to spend twelve hours in the chapel as a private preparatory ritual, which then evolved directly into the performance action at Catalyst Arts.[39]

The ritual of 'observing' at the Chapel of Adoration was followed by the second part carried out at Catalyst Arts in central Belfast. Working off stepladders Johnston drew on two large windows. A video monitor had been installed on the wall between the windows. The video played a looped clip of archive footage featuring Jane Ewart Biggs, the wife of Christopher Ewart Biggs, who had been assassinated by the IRA in his role as the Ambassador to Ireland. In this footage Jane Ewart Biggs 'forgives' the Irish people for murdering her husband. Throughout the broadcast she remained composed and tightly controlled in manner and voice, however the footage also included an off-cut fraction of film from the moment when she had believed the camera had been turned off. This section of footage was not intended to be broadcast, but showed her momentarily collapse in the chair. Johnston was intrigued by this fleeting moment of fragility and developed her action for the Catalyst space in response.

> The action involved: holding a small container of saturated sugar solution which I repeatedly dipped my fingers into, then touching my throat I concentrated on repeating Ewart Bigg's words inward, silently, before drawing the sensation of the words trapped beneath the utterance.[40]

As Johnston moved along the windows she would occasionally return to panes where the solution had dried and blow chalk dust from a sheet of paper, then burnish the chalk into the traces, bringing the hidden marks back into visibility.

Composure, was one of 20 performances made as part of *The Rooms Series*, which Johnston produced over a five-year period. Each work in the series involved 'rituals' of observation inside both private and public spaces where the artist undertook between 12 to 48 hours of being unobtrusively present in situations; piecing together a choreography of behaviour

'...the accumulative performance reached a moment of finality realised through the body as transgressive metaphor with the textual, phonetic and vernacular rendering of the words 'Norn Irn' being cut into the flesh of my arm.'

table; the space completely converted into an overwhelming array of residues and historical detritus.

Suzanna Chan has observed that she felt Johnston's work 'sought to unfold questions of if and how an artist can represent and bear witness to the trauma of others?'[45] The same can be said of the *Triple AAA* performance. The duration and repetition of the work over several days allowed an unfolding to occur. That the work was embedded with a sense of bearing witness to the trauma of others is also true as experienced through listening to the litany of names of those who died during the Troubles. This was obfuscated (the recording played backwards) in an attempt to draw attention to the ambiguity of behaviour, social interaction, codification language and information particular to Northern Ireland. As to the position of the artist in this context: we were concerned with how we could bear witness to this history through the prism of our own experiences and the use of the materials we had brought into the space. A central desire was to see how experiences might be converted through the use of historical archival documents, associated physical gestures and materials to establish a topography of conflict in the art space environment. Central too was how this might reveal behavioural, political and social 'ambiguities and polarities' for the purposes of creating dialogue, debate and testimony.[46] These central concerns cohabit a creative practice rooted in a history of art making with a specific identity in Northern Ireland that also has as its co-respondent a conversion into teaching and pedagogy. In *Triple AAA* this was revealed through the artist as archivist; acknowledging that creativity and pedagogy in 'conflicted space is inextricably interconnected with practices of documentation and archiving and the way these practices shape memories and inform the re/construction of histories.'[47] There are references here too regarding Beuys, and the affirmation that fundamental to his art was his teaching.[48] This

Opposite top: Sandra Johnston, *Composure*, 2004. Photo courtesy of the artist.
Opposite bottom: Nick Stewart, *All Over Walls*, 1991. Photo courtesy of the artist.

holistic view shared by *Triple AAA* with Beuys confirms the 'importance of teaching within the practice of the artist [...] whose actions in pedagogy and art are intertwined in the same cultural critique.'[49]

For each artist in *Triple AAA* a resolution of sorts was defined by the intensity and focus of five days excavation, interaction, navigation and perishable reduction. For me the accumulative performance reached a moment of finality realised through the body as transgressive metaphor with the textual, phonetic and vernacular rendering of the words 'Norn Irn' being cut into the flesh of my arm. Recalling that initial transgressive act of art immolation *Art Is Not A Mirror It's a Fucking Hammer*, this final 'akshun' at the conclusion of the *Triple AAA* performance brought to an end my own engagement with performance art specific to Northern Ireland.

So it was that at Catalyst Arts in Belfast, during September 2013, *Triple AAA* revealed an exhumation and exhaustion of personal iconographic materials and concepts. It was here that testimony was revealed and a form of conflict resolution occurred through, in, and of radical art that was defined by a strategy, pedagogy, and history of ritual and catharsis particular to performance art made in Northern Ireland.

I SAW YOU ON THE STREET WHERE I WAS BORN

By concentrating on societal ills such as conflict and imbalances of power it might be suggested that certain performance artists' attempt to evoke trauma inherent within their observers' psyches and elicit a purging of these repressed memories. This may be the case with variations and subtleties when regarding performance art produced in Northern Ireland. However, this is only one of many interpretations. It is clear though that in these performances ritual and catharsis were utilised as a means of public testimony, and that context, time, space, repetition, codified enactment, recall, and memorialising converted into acts of transformation.

Because we are discussing performance artworks made 'live' in real time our means of recall is through witness, testimony, personal retrieval, memory, and collected documentation. It is also foremost through lived experiences, and through the work of the artists sampled here, and through numerous other artists in Northern Ireland who have engaged in performance art as a political act of protest, mediation, transformation and empowerment under extreme circumstances.

These 'acts' and their attendant recollection through memory, recall and physical documentation can be transmitted through time to the present and therefore be renewed.

The work was always about bringing the contested memory of places through to a point of reckoning in the present tense, finding something in the present that indicated the past but would not necessarily be ensnared by the trauma that had occurred there.[50]

Current performance art in and about Northern Ireland that reflects upon the past adds to the contemporary process of conflict transformation in the form of art as testimony.

I would contend, and with the examples cited as evidence, that without the power of testimony evident in these performances we are unable to summon images of past traumas that are needed to evoke the catalyst of recovery.

Conventional art mediums failed at a specific time and in the specific location of Northern Ireland because conventional practice separated art from everyday experience by operating in traditional terms, in neutered spaces such as galleries and art institutions. From 1975 onwards performance art in Northern Ireland gained momentum because it placed the artist at the centre of art making and evidenced the 'live' or 'living' process of making art as it actually took place. In so doing, it created focus for the artists' actions and their placement in relation to a specific landscape of civil conflict. This in turn allowed artists, and by extension the public, to inhabit a liminal space where conflict might be converted into its opposite through performance art that utilised ritual and catharsis as a means for transformation in an 'experimental exercise of freedom' on our own doorstep.

1. André Stitt, *Amnesia*, performance text (2013).

2. Alastair MacLennan, *Performance* magazine, 37 (1985). p. 11.

3. A phrase coined in the late 1950s by Brazilian critic Mario Pedrosa who applied it to a range of artists motivated to abandon traditional art forms such as painting and sculpture for a new aesthetic that connected directly with political, cultural and social concerns through a performative practice.

4. Slavka Sverakova, 'Performance Art in Ireland 1975-1998', in *Art Action 1958-1998*, ed. by Richard Martel (Quebec: Editions Intervention, 2001). pp. 195-211.

5. Eamon Melaugh (1972) <cain.ulst.ac.uk/melaugh/portfolio4/f4p16.htm> [accessed 10 January 2014].

6. I use the term 'multi-artist' as a description of Beuys's multi-faceted artistic personality and practice. Beuys was adept at interweaving and inhabiting several roles and personalities within his life as an artist. This included his self-mythologising and the development of a personality cult that in many ways he helped foster. He inhabited a multitude of roles including that of social, spiritual, and political thinker and teacher who tended to illuminate his theories with a myriad of practical artistic outcomes that included elements of the charlatan, pseudo healer/shaman, conman, and trickster. see also C. G. Jung, 'On the Psychology of the Trickster' in Paul Radin, *The Trickster: A Study in American Indian Mythology* (New York: Schocken, [1956] 1972), pp. 195-211.

7. Art and Research Exchange (A.R.E.). Originally the organisation materialised as the Northern Ireland workshop of the Free International University (F.I.U.), established in Germany some years earlier by Joseph Beuys and the Nobel Prize winning author, Heinrich Böll. The FIU, as its title suggests, had aspirations to become a global network of creative groups and individuals involved in interdisciplinary research and creative development, crossing boundaries between art and community, politics and economics, history and culture.

8. Chris Coppock, 'A.R.E. – Acronyms, Community Arts and Stiff Little Fingers', *The Vacuum*, 11 <http://www.thevacuum.org.uk/issues/issues0120/issue11/is11artartres.html> [accessed 3 December 2014].

9. Liam Kelly, *The School of Art + Design/Belfast 1960-2009* (Belfast: Ormeau Baths Gallery, 2009) p. 39.

10. Alastair MacLennan, *Is No* (Bristol, Arnolfini, 1988), pp. 82-3.

11. Linda M. Montano, *Performance Artists Talking In The Eighties* (Berkeley and Los Angeles: University of California Press 2000), pp. 385-6.

12. Andrew Pendle, *Beyond Art* (Dublin, Theatre Ireland, 1984).

13. Thomas J. Scheff, *Catharsis in Healing, Ritual, and Drama* (Berkeley and Los Angeles: University of California Press, 1979).

14. Alastair MacLennan and André Stitt, recorded interview in the collection of André Stitt (New Zealand: Dunedin College Art, 2011) n.p.

15. Alastair MacLennan, *Vox*, 7 (Dublin, 1981). I'm using a primary source in this instance. MacLennan has created many statements or manifestos focusing on resolving 'conflict' through 'skill' and 'action'. As with many of the artist's public pronouncements they often contain repetitions or variations reiterated in extended form, depending on what is conceptually pertinent at the time. In a sense they may correlate to ritual Zen style aphorisms. Other examples of the 'conflict', 'skill', and 'action' versions can be found in various publications including *Is No* (Bristol, 1988), Arnolfini (1984), and *High Performance* magazine, 7.1 (1984), pp. 58-61.

16. <http://www.britannica.com/EBchecked/topic/504688/ritual/66240/Functions-of-ritual> [accessed 16 December 2014].

17. MacLennan uses the term 'Actuation' for his work. '…an "actuation" activates a space… it activates energy latently lying there… it effects demonstrative interfusion of energies lying seemingly dormant.' Alastair MacLennan, unpublished email communication with André Stitt, 1 June 2011.

18. 'Akshun' or 'Akshuns' is a term I have used since 1977 to denote the 'type' of performance art I make. Basically it is a northern Irish phonetic translation of the word 'Action' as in 'live action' or 'action art'.

19. Neil Jefferies, '*On Through the Not So Quiet Land*' (unpublished master's/doctoral thesis, Cardiff Metropolitan University, 2008).

20. André Stitt, *Early Akshun, Belfast 1976-1980* (England: Spacex, 2008), pp. 204-27.

21. John Carson, unpublished email communication with André Stitt, 29 November 2013.

22. Ibid.

23. Stitt, *Early Akshun*, pp. 204-27.

24. Rona M. Fields, *Society Under Siege, A Psychology of Northern Ireland* (Philadelphia, Temple University Press, 1977). When first editions of this book where imported into the UK they were confiscated. Apparently under orders from the British government, UK Customs later 'pulped' copies. Effectively censoring the publication from public use and knowledge, several 'alternative' and political bookshops were also raided and the book removed.

25. Ibid.

26. David MacLagan, *Ritual and Performance in Neither Time Nor Material, Nick Stewart, Performance, Installation, Drawing, Video 1982-1995* (Derry/Londonderry: Orchard Gallery,1995), n.p.

27. Nick Stewart, unpublished email communication with André Stitt, 29 November 2013.

28. Ibid.

29. Ibid.

30. Ibid.

31. MacLagan, *Ritual and Performance in Neither Time Nor Material*, n.p.

32. Moira Roth, 'Live Art in Derry', *High Performance*, (1988).

33. B. C. Alexander, *Victor Turner Revisited: Ritual As Social Change* (Atlanta, Georgia: Scholars Press, 1991), pp. 17-18.

34. Sandra Johnston, unpublished email communication with André Stitt, 16 December 2013.

35. Ibid.

36. Ibid.

37. André Stitt, *Small Time Life* (London: Black Dog, 2002), pp. 84-5.

38. Sandra Johnston, *Beyond Reasonable Doubt, An Investigation of Doubt, Risk and Testimony Through Performance Art Processes in Relation to Systems of Legal Justice* (Berlin: Lit Verlag GmbH., 2013), p. 147.

39. Sandra Johnston, unpublished email communication with André Stitt, 16 December 2013.

40. Ibid.

41. Ibid.

42. Ibid.

43. Kirstin Mey and Grainne Loughlan, *Research in Art & Technologies*, Report No. 2, 06/06 - 4/09 (Belfast: Interface, University of Ulster, 2009), pp. 8-9.

44. Julie Bacon first used the term in 1999 referring to the exploration in interdisciplinary performance and installation works that she was making. This concerned itself with the relationship between 'live' presence in the art work (that of the artists and others) and the processes of historicisation.

45. Suzanna Chan, 'Performance Art in Ireland', *Circa* 111, (2005), pp. 68-9.

46. Heike Roms, *Performance Archives Performance, Flashes from the Archives of Oblivion, curated by André Stitt* (Cardiff: exhibition catalogue, 2007).

47. Mey and Loughlan, *Research in Art & Technologies*, pp. 8-9.

48. Kristina Podesva, *Pedagogical Turn: Brief Notes on Education in Art*, Filip 6 (Canada: Projectile, 2007), <http://fillip.ca/content/a-pedagogical-turn> [accessed 16 December 2014].

49. Roddy Hunter and Judit Bodor Hunter, 'The Art of Action in Great Britain', in Deidre Heddon and Jennie Klein (eds.), *Histories and Practices of Live Art* (Basingstoke and New York: Palgrave Macmillan, 2012), pp. 77-8.

50. Sandra Johnston, unpublished email communication with André Stitt, 16 December 2013.

KARINE TALEC

BBEYOND AND THE ART OF PARTICIPATION

In Northern Ireland artists started making performance art in the mid 1970s, a time of social and political unrest, as this art form seemed to provide a compelling way of addressing concerns about living in a society deeply troubled by questions of identity and division. Since then, performance art has grown from strength to strength in Northern Ireland. Over the years, it has benefited from the driving influence of leading figure Alastair MacLennan in particular and from the self-determination of artists like the now well-established Bbeyond. Through the development of an extraordinarily international frame of reference and a unique collaborative model of practice, this organisation has played a major role in promoting performance art in Northern Ireland and abroad over the last thirteen years.

Opposite top: *Bbeyond Monthly Meeting*, Londonderry.
Opposite bottom: Bbeyond. Photos courtesy of Bbeyond.

Until the 1990s, the performance art scene in Northern Ireland was steered by individual artists, with periodic events happening in the Art and Research Exchange (A.R.E.)[1] and the Crescent Arts Centre in Belfast.[2] In 1994, artist-led Catalyst Arts Gallery ran the first FIX event, the longest running live and performance art biennale in Europe. That year various projects were also organised in Berlin and Poland by Alastair MacLennan and Brian Connolly.[3]

During an artist talk in Catalyst in 1998, Polish artist Artur Tajber expressed his interest in more regular Live Art events being coordinated between Poland and Belfast. Artists Brian Patterson and Malgosia Orysiak[4] started discussing the idea of curating such events as a way of encouraging collaboration between artists on a local, national, and international level. Along with Alastair MacLennan, Brian Connolly, and Rainer Pagel[5] they decided to establish a new organisation that would develop and promote performance art in Northern Ireland and create links with performance artists in other countries through exchange projects.

In 2001, Bbeyond was officially launched with their first event, *Place In The Market*,[6] taking place at St George's Market, Belfast, with the participation of internationally renowned artists such as Artur Tajber, Roi Varaa, and Valentin Torrens.[7]

Choosing a busy city centre market as the location for their first event led the work to raise questions around notions of consumerism, value, art as commodity, and artist as worker, but essentially the group felt that it was ideal to engage directly with the wider public and inject poetry into everyday life. This aspect of the work was crucial to the collective who viewed the essence of performance art to be 'participat[ing] in life and the world around us, not just in art.'[8]

Over the following years, with minimal funding and resources, no gallery or office space as such, but considerable drive and determination, this handful of individuals curated over 155 local events and international exchange projects, with 1,654 performances by 341 artists from 32 countries.[9]

In 2006, performance workshops were added to the exchange project format as a way of learning and exchanging with other artists. One workshop in particular had a significant impact on Bbeyond. Led by German artist Boris Nieslony for a week in February and March 2007,[10] this workshop prompted Patterson and MacLennan alongside a group of young artists to perform simultaneously rather than individually.[11]

BBEYOND'S MANIFESTO, 2001:

Bbeyond is a new organisation set up in Belfast to promote the practice of Live Art.

Our aim is to raise people's consciousness of Live Art as being integral to the world around us, inspiring reflection and enriching the experience of the viewer.

We will encourage an interchange of actions and ideas through nurturing existing networks and developing new ones.

We envisage Belfast as a host for challenging and seminal events, for which we intend to use natural and artificial structures and public spaces, thereby extending audience exposure to various types of Live Art.

Apart from facilitating and organising events, we want to contribute towards the exploration of the diverse and polyphonic modes of this art practice. In the course of the organisation's development, we plan to launch a publication/website as a forum for discussion and critical writing.

Ultimately, we want the company to be a source of connections with local, national, and international artists and Live Art groups, sharing awareness of activities here - and beyond.

Interested in this way of working together, they decided to repeat the experience and on 21 June 2008 the first *Bbeyond Monthly Meeting* occurred.[12] The event has been running every month, with about 80 meetings organised in the six years since that date.[13] *Bbeyond Monthly Meetings* have generated a lot of interest over the years and have become a model of collaborative practice, which is now being duplicated in other parts of the world.[14]

The meetings generally happen in a nominated public place such as a street, a park, or a square, where the group of artists perform simultaneously for a number of hours. The performances are self-led,

unrehearsed, and improvised, with an emphasis on creative play and freedom. This open-minded and non-judgemental platform has enabled individual artists to experiment with creative ways of coming together and exploring diverse collaborative and live/performance art possibilities in response to context and place.

Since joining Bbeyond in 2007, Belfast artist Sinéad Bhreathnach-Cashell attends the *Monthly Meetings* as a way of invigorating her practice and opening up new ways of working.

'I value the Monthlies as a regular informal situation to play with chance encounters, open up ideas, break habits and discover novel ways of relating to people, materials, space, gesture and time.'[15]

The performances are autonomous, evolving alongside each other, singular yet part of the whole. By opening up to the possibility of accepting and responding to someone else's actions, an ethics of encounter emerges.

A recent member of Bbeyond myself, I participated in the May 2014 *Monthly Meeting* in Castle Gardens, Lisburn. During this group performance Bbeyond member Christoff Gillen extended lengths of coloured wool across the chosen space, thus creating a web-like structure that acted as a visual link between the participants. The yarn also served as a physical (inter)connective material that the artists could experiment with, respond to, and be moved by. I attached a number of these threads to the sticks I had placed around my head and subsequently could feel every tension, pull, and movement generated by other artists in contact with the wool. On a broader level, I see the web as a metaphor for the artistic and conceptual articulation of the *Monthly Meetings*. While enjoying individual creative freedom, the artists are invited to negotiate the presence and actions of others and remain open to the possibilities of encounter that such a shared space-time situation actuates.

Bbeyond's decision to perform as a group in the public sphere is also a political act that puts into practice the group's philosophy of 'Art in Life, Life in Art'. Living in a post-conflict context of heavy surveillance and division, many artists in Northern Ireland feel compelled to question the priorities of public space. 'Performance art in the public space has the power of making visible the nature of a place. By the way people react, performance art reveals the nature of a context, of a society', explains

Opposite top: *Bbeyond Monthly Meeting*, March 2011, St Anne's Square, Belfast.
Opposite bottom: *Bbeyond Monthly Meeting*, May 2014, Lisburn.
Photos: Jordan Hutchins.

Brian Connolly.[16] These poetic embodied experiences can be both liberating and healing, their connective nature encouraging a reflection on ideas of community, participation, and dialogue.

Recognised artists such as Alastair MacLennan, Sandra Johnston, Brian Connolly, James King, and Elvira Santamaria Torres are part of Bbeyond, yet the organisation welcomes all artists and non-artists interested in performance art, whatever their age, race, gender, religious beliefs, level of experience or style. 'We welcome all people, from all backgrounds. We see that as a viable way of doing art.'[17] This has been invaluable in giving the younger generation of artists a chance to experiment with the art form and to connect with well-established practitioners.

The supportive and altruistic ethos nurtures the potential in artists, creating intergenerational opportunities to experience, develop and present practice, inviting artists to shape their own pathway in a community of practice.[18]

After graduating from Belfast School of Art in 2008, artist Anne Quail found that the open, sharing and informal set-up of the *Monthly Meetings* format fostered the newcomer.

I needed a place to sound out ideas, as well as build the confidence to perform to an audience; it was six months after joining the monthly meetings that I did my first solo performance. Bbeyond has a generosity of spirit, which I have not encountered before in the art world, providing real world opportunities and support to develop my practice.[19]

On 22 and 23 February 2014, the organisation held a Bbeyond Development Weekend[20] to reflect on future directions for the collective. Adhering to the group's principles of trust, inclusion, collaboration, and freedom, all members[21] were invited to participate and address issues such as sustainability, structure and archiving. Some of the key findings suggested that Bbeyond secure an office space, hire administrative and financial support, and create members sub-committees to help with tasks such as fundraising, online presence, and outreach programmes.[22]

Only by responding creatively to such constraints and challenges will Bbeyond stand a chance to sustain itself and continue to provide support and opportunities to local and international artists, building an ever stronger artistic network (web) that extends beyond the confines of style, identity, culture, and place.

1. A.R.E. was formed in 1975 as the Northern Ireland initiative of the Joseph Beuys's Free International University. A.R.E. was co-founded by artists Belinda Loftus, Alastair MacLennan, Rainer Pagel and others.

2. Brian Connolly also organised the Available Resources Project in the Orchard Gallery, Derry in June and July 1991.

3. Artists Alastair MacLennan, Brian Connolly, Maurice O'Connell, Sandra Johnston, Sean Taylor, Amanda Dunsmore, Heather Allen, Victor Sloan, Anne Tallentire, Noel Molloy, and Fran Hegarty participated in the *Irish Days II* event in Ulstka, Poland, and in Berlin, at Jurgen Schneider's venue, the Unwhar Gallery and others.

4. Formerly known as Malgosia Butterwick, Orysiak was involved with Bbeyond until 2004 when she moved back to Poland.

5. Rainer Pagel is currently Secretary of Bbeyond. Belfast artists Brian Kennedy and Peter Richards were also involved with the setting-up of Bbeyond.

6. *Place In Market* took place over two weekends between 12 and 19 October 2001.

7. Brian Connolly, Frances Mezzetti, Ciaran O'Doherty, Peter Richards, Helen Sharpe, Dan Shipsides, Artur Tajber, Valentin Torrens, and Roi Vaara performed at the event. Heather Allen presented a performative video action, Anna Peschkin and Marek Pisarski presented a video of an earlier market performance in Poland.

8. Malgosia Orysiak (Butterwick), 'Live Art, Live Audience', *Visual Artists' Ireland News Sheet*, November (2001).

9. Figures accurate in October 2014.

10. In the Crescent Arts Centre, Belfast.

11. Boris Nielsony is co-founder of Black Market International, an artist collective that has been experimenting with this group format since 1985.

12. This followed up on Sinéad O'Donnell's Ex-Site events, which started the group performances format in Belfast.

13. The June 2014 *Monthly Meeting* (on the 6 year anniversary date) was Bbeyond 77th *Monthly Meeting*.

14. In Essen, Germany, in Bergen, Sweden, and in Québec and British Columbia, Canada.

15. Sinéad Bhreathnach-Cashell is Chair of Bbeyond. Karine Talec in unpublished email communication with Sinéad Bhreathnach-Cashell (current Chair of Bbeyond), 7 December 2012.

16. Brian Connolly, from Karine Talec, *Performance Art in Northern Ireland: Re-thinking the links between Art, politics and the aesthetics* (2012) unpublished.

17. Brian Connolly, unpublished email communication with Karine Talec, 7 December 2012.

18. Sinéad Breathnach-Cashell, unpublished email communication with Karine Talec, 1 April 2014.

19. Anne Quail (b. 1983) graduated from a Master of Fine Art at the University of Ulster in 2008. Her practice ranges from durational performance to video installation and video.

20. Bbeyond Development Weekend: *What Next for Bbeyond?*, University of Ulster, Belfast, 22-23 February 2014, with Lois Keidan from Live Art UK and Boris Nielsony as keynote speakers.

21. In February 2014, the collective comprised of 25 subscribed members.

22. Until then Bbeyond's administration and events organisation will continue to rely heavily on co-ordinator Brian Patterson.

DUBLIN AND PERFORMANCE ART, TWENTY YEARS OF ACTION
1970-1990

Performance in the visual arts in Ireland had a watershed moment in 1972 with the ritualistic performance of the 'birth' of PATRICK IRELAND. In November 1972 Brian O'Doherty transformed himself into PATRICK IRELAND in his *Name Change* live performance for the Irish Exhibition of Living Art in Dublin's Project Arts Centre. I did not witness this performance, as I was six months old. However I choose this performance to open the essay as it posits live performance as ephemeral, indelible, and irreplaceable action.

Opposite: Kevin Atherton, *In Two Minds*, 1978. Photos: Nigel Rolfe.

Ephemerality and immateriality have always been important aspects of performance art practice. Live performance is often a chaotic beast, with the collision of the fluctuating unknowns of action, site, time, and audience. Each iteration of a live performance is unique and unrepeatable.[1] This essay explores instances of live performance practice made with the artist as performer. I do not, I caution, look to uncover the 'truth' here of any live performances that were made in Dublin during this period. Rather than retrospectively describing live performance actions I did not witness, I attempt to describe the current weight and context of some ephemeral art works that occurred in Dublin during my time frame of 1970-1990. My approach is as a researcher, as an archeologist, but most of all, as a collector of stories.

On Wednesday 29 November 1972 in a darkened Project Arts Centre, the artist Brian O'Doherty, clad in white with a white stocking pulled over his face, paced the gallery making an 'Óm' walk.[2] He left the space. He re-emerged on a stretcher carried by the artists, Brian King and Robert Ballagh, also dressed in white. They placed the liminal O'Doherty/IRELAND body onto a table. King and Ballagh began painting the body. Green paint from the head down. Orange paint from the feet up. Transforming the body, briefly, into the Irish Tricolour. They continued painting along the body. The different paints crossed over each other. The colours mixed. The paint on the silent body became a muddy, scrambled, chaotic mess.

In 1993 Peggy Phelan wrote a keystone text on live performance art practice; 'The Ontology of Performance', where she proclaimed: 'Performance's only life is in the present'.[3] Phelan's seminal essay focuses on the 'manically charged' present of a live performance. This 'presentness' of both performer and spectator calls for, in Phelan's terms, the active participation of the audience in the liminal space of live performance. Given a time travel capsule I would dial Project Arts Centre 29 November 1972 and willingly witness, aid and abet this highly charged action. I have a different means, at this 40 year distance, of engaging with this event. Time has passed, and so inevitably our reading and perspective on past events is layered by what has occurred in the intervening period.[4] The descriptions of the action, gathered through reviews and written descriptions of the performance, and the surrounding political context indicate a provoking event occurring during a potent time in the history of this island. Performance lives in the memory of the event. The immateriality and ephemerality inherent in live performance opens the door to our memory and imagination when considering past performance work. These memories, imagined or otherwise, are created by the artist, the attendant witnesses and subsequent audience engagement, encompassing both verbal and written accounts of the live performance.

Name Change was fuelled by the political urgency of Derry's Bloody Sunday (30 January 1972).[5] The immediate reaction in Dublin to Bloody Sunday was so powerful and angry that citizens of Dublin burnt down the British embassy. With *Name Change*'s symbolic action O'Doherty hoped to 'create a new identity that would rhyme in some strange dissonant way with the events in Derry'.[6] The birth of PATRICK IRELAND was certified by a proclamation that read:

> The artist Brian O'Doherty undertakes to sign his artworks PATRICK IRELAND until such time as the British military presence is removed from Northern Ireland and all citizens are granted their civil rights.[7]

Undoubtedly, the Troubles have had a deep impact on art making in Ireland. André Stitt speaks of how conventional forms of art making failed to express the experiences happening outside the door of his studio.[8] Stitt emerged from Belfast Art College in 1976 making action-based provocative and politically challenging works he terms 'Akshuns'. Stitt regularly traveled to Dublin to perform. He first presented a live performance, *A.K.A. F/ART*, in Dublin in 1979 for that year's Irish Exhibition of Living Art. His work, driven by moment-to-moment decisions, is filled with unpredictability, danger, and chaos. Stitt frequently investigates themes of violence, oppression and inequality. In 1984's *Exhibition of Living Art* Stitt performed *LOVE CRIMES* at the Project Arts Centre. Stitt's handwritten score for this work proposed a structure of actions that included:

> Place gun and dice on screen
> Razor – wine as aftershave
> Soap + water washing balls
> Fire blow!! at audience,
> Danger.[9]

I imagine the performance; the threat of the gun, of the razor, of the fire. I picture the actions made directly on the body of the artist; washing (I assume) his own balls, splashing his freshly shaved face with wine. I fantasize (for that is all I can do) about the sting of wine on raw skin. I imagine the power in the humiliation of washing your private parts in public. I picture myself sitting around the floor of Project. I am watching the spectacle of actions on the artist's body. I dodge the flames of fire he spits in my direction. My imaginings oscillating to subjectivity as the performance implicates my own body.

Amelia Jones argues that the firsthand experience of live performance is not to be privileged above other modes of documentary engagement. She contends 'there cannot be a definitively "truthful" or "authentic" form of the live event even at the moment of its enactment'.[10] The story of the performance works I draw here spring from the live performances but, I must caution, re-telling is a highly nuanced re-presentation, layered by the aura of the events, the geographical and political site of their occurrence and the distance of time and the audience from the live performance.

The site of live performances in this essay is the geographical location of Dublin. Yet the site of Dublin cannot be extracted from the turbulence of the political context of the country as a whole. The practice of Alastair MacLennan is significant: a teacher in Belfast College of Art from the mid 1970s, MacLennan asks his audience to witness and co-inhabit the visceral territories he explores. MacLennan regularly performed live in Dublin throughout the 1970s and 1980s. In 1988 for example, MacLennan made a seminal work, *The Burn*, in the shell of the building adjoining the old Project Arts Centre. I witnessed this performance first-hand as a secondary level student. In this eight-hour non-stop actuation,[11] MacLennan moved slowly around the burnt out shell of the building amid the rubble and specifically placed objects, including pigs heads and burnt flags. I have hazy memories of the detail of the performance, including how long I observed it. I cannot offer a definitive account of this performance, but I can describe my memory, jumbled and nuanced by time. I remember the sensation of astonishment at MacLennan's live body as art material. The slowly moving, half seen body of MacLennan cut a deep mark in my fledgling psyche. He electrified a site-specific installation with the human body's intervention and in so doing proposed the infinite possibilities of the silent live body.

Let me turn the focus and context of this essay to live performance practitioners living in Dublin during this period. The arrival of Nigel Rolfe in Dublin in 1974 also had a catalytic impact on performance art practice in the country. Rolfe's significant practice uses a variety of materials; sculptural form, still and moving image, sound and, critically, his body as material. He has a considerable international reputation, performing and exhibiting his work around the globe and, for a time, performing with the

Opposite top left: Nigel Rolfe, *The Rope*, Cork, 1983.
Opposite top right and bottom: Nigel Rolfe, *Cross In Face (Two Beds)*,
ROSC University College Dublin, 1980. Photos courtesy of the artists.

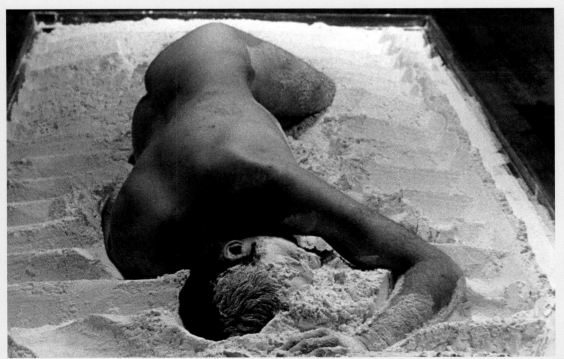

> 'The installation involved a network of cables suspended from the ceiling... counterbalanced by chairs, paint and sand bags. Through this construction Brisley maneuvered his body, suspending himself, literally, between the wall and the floor.'

instrumental *Black Market International* performance group. Rolfe has described his practice as 'sculpture in motion', and his website states 'the central contention of Rolfe's practice is that art making is a live and vital engagement'.[12] This contention is evident right from his emergence on the Dublin art scene. Rolfe lectured at the National College of Art and Design and was a highly influential figure, teaching such artists as Alanna O'Kelly, Áine Phillips, and Gearoid Dolan, to name but a few. From the moment of his move to Ireland Rolfe's output was prolific. He toured Ireland performing in sheds, town squares, and galleries. Rolfe even performed *Zebra Man* on the national broadcaster's long established and highly influential live television programme, *The Late Late Show*. He held his first solo exhibition, *Balance Structures,* at Project in 1976 and became the visual arts director at Project from 1977-79. Rolfe's programming in Project was scene setting, inviting both national and international performance practitioners to exhibit. In 1979, for example, Nigel Rolfe invited Stuart Brisley and PATRICK IRELAND to perform with him for *Attack/Defense – Working in Darkspace* in the then derelict Project Arts Centre. Brisley, a seminal figure in British art and performance art practice internationally, made *Between the Wall and the Floor* for this exhibition. The installation involved a network of cables suspended from the ceiling of Project, counterbalanced by chairs, paint and sand bags.[13] Through this construction Brisley maneuvered his body, suspending himself, literally, between the wall and the floor.

At 2pm on 3 September 1980 Rolfe performed *Bed* for that year's ROSC International Exhibition of Modern Art. Over a period of time Rolfe's naked body was slowly immersed into a trough filled with white and red dust configured into drawn motifs.[14] Rolfe's body re-distributed the coloured dust, in the process marking the place of the body in the sculptural installation, and in turn, marking the pigment on the body of the artist. The black and white photograph of the performance frames Rolfe's face. Eyes closed, two thick white lines of dust made a cross of white over his face.

I imagine it was difficult to breathe with that dust touching his nostrils. I imagine the dust got in his eyes. I imagine he has released himself to the performance and vaguely notices these practical bodily concerns. The image speaks volumes: a death mask on a young warrior.

From 1983 Rolfe began exploring rope as a material making, arguably, his most iconic work in the oeuvre of Irish performance art. *Rope Piece: The Rope That Binds Us Makes Them Free* was a live iteration from a series of rope works during which Rolfe wraps thick creosote doused twine around his head, in a repetitive, considered, slow bind. In so doing he cuts off our view of his face, barricading his eyes and blocking his airwaves. The stories of near asphyxiation abound around this performance. He nearly passed out, or, we imagine he nearly fainted. Reading and hearing about this endurance-orientated, dangerous performance we conceptualise the incarceration underneath the rope. We guess the difficulty in breathing, the lack of oxygen, the pungent smell of creosote, the weight of the growing ball of rope. Hands raised, he continues to wrap, his head becoming an oversized ball of twine. He sits on a chair, in the photograph I access, his viewable body is inactive save for the hands that bind him.

The Rope That Binds Us Makes Them Free is a title describing a series of works, including postcards, photographs, moving image, and live performances. In drilling down into documented descriptions of the live performances, two descriptions, contained in the National Irish Visual Arts Library archives are interesting to consider. Firstly, John Hutchinson, in a catalogue published to coincide with Rolfe›s 1986 exhibition at the Institute of Contemporary Art, London, sets the performance as Rolfe›s most ambitious project to date and describes it as:

A map of Ireland and the shape of a man's body were stenciled onto a white cloth, and coloured green and orange. Rolfe lay naked on the silhouette and then ‹undrew› them, accompanied by a slide presentation that juxtaposed images of ancient Irish monuments and a brief poetic text. These central features were complemented by three videotapes, which showed a female Irish dancer, the artist binding his head with a length of rope and being struck in the face by a torrent of water.[15]

And secondly Andrew Graham-Dixon writing in the *Sunday Times*, again in 1986, described a performance of *The Rope That Binds Us Makes Them Free* at the Laing Art Gallery in Newcastle as:

Rolfe sat centre stage and proceeded to bind his head in thick sisal twine; by the end of the performance his features were completely obscured and he had turned his head into a football-sized ball of malted cord.[16]

The two texts describe different live performances, distinct and yet interrelated works. The key action of this work that has filtered through the intervening years is one of Rolfe binding his head in the cresote soaked twine. To engage with this work, at this distance, we must insert our own agency in the meaning making. Even with the assistance of written documentation, the live performance is illusive, shifting from a large scale live installation, to simple man-and-action live presentation made interrelated by the title and the use of the potent rope.

Rolfe found the rope in an abandoned cottage in County Leitrim. A cottage where the inhabitants woke one morning, had tea at the kitchen table, walked out, closed the door behind them and simply never returned. The cottage contents were fossilized where they stood. Why was the house abandoned? Was it through catastrophic accident, emigration, or sheer neglect? An abandoned cottage implies an abandoned village, town, and country. Rolfe writes '[f]rom one of the cottages [in Leitrim]...I took a ball of twine...To bind my head...To capture, to contain, to smother-perhaps a symbol of Ireland.'[17]

Rolfe's work has consistently explored and engaged with issues of oppression and miscarriages of justice. In 1984, for example he made a work dealing with the death of the 15 year old Anne Lovett while giving birth to her son beside a grotto in County Longford, sparking a national debate on the status of unmarried mothers in Ireland. Further, his 1986 performance *Island Stories* was a responses to the death of Sean Downes, hit by a plastic bullet on another internment commemoration rally on the streets of Belfast. Rolfe used a bodhran to beat out the heart of the nation in this powerful performance.

The reception of performance art is a creative and relational process; its live manifestation offers a unique embodied relationship to the work. An exciting and potent part of live performance is the mythology that develops around these one-off temporal events: the creative reverberations that come from the audience and the documentation. The audience ripples in circles, from the viewer at the live performance, to the receiver of the second-hand account, to third-hand accounts and so on. Joseph Beuys's famous

Opposite: Alanna O'Kelly, *One Day... In Time (Extracts from Una O'Kelly's Diary November 1981-1988)*, Orchard Gallery, Derry. Photo courtesy of artist.

> 'Beuys's belief that art and creative practices hold transformative power in contested situations may be layered into readings of many of the works described here.'

invitation 'everybody is an artist' rings true in the context of this exploration of performance practice in Dublin in the 1970s and 1980s. What I am describing are post-structural phenomena that allow for a multiplicity and elasticity in the construction of meaning.

Between 1974 and 1984 Joseph Beuys visited Dublin many times.[18] In 1974 he showed a series of drawings entitled *A Secret Block for a Secret Person in Ireland* at the Hugh Lane Municipal Gallery. He also presented a performance lecture during the exhibition, leaving behind a series of chalk-board drawings made during the lecture, which are now part of the Hugh Lane's collection.[19] Throughout this period Beuys made concerted efforts, aided by Dorothy Walker, to establish Dublin as the Headquarters of his fledgling Free International University (FIU). Indeed, the Royal Hospital Kilmainham, now the home of the Irish Museum of Modern Art, was offered to Beuys as a possible site for the FIU. Aside from his formal performances in Ireland, his social sculpture practice created through dialogue and exchange, has had a longer-term impact on practice here. Christa Maria Lerm Hayes's engaging publication, *Beuysian Legacies in Ireland and Beyond,* proposes that Beuys left a legacy of performative possibilities in Ireland. She writes '[h]e practiced art as applied or active/activist anthropology'.[20] Beuys's belief that art and creative practices hold transformative power in contested situations may be layered into readings of many of the works described here.

Another international practice seen, briefly, in Dublin during this period was Marina Abramović and ULAY's *Rest Energy.* This four-minute, ten-second work was first performed for ROSC 1980.[21] During *Rest Energy* a bow and arrow is held taut by the performers' body weight, the arrow pointed directly at Abramović's heart. One slip or break in concentration and the arrow could pierce her heart. This short, minimal, tense performance was experienced in this exhibition alongside the long and painterly action of Rolfe's *Bed.*

Beuys's 1974 performance at the Hugh Lane Municipal Gallery interestingly was around the corner from the Grapevine Arts Centre. It was later to become the City Arts Centre but the Grapevine was, for some time, located in an old tenement house in North Fredrick Street, literally two minutes walk from the Hugh Lane Gallery. The Grapevine worked on developing a different perspective on culture, one that was inclusive and challenged cultural orthodoxies. One of the founding members of the Grapevine, Jackie Aherne, made a live performance *Hag* during this period. *Hag* was presented in a darkened space and used lighting, voice-over and the artist as performer. I have no documentary evidence of this work beyond a story told to me. That story described a 'creature' emerged out of the shadows, moving large, constructed arms, up and down, up and down, back and forth and back and forth. The voice-over described the monotonous jobs of cleaning a house or stacking shelves. The artist Pauline Cummins told me this story and cites this feminist and equality-driven performance as an inspirational one for her practice.[22]

This work now lives lodged in a place between fact and fiction. Storytelling, representation and historicisation ripple around live performance artworks, most particularly as we attempt to remember them at a distance of 30 or 40 years. The contemporary art theorist Mechtild Widrich interrelates storytelling of live performance experience with an Austinian speech act.[23] In 1962 John L. Austin, British philosopher of language, developed the theory of speech acts. Austin termed the word performative to describe how, in uttering a sentence, action occurs. He cites the example of a marriage ceremony: at the moment when the woman is asked, 'do you take this man as your lawfully wedded husband?' Uttering the response 'I do' is the moment the marriage becomes legally recognised. The speaking of words makes an event occur. Austin states 'it seems clear that to utter the sentence [...] is to do it. I propose to call it a performative sentence or a performative utterance'.[24] Through this reading, Aherne's performance 'becomes' as a result of my conversation with Pauline Cummins. *Hag* offers an infinite loop of performance possibilities as the story is told and the work is (re)imagined.

John Carson was the visual arts organiser at the Grapevine from 1984 to 1985. Belfast born Carson often works with video projection and text. He sees art as a form of enquiry and his work is filled with acerbic humor, wit, and irony. His 1985-87 performance *Off Pat* interplays stories, songs and slides. In a deadpan performance, presented in the vein of a TV anchorman, Carson told stories and anecdotes on 'art, law and order, manliness, drunkenness, prejudice, boredom, tradition, religion and politics'

sometimes spoken and other times sung, in a voice fit for the shower.[25] Mic Moroney described his work as having 'a knack for pointing up alienation and absurdity'.[26]

Alongside the Grapevine Arts Centre, the Project Arts Centre and the Irish Exhibition of Living Art were the venue for many exciting and essential performance art works from this time. In 1985 for the Irish Exhibition of Living Art a young Anne Seagrave performed in the Project. Seagrave's performances range from vocal and movement pieces to monologues with multimedia presentations. She employs a multi-perspectival approach to issues of dislocation, inequality, confusion, and feminist inflected subversion. Her monologues are witty and personal and her performance exacting, using clear and repetitive gestures. In 1988, again at Project, Seagrave performed *The Centrifugal Theory*. The voiceover tells us;

> My eyes never close
> as my eyelids are gone.
> I catch sight of them
> flying off
> in the direction of Omagh.[27]

The Centrifugal Theory could be referencing the 1987 Enniskillen Remembrance Day bombing, but from my 2014 perspective I immediately think of the 1998 Omagh bombings. Other women artists emerged during this period: Alanna O'Kelly, Pauline Cummins, Anne Tallintire, and Louise Walsh, to name but a few. Their significant contributions are discussed thoroughly by Kate Anotsik Parsons elsewhere in this publication.

When French philosopher Roland Barthes claimed 'the death of the author'[28] he announced the birth of the audience. The audience become interpreters or co-creators when experiencing live performance, the emancipated spectator of which French philosopher Jacques Rancière writes.[29] In a repost to Phelan's 1993 statement '[p]erformance's only life is in the present', described at the beginning of this essay, Christopher Bedford, director at the Rose Art Museum Massachusetts, proposes a viral ontology of performance stating, 'there is no performance outside its discourse'.[30] The descriptions, or rather storytelling of these artworks ultimately re-contextualise the works. The 'truth' of these live performances remains

Opposite top: Sean Taylor and Amanda Dunsmore, *Wailing Wall*, 1996.
Opposite bottom: Brian Connolly *Virtual Reality Googles* as part of *Market Stall Performance* St George Market Place, Transylvania, during ARES Festival, curated by Gustav Uto and Sinéad O'Donnell and funded by the British Council, 2006. Photos courtesy of the artists.

evasive. A live artwork occurred, the instability of these works now becomes an opening for their extension through interpretations, descriptions, and stories, in a relational, post-live performance life.

In 1978 Kevin Atherton performed *In Two Minds* at the Project Arts Centre. A work initially conceived as a deconstruction of video art, the piece now speaks to the movement of time and the distance of years for performance art practice. In 1978 Atherton pre-recorded himself asking a series of questions. An hour later he projected this recording and sat before it, answering his hour-old self's questions. Interestingly, Atherton revisited this performance in 2011 and traversing the 33 year gap, he conversed live with his 27 year old recorded self. Atherton re-enters the work with the passage of years to create a new version of the live performance. *In Two Minds* presents two versions of the performing Atherton inserting a time delay in the encounter. Further, with Atherton's re-performance of the work, stretching the time delay between each Atherton, we are alerted to the passage of time. A timeline of present (the live performance) and past (the pixilated performance) is offered for consideration. The possibility of further re-performances drops into our imagined future timeline. The performance becomes an open work, an incomplete and infinite loop.

Performance art is a time-based art form but not a time-dependent one. The performances considered here exist beyond the time of their presentation. French philosopher Henri Bergson describes our experience in time as a maelstrom of experiences we remember. 'Wherever anything lives there is, open somewhere, a register in which time is being inscribed.'[31] Remembering live performance is dependent on the stories told about and around it, that is, it is dependent on the audience, past, present, and future. These live performances allow for a performative and creative engagement at this time distance, from their iteration in the Dublin Art Scene of the 1970s and 1980s. I have attempted to open a collective register on these live performance works and describe their inscriptions. This process of description gives a further and different life to these performances. The live performances made by and on the artist's bodies and witnessed in Dublin during this period were potent, were visceral, were vital, and are nodes of inspiration and influence for this generation.

1. Amanda Coogan, *What is Performance Art?* (Dublin: Irish Museum of Modern Art, 2011).

2. A walk based the seventh century Irish Celtic alphabet, Óm or ogham, made by carved lines on vertical stones. O'Doherty/IRELAND translated these lines into performed walks.

3. Peggy Phelan, *Unmarked: The Politics of Performance* (London: Routledge, 1993), p. 146.

4. PATRICK IRELAND was buried in the grounds of IMMA on 20 May 2008.

5. Bloody Sunday was an incident on 30 January 1972 in the Bogside area of Derry, Northern Ireland, in which 26 civil rights protesters and bystanders were shot by soldiers of the British Army. 13 males, seven of whom were teenagers, died immediately or soon after of injuries they received that day.

6. Brian O'Doherty, *The Dying of PATRICK IRELAND*, dir. Sé Merry Doyle (A Loopline film, 2010).

7. PATRICK IRELAND, *Name Change*, 1972, Irish Museum of Modern Art Collection.

8. André Stitt, *Lecture for Points d'Impact*, Performance Art Festival (Centre for Contemporary Art, Geneva, 2009).

9. André Stitt, *Homework: Photos + Scores + Statements + Notes for Akshuns*, 1976 – 2000, (Cologne: KRASH–Verlag, 2000).

10. Amelia Jones, '"The Artist is Present": Artistic Re-enactments and the Impossibility of Presence', *The Drama Review*, 55.1 (Spring 2011), 16-45 (p. 19). Also see Amelia Jones, '"Presence" in Absentia: Experience Performance as Documentation', *Art Journal,* 56.4 (1997), 11-18.

11. MacLennan's term for his practice of inserting the live body in his installations.

12. Nigel Rolfe, 'Information', *Nigel Rolfe* <www.nigelrolfe.com> [accessed 27 November 2014].

13. Stuart Brisley, 'Between the Wall and the Floor, 1979', *Stuart Brisley* <http://www.stuartbrisley.com/pages/27/70s/Works/Between_the_Wall_and_the_Floor/page:35accessed5/4/2014> [accessed 5 April 2014].

14. Time unspecified.

15. John Hutchinson, *Nigel Rolfe, Exhibition Catalogue* (London: ICA, 1986).

16. Andrew Graham-Dixon, *Sunday Times*, 2 March 1986.

17. Roselee Goldberg, *Performance; Live Art since the 60s* (New York: Thames & Hudson, 2004), p. 54.

18. A footnote in Sean Rainbird's *Joseph Beuys and the Celtic World* notes an unpublished manuscript by Dorothy Walker, *Joseph Beuys and Ireland 1974-1984*, copy in Tate Gallery Record (London: Tate Publishing, 2005).

19. This performance could have been on 24 September 1974, Beuys's diary entry for that date has 'Dublin' written diagonally across the page (source as above).

20. Lerm Hayes, Christa Maria, *Beuysian Legacies in Ireland and Beyond* (Germany: LIT Verlag, 2011), p. 14.

21. Biesenbach, Klaus, *Marina Abramović The Artist is Present* (New York: The Museum of Modern Art, 2010), p. 134.

22. Unpublished interview between Amanda Coogan and Pauline Cummins, 29 March 2014.

23. Mechtild Widrich, 'Can Photographs Make It So? Repeated Outbreaks of VALIE EXPORT'S Genital Panic since 1969', in Amelia Jones and Adrian Heathfield (eds.), *Perform, Repeat, Record* (Bristol: Intellect, 2012), pp. 89-103.

24. John L. Austin, *How to do things with Words* (Massachusetts: Harvard University Press, 1975), pp. 5-6.

25. Dorothy Walker, 'Pentonville Performances', *Irish Arts Review* 4.2, (Summer 1987), p. 61.

26. Mic Moroney, 'Laughter in the White Cube', in *0044 Irish Artists in Britain* (Ireland, Gandon Editions, 1999), pp. 32-37.

27. Anne Seagrave file held in National Irish Visual Artists Library, Dublin [accessed 12 December 2014].

28. Roland Barthes, 'Death of the Author', (1976) in *Image, Music, Text*, (New York: Hill and Wang, 1978), pp. 142-48.

29. Jacques Rancière, *The Emancipated Spectator*, trans. by Gregory Elliott (London and New York: Verso, 2009), p. 2.

30. Christopher Bedford, 'The Viral Ontology of Performance', in *Perform, Repeat, Record, Live Art in History*, Amelia Jones and Adrian Heathfield (eds.), *Perform, Repeat, Record* (Bristol: Intellect, 2012), p. 77.

31. Henri Bergson, cited in Bertrand Russell, *History of Western Philosophy and its Connection with Political and Social Circumstances from the Earliest Times to the Present Day* (London: Routledge 1961), p. 759.

THE DEVELOPMENT OF PERFORMANCE AND SOUND ART IN CORK

The interview is held in the offices of the National Visual Arts Library (NIVAL), Dublin, on 18 February 2014. The contents of Danny's folder that exists in the NIVAL repository and a folder relating to performance art lay open on the table. Danny also brings some artifacts and documents from his personal archive to the interview.

Opposite: Danny McCarthy, *Healing Memories*, Mallow Arts Lab, 1990. Photo: Stephen Murphy.

MEGS: As I looked through the collection in the ALA[1] relating to sound and performance art, there's a lot of posters there from the Triskel in Cork – you can tell that they are maybe from the mid seventies or eighties but you're just not sure, as what's missing from some of the posters is the year! It's something people forgot to put on! As a founder of Triskel could you tell me about the foundation of Triskel?[2]

DANNY: I was a co-founder of Triskel with Patrick McQuoid because I had originally started an organisation called *Mallow Arts Lab* in Mallow. That would have been about 1973, 1974. That was a multi-disciplinary thing with visual art, music, film, and poetry, and we published broadsheets, poster poems, and books, all in this small town. It built up quite an audience for poetry; we had 200 people at poetry readings! In Cork then there was the Tubular gallery, the first private gallery in Cork; it was on Paul Street. Patrick McQuoid used to run it, and I got very friendly with him and exhibited with him. Eventually, Tubular closed and Patrick wanted to set up an arts centre, so we got together and worked on that, in a place called Beasley Street. It was just off South Mall and within the first five or six months, we had our first performances, with Nigel Rolfe, Margaret Gillen, and myself. Then we moved from Beasley Street up to Bridge Street, where we had a basement that was quite ideal for performance. There were concrete floors and pillars so you could muck around a little bit. I remember one weekend of Alastair [MacLennan] being down and he'd brought fish from Belfast and tied them to the pillar. By the time the weekend was over, the fish fell to the floor and all these maggots were crawling around the place. In a basement, the smell was totally obnoxious, you know! [*Laughing*].

Gradually the name Triskel as a venue for performance got known. Alastair and myself became very good friends. Alastair would put artists coming over to Belfast in contact with us, and if they wanted a gig in Cork we'd try and accommodate them. Dale Frank, an Australian artist, performed in the early days of Triskel – he came from Belfast to Cork.

M: There definitely seems to be a correlation between Belfast and Cork in the development of performance in Ireland.

D: There was more a correlation between Belfast and Cork than anywhere else in Ireland. Once Nigel Rolfe stopped presenting work in the Project [Arts Centre] there wasn't anyone in Dublin doing it. And it just kind of faded back.

M: So you and Alastair would've kept in close contact about who was coming over and artists who were performing in Cork would go on to perform in Belfast or vice versa?

D: Oh yeah. It was an era so totally different to now, that it's almost hard for people to understand and grasp. To get any information on anything was very, very difficult.

M: So the performance scene was really reliant on these personal connections that you were making and corresponding with; letting each other know what events were happening and what artists were here…

D: Yeah, and then in the early eighties, about 1982, there was a big exhibition of Irish Art called *Hibernian Inscape,* which was curated by an art critic called Paul Overy, who was with the *Guardian* newspaper at the time, so he was a well respected critic. The exhibition was travelling to Glasgow and he decided it would have this Live Art element. We were in a place called *The Third Eye Centre,* a big arts centre in Glasgow. I think it was for about two or three weeks, with Live Art going on there. I did a piece called *The Harp That Once*; it was a heavy political piece based on the situation in Northern Ireland. The space itself suggested to me the shape of a harp. There was a pillar in the middle and there were two pillars down this end, so I joined them up and made strings out of barbed wire. The piece consisted of a tree in the middle and it consisted of me reaching and plucking the leaves off the tree and pinning them onto the barbed wire dressed in a normal suit and shirt and that. Then when all the leaves were broken off the tree, I picked them off the barbed wire and replaced them on the barbed wire with white crosses. And at the same time a Thomas Moore melody, *The Harp That Once, The Sound of Beauty,* was played and sung by a tenor from the Cork Operatic Society recorded on a loop tape. It was quite a beautiful song, and at the same time we had this tragedy going on [in the north]. And a funny thing was we were kind of wary about it being heavily political in Glasgow, but there were headlines in the newspaper 'Lord Mayor in furore, over art in arts centre' and I was going 'fuck it, that's us. We're in trouble.' But what were they giving out about but Alastair walking around in the nude! I also remember I got a fantastic review for that in *Performance* magazine, which was an English magazine.[3] It described my piece as Wagnerian by comparison to Nigel's and Alastair's, which was a pretty big deal at the time and I still have the magazine. [*Laughing*].

Again at that time, going to Scotland, going internationally was a big thing, you know? Now people take no notice of travel at all. Artists all go international. But then it was big. I don't know what you'd equate it with right now.

M: So it really elevated the status of performance art?

D: Yes and for the artist as well – that your art was good enough to be selected for that kind of thing. Then another interesting thing that came about was the editors of an American magazine called *High Performance* – Linda Frye Burnham and Steven Durland – came over and they wanted to talk to us and see the Cork scene. They went to Belfast and they called into Nigel in Dublin and they wrote about it. But interestingly they had with them a fella called Paul McCarthy, and he ended up doing a performance in a space called Art Space in 11 Leitrim Street in Cork, which was the first artist-run studios in Cork. Art Space was run by Mike Murphy, Catriona Hearne, and Breda Lynch. But they let us use that space because in Triskel – there was carpet on the floor so it wasn't terribly suitable. I had previously done a piece there called *Referendum Addendum,* which was about the abortion referendum at the time. That was around 1983.[4] The piece consisted of a tree with dolls heads hanging over the tree and all the dolls heads were filled with red ice. On the ground there was a large sheet of white plastic in a circle, and as the dolls heads started to melt, it started dripping onto the plastic. My performance consisted of trying to mop up the mess. And at the same time, there was a shadow of the tree being cast onto the wall behind it. So there were the heads and the dripping. It wound up eventually that the heads had run out of ice and I had cleaned it up. Then I broke the branches off the tree and I put one head on the bit of the remaining branch and created a phallic symbol on the wall. The idea behind it was that this referendum was not going to solve a thing at all, that we're going to be haunted by the shadow of it forever. So there were pro-abortion people there and anti-abortion people.

M: In the audience?

D: Yeah, in the audience. They had come as groups. The pro people were attacking me as being anti-abortion and the anti-abortion were attacking me for being pro-abortion. And I suppose the important thing was I said 'Don't talk to me, talk to each other, dialogue is the only way it can be solved.' But that was one of the first pieces done there and it was reviewed.

'Then there was a large fish made out of metal on the wall. There was almost like a sardine tin that you opened up and inside there was a live goldfish that was fed every day by Paul O'Reilly, the gallery director at the time.'

We got that space for Paul McCarthy. So we let him do a piece there; his first performance in Ireland.

M: You let him? [*Laughing*].

D: Well, his star hadn't risen at this stage. He was just another jobbing performance artist. We had André Stitt a year or two before that and we were saying 'jeez this guy is really influenced by André Stitt.' [*Laughing*] You know, with the ketchup and the mustard and all this kind of stuff. He had no fame at all at this stage. I asked Linda Frye Burnham two years ago to see if they had photographs of it. She said they had millions of photographs but they never went through them to sort them. This was a solid glossy magazine, and that whole issue was dedicated to Irish and English performance art. There's an article specifically on Cork performance written by Anthony Sheehan at the time. At the time it was quite an important magazine internationally. I'll show it to you…

M: It's in perfect condition!

D: It's probably the only one in the country unless they have one here… that issue put other people in touch with us. For example, we had the Basement Group from Newcastle in England, they came over and did a tour of Belfast and then came to Cork. Cork had a great reputation for live work getting reviewed. We had a wonderfully dedicated critic here called Hilary Pyle who reviewed most of the performance art and sound events in the *Cork Examiner* and the *Irish Times*. You could do a work in Dublin and be ignored, and in Cork get reviewed. That also attracted a lot of artists our way. We had Roland Miller and Shirley Cameron, two very influential artists from England. Also Nick Stewart, Angela McCabe, Brid O'Brien, Julie Kelleher. Recently I came across in my archives a letter of application from Willie Doherty to do a performance, which he did, and a fine piece of work it was too. Nigel Rolfe was a regular as was Alastair MacLennan. Artur Tajber from Kracow was a regular Polish visitor. Brian

Connolly and Martin Wedge, Colette Lewis, Mary Duffy, Augustine O'Donoghue, Robert Ayers, Pauline Cummins, Sandra Johnston, Ouch Electro, Frances Mezzetti, the list could go on for pages, as there were literally hundreds of performances.

M: So *High Performance* magazine and the critical attention from Hilary Pyle really started to bridge connections?

D: Well I did the first performance ever in EVA.[5] EVA wasn't taking proposals for performance at the time, but I had won first prize in EVA in the sculpture section in 1981 selected by Pierre Restany, the renowned critic. Then they decided to have an exhibition of EVA prize winners and artists selected their own work, so I did a performance and installation. So that at least I got performance in the door there, you know.

M: So you got in the little crack…

D: Yes and I think that was important. I did the performance at the opening. The title of it was *You Don't Have To Be An Artist To Draw Conclusions* and it was based on the fishermen's struggle off the coast of Ireland at the time and the way they were being exploited. Foreign boats were taking the catch, and people were risking their lives. So I worked with the fishermen in Castletownbere and collected statements from them, and printed them on the wall. Then there was a large fish made out of metal on the wall. There was almost like a sardine tin that you opened up and inside there was a live goldfish that was fed every day by Paul O'Reilly, the gallery director at the time. The performance consisted of me just sitting there with a fisherman's net hanging over my head and with a plate in my hand and a mackerel dusted with gold on it. I sat there for the four hours of the opening. But that was actually the first performance ever in EVA.

M: That's an interesting trajectory from sculpture to the body in space, and I suppose it sounds obvious now that you're mapping it out, but I think a lot of artists now deal with the medium from a completely other angle…

D: Yes, after working with Triskel and pushing performance art there, I was interested in getting it exposed through spaces as well and slipping performance in the back door. 1985 was another big year because it was Cork 800.[6] There was an exhibition held in Cork called *CAN* (*Cork*

Art Now) and we were on the organising panel of it. Vera Ryan was the selector and I proposed to do a performance at the opening called *The Daughters of Vasectomy,* which was a group performance about people who existed on the fringes of society. Because I was doing that, I came up with the idea for *Performance Art Now* (*PAN*), an event at the Crawford Art Gallery that included a seminar on performance art. That was 1985. We had Mutus Liber from Turin with a three person performance group, Rodger Doyle from Dublin talking about sound and performance and Alanna O'Kelly was down and she did a very powerful piece. It was one of her early keening pieces.[7] We also had a panel discussion.

M: And how unusual would that have been in Ireland at that time, to have a specific seminar on performance in a place like the Crawford?

D: It would've been totally unusual. It was the first one ever in the country that I'm aware of. I recall I had a heated debate with Paul O'Reilly, director of EVA at the time, because performance art wasn't listed in the EVA submission forms – they listed painting, drawing, sculpture, graphics etc. – and the result was it was listed the following year. As well, we started doing performance in Mallow because there used to be an arts festival there every year. I was still involved, so we'd get performance artists Nigel Rolfe, Michael Shanihan, Fergus Kelly, and myself. At the same time there was performance happening in Kenmare, County Kerry. They had a festival down there called *Cibeal Cincise.* A Cibeal is a gathering when farmers get together to help each other.

M: We call it something different in the west, we call it a Meitheal.

D: A Cibeal is pretty much the same thing. But they used to bring down very good groups and exhibitions to that, and they started doing performance there as well in the square in Kenmare.

M: And how did local audiences respond?

D: I did a piece called the *Nemeton At the End of the Sea* because there's this sacred stone circle outside of the town and Kenmare is *Ceann Meara* translated it means 'end of the sea'. Nemeton is a Celtic word for sacred space.

I did the performance at 11 at night in the square in darkness. I had built a large stone circle with a mound with a tree in the middle of it. I was coming down this laneway with a lighted torch and I was trying to set fire to the tree. Even though I had soaked the tree in petrol earlier the branches weren't lighting. Obviously it had seeped down into the roots. So these young fellas there were saying 'give it to me, I'll light it for ya!' And at that stage when you're doing a performance you know you that have to either involve them in some way or they'll ruin everything for you. So I handed one of them the torch and he couldn't light it. So he passed it to his next mate and he couldn't light it either. So then I took it off him and I just touched the tree at the bottom and the whole thing flared up. They were on my side then! I was walking around, using smoked mackerel and this other fella in the audience was half-pissed and he was shouting 'give us a bit of fish and chips' so I walked over to him with the fish in my hand, a full fish, and took a bit off, it being smoked mackerel it came away no problem and I handed it to him. He completely shut up and then disappeared. Now again there's no documentation of it, we couldn't photograph it at that hour of night, not with the cameras that I had anyway. When I finished my thing, the crowd went up the Park Hotel where the Pogues were playing. We were all staying at a castle just outside of Kenmare. The singer Dolores Keane was there, Jimmy Mc Carthy, the Pogues were all there, it really was the cream of Irish music there at the time all under one roof… it was interesting I think, performance going on in small places. I also organised some in Midleton where I lived as well.

M: So you'd get crossovers with other types of performance?

D: Yes, you didn't have an art audience as well, where as if you did it in Dublin and Cork you had aficionados going to it. Then in 1988 I got to curate a show in The Project. I really wanted Irish artists and Irish performance internationally exposed, so I invited Steve Durland back to do a piece in the show, knowing that he would then write about it as well.

Jenny Haughton was the head administrator of SSI (Sculpture Society of Ireland) at the time and she understood the need for political strategising. André ended up on the cover with his piece!

It was interestingly one of the first times red tape started creeping into performance with insurance and all this kind of thing. I remember I was in charge, and I had asked Alastair if he would do a performance. He wanted to work in the building beside The Project which was kind of derelict, with steel beams and that kind of thing, but The Project didn't want him in there because he wasn't insured. He was willing to sign the liability disclaimer but they wouldn't allow him. Eventually Jenny had to go get public liability insurance to allow him to work in there. You know, it was my first encounter of this kind of bureaucracy. Steve Durland also did a performance where he asked us to order a meal for two to be brought to the gallery that night. He set up the table for two and as he sat down to eat the meal as the audience came in. Everyone got a number, a number was then pulled out of a hat and that person was invited to join him in the meal. The performance consisted of us watching the two of them having a meal and listening to their conversation. It was a very simple piece and there's so much of this kind of school of work now in contemporary art…

Again at that time you didn't have the money to put people up in a B&B so you'd put them up in your house and we became really good friends and were in touch for years. It was interesting how people were coming in and out that way. You were acting as a host as well as a curator. For example Richard Martel, the performance artist from Québec. His knowledge of performance art is so huge, he has the best library of performance art I've ever seen. He actually did a big publication on performance art *Art Action 1958-1998* in which there's a whole section on Ireland as well.[8] Again, I think it was through Alastair that he got in touch with us to do a performance in Triskel. And like André Stitt, he appreciated what was going on in Cork. He knew there was a commitment and a dedication to the work, because he was doing the same in Québec.

M: It seems like for so long, people were working to develop performance and keep it live by continually sharing it and getting others involved. It's so interesting that Cork, Belfast, Québec, and Italy were connected centres of performance that were geographically spread so far and wide, but really you were working together. You can see through the years, because you've been involved in the Cork Artists Collective[9] as well with Mick O'Shea and Irene Murphy and the Guest House[10] and the National Sculpture Factory[11] as a board member, that through the years, you've gotten a huge amount of other people involved in performance, that's part of your work.

D: Well, that was part of it. I suppose I was kind of good at organising things and I'd get people involved in the organising. I wouldn't be doing it for my own sake as such. It was to give people the opportunities to do the work and try it and experiment with it. I think for me that was quite vital to provide those opportunities for people as it was not being encouraged or fostered in art colleges at the time.

M: It might be good to mention the names of some of those events. I know there was *Electric Rain,* were you involved in that?[12]

D: No, *Electric Rain* was organised by Irene Murphy an amazing performance artist and some others.[13] But I was on the board of Triskel, the National Sculpture Factory and *Art Trail*[14] and involved in *Sound Works,*[15] so I would've been pushing for performance through that.

M: So you developed a very strong peer network, you can see how the Guest House would've evolved from that kind of ethos of hosting.

D: Well, yes, Mick O'Shea and Irene both really built up the Guest House. My involvement has been performing there rather than any official capacity and recommending people to come.

M: I think the Guest House is a really nice ethos for a space. You can see how younger artists have all moved through it. It's given them a starting point to produce live work as well. I know the Guest House was established during Cork European Capital of Culture in 2005. What was the scene like in Cork for performance and sound before that? What was the impact of it?

D: The scene for sound art was very strong before Capital of Culture. It was from the mid 1980s on that sound started to have its own independent voice. And then in the 1990s *INTERMEDIA Festival* kind of took over.[16] *INTERMEDIA* came about because we were doing lots

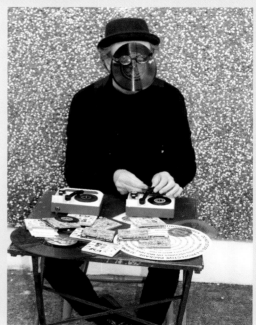

of different events with video, performance, sound, sound poetry, and performance art over the year, but we (Tony Sheehan and myself) decided we would focus it into an intense period so all the work would get focused on by the audience and the press. *INTERMEDIA* as an event was hugely important and ran for around ten or twelve years. It had artists coming from all over the country and Europe and beyond as well. It had an invited section and an open submission. The open submission was selected by an outside panel, whereas I tended to select the international artists helped by Triskel's amazing curators like Fiona Kearney, Valerie Byrne, Declan Rooney, and Garry Sheehan. Looking back over the old catalogues it's amazing the quality and amount of artists we presented. I recall the last *INTERMEDIA* we had a performance by Aoife Desmond which was so full we had to turn people away and Aoife repeated it two hours later.

M: Cork has got two music schools. That in itself creates a certain context for sound art doesn't it?

D: They're both very different but very open. We've played in Cork Institute of Technology's School of Music quite a few times now, and University College Cork's Department of Music is more experimental with a focus on modern contemporary music. I lecture in a module there called *Sounds Like Listening,* which consists of an introduction to sound art, improvisation, and my practice of listening. It shows how good and progressive the college is in that this module started about ten years ago.

M: Can you tell me about the start of sound art in Cork?

D: After a *Sound Works* concert one night this guy, Sean ó hUigin, who was from Canada, asked me for my telephone number. He called me three or four days later and he wound up having a huge influence on Cork. He had been very involved in the whole sound poetry scene in Canada and London and had appeared in a lot of the international concrete poetry festivals, this guy was pretty world-round famous. He's still in Cork, he had changed his name to the Irish version of it, Sean ó hUigin. But every time I met him he'd have a new book or magazine or cassette for me. He was bringing all sorts of tapes of contemporary Canadian, American, and English sound art. He gave me an enormous archive of cassettes and books. He's in a nursing home now, but I gave a big bunch of it to the Guest House so it's available for research and study. Sean's material and work was a huge influence to us. That helped found the knowledge of the sound scene as well. One must remember there was no internet then.

M: At the time you just didn't have the same circulation of that work…

D: No, not all. Sean was subscribing to a magazine called *Music Works.* And one of the editors there was a friend of his and he used to have people visiting him here like Paul Dutton, who was one of the leading sound poets in the world. So artists would come visiting Sean and we would put them on in Triskel…

M: So again, it's all very much these personal connections that were feeding the scene in Cork at that time.

D: It was kind of the only way that things could happen at that stage.

M: Well the visibility of this kind of scene… well really the scene was invisible.

D: At that stage it was totally invisible, and record shops just wouldn't have that kind of stuff. Anyway I got involved in *Art Trail* and I started doing events for them. Colette Nolan also did some sound art for *Art Trail* and gradually it just began to increase. *Art Trail* produced two of the *Sound Works* events and Julie Forrester and myself edited and published a book plus CD *For Those Who Have Ears.* So sound art was growing quite strongly. I approached Capital of Culture with the idea of working with David Toop on a project called *Sound Out* to bring in international artists to make outdoor work in Cork city. *Sound Out* came about through a project that the National Sculpture Factory had run called *Daylighting in the City,* which got four artists from Cork and four artists from Belfast to respond to the so-called dockland development. It had some performers in it such as Cindy Cummings, a dancer, who did a performance at it.

I had come up with a sound-installation for it by accident almost. I was walking down to the Sculpture Factory and while I was passing the quays there were fishing boats coming in for the evening because the forecast was bad. Their engines were running together, so there was this incredible hum and it was quite beautiful. In the Sculpture Factory, Mary McCarthy [Director] showed us the plans for the docklands development, and I spotted that they wanted to put a walkway where the two channels of the rivers meet and that it would stop the boats coming up. I realised then that sound was going to disappear from that area, so that immediately gave me my idea for what I wanted to do. I went back the following day and recorded the sound of the boats. I did that all along the quay right up into the City Hall. I made a compositional piece with the sound of the boats called *(Re)Locating the Sound Scape* because that sound was going to disappear from the place. I installed the whole thing with the old Tannoy speakers that would usually be used for the *Corpus Christi* processions and that kind of thing, so they were already a natural part of the landscape rather than imposing speakers in the landscape. The piece took over two city quays. It's still the largest electronic based outdoor sound installation that has been done in Ireland.

M: I read something you mentioned on your work, and I thought the idea of an acoustic ecology is lovely. The idea that sounds in our environment are being removed and lost all the time.

D: Exactly. I have another piece that's similar but it's a permanent piece in the Crawford Gallery, the foghorn piece called *Found Sound (Lost At Sea) 11.1.11*. It reminds people that the sound of the foghorn disappeared from the Irish coast on 11 January 2011.

M: It's an interesting thing to think about; listening in space all the time. Those sensory things that perhaps you don't pay attention to all the time.

D: Three or four weeks after the *(Re)Locating The Soundscape* piece I met someone and she said to me 'I pass Lavitts Quay everyday and I still listen out for your piece; you made me listen to the city for the first time.' And that kind of struck me, it was a really good compliment for me to get for my work. That then sparked the idea for me to do the *Sound Out* exhibition. I am very friendly with David Toop and David has a big international name so I applied to the Capital of Culture people and they gave us the money to do it. We said if we wanted to do this properly we'd take just four artists so that they could totally engage with the city. Max Eastley built a kind of a sound sculpture, an Aeolian harp operated by wind located on a pillar going into University College Cork. Christina Kubisch installed a piece called *The Battle of the Birds* on a tree on North Main Street that was operated by solar power. Scanner (Robin Rimbaud) did a piece using street names of Cork that he later did in Beijing (with Chinese street names) questioning 'why is this place called Patrick Street? Why is this place called Oliver Plunkett Street?' so he got

'So the exhibition consists of you going to a central point and you get a map and the map then would have these little points marked and you'd walk around and you'd stand there and listen. A simple, wonderful idea.'

Cork voices to read them in both Irish and English. That really engaged people. Akio Suzuki, a Japanese artist, did a work called *Oto Date* where he walks around the city and finds interesting places to stand and listen, and when he finds that place, he stencils a set of ears on the ground. So the exhibition consists of you going to a central point and you get a map and the map then would have these little points marked and you'd walk around and you'd stand there and listen. A simple, wonderful idea. So we did a catalogue of that and a CD of it as well, that was big. It was the first major sound art exhibition in Ireland.

M: I'm interested in the idea of sound installation, and that transition then into sound performance – the two developing side by side.

D: Yes they did, it's interesting as well that sound performance is almost like improvised music and that kind of crossover. Mick O'Shea and myself founded *The Quiet Club* in 2006 and we make sound performances in collaboration with up to 15 or 20 people and it varies. *The Quiet Club* has been really, really good for us, we've done stuff all over the world with it, China, USA, and everywhere with it.

M: How do you see the performance and sound art scene after the City of Culture up to now? Now we're in another recession crisis, but more and more young artists are getting involved in sound and performance all the time; a whole new generation?

D: Yes, well I curated a CD for *Art Trail* called *Rediscovering Locality (A Sonology of Cork Sound Art)* and there are 18 different acts on it. Kevin Tuohy, Vicky Langan, Harry Moore, Paul Hegarty, John Godfrey, Karen Power, Dan Guiney, Tony Languois, the list goes on… It's quite phenomenal. I remember one of my students at the time saying it's kind of a 'golden age of sound art'. And it was really. I mean you'd be turning people away from performances or there would be standing room only.

Then there's the *Bend it like Beckett*, which was another Art Trail CD I curated. There's a hundred pieces on that CD with loads of international artists involved as well as Irish.

M: And how important do you think is the live element of it now? The performance scene in Cork seems to have transitioned into a live sound scene now.

D: Well both are happening because it kind of grew. Mick and myself approached Crawford Art Gallery about three years ago and we asked them if we could run something on a Saturday afternoon. They said fine. So we set up inside the sculpture gallery and we were playing along with Anthony Kelly and David Stalling. Irene Murphy did the photography. We did some posters and advertisements and we doubled the footfall in the Crawford on a Saturday afternoon. Instead of having 200 they had 400. We did a four-hour performance and people could come and go. Afterwards the Crawford came back and said to us 'would you be interested in doing some more?' We brought out a CD and a booklet on it. So then we came up with the idea of doing a collaborative project Strange Attractor. We said we'd do a month's residency in the Crawford's contemporary galleries but we wanted to do a kind of build up towards it. So for nine months we brought a different artist in every month to play with us and we worked our way through the whole building. We had Mary Noonan [a dancer], David Toop, Stephen Vitiello, Steve Roden, the crème de la crème of sound artists like Rhodri Davies, Lee Patterson, and Jed Spear. We played with these artists for four-hour performances, over the period of nine months. We were getting good crowds for all these things. We also did some installation-based work and used it as a residency and workspace as well. At this stage we had Irene Murphy working with us as well. She set up the space in the middle like a sitting room or a resource area. We had books, a record playing area, we could make a cup of tea. We started meeting there at lunchtime to perform together, and an audience started to grow. We wound up then inviting all the younger generation locals, to come and play with us for the hour at lunchtime. So they were coming in every day, and people were eating their lunch in there and having their coffee. The Crawford were delighted with it. Anthony and David would come in at the weekend and we'd have a Saturday evening concert. So it grew wonderfully and organically. Luckily then as well when Jed Spear from Boston came over and the idea of bringing it to America emerged. So the idea was that we'd go to Boston for two weeks as a residency at Mobius,[17] and he'd get local artists to come in and play with us. Then we called Stephen Vitiello and we said to him, 'we're coming to Boston, could you get us a gig in New York?' He wound up getting us a gig in New York in this place called Harvestworks, which is historically huge. It's on Broadway. They've presented work by John Cage and the crème de la crème. But he got us in there. It was like going to England to play the Royal Albert Hall! We were treated like royalty really.

M: Is Anthony still running *Aphasia Recordings*?[18]

D: It's called *Far Point Recordings*[19] now but it's the same people involved.

M: In the current context of shrinking resources, how important are spaces like the Guest House, and the Cork Film Centre for people working in sound in performance in Cork?

D: The Cork Film Centre was of huge importance to people working in video and film. We did a sound work there not too long ago. That it's gone due to loss of funding is a huge loss. The Guest House will keep going anyway despite funding cuts. And the National Sculpture Factory is going fine. We do an annual NSF event called *Sonic Vigil* at St. Anne's Church in Shandon and it works very well there. This year – 2014 – we're making it a three-day event rather than a one-day event. There will be a series of talks, workshops, and concerts. One will be by CAVE (Cork Audio Visual Ensemble). We're going to have a special Sonic Vigil broadcast on the Irish radio station, Lyric FM, with presenter Bernard Clarke. So far we have released a four CD box-set, a blue vinyl LP, and a USB key in the shape of a cassette; it's a really lovely design. This year we launch a DVD by filmmaker Max Le Cain of last year's event. So that kind of attitude is still here in Cork. We'll do it without money and it's important that the works are recorded.

M: There's another generation that want to keep doing it too.

D: And it's not just an art world thing, it's students of music as well coming together. I've been working with people like John Godfrey and Karen Grant from the School of Music, and he would also encourage students there. John and the Quiet Music Ensemble will be doing a piece of mine in concert in UCC called *Listen, Listen Again, Listen Better* which consists of five enamel bowls and 50 stones, and the musicians go up and pick whatever stones they want and put them in the enamel bowl. Then they put a magnifying glass over the top of the bowl, which magnifies it and that is their score. They played it at the Hilltown New Music

Festival, which surprised me and it sounded wonderful. They were superb improvising musicians and they improvised from the score I made.

M: In terms of the legacy of sound in Cork, what do you think the future holds? How do you see it progressing?

D: I think it has attained a big international reputation, which is great and it means people of an international status want to come to Cork to perform. They know about what's happening in Cork, it's spoken about internationally. Mick O'Shea and myself are working on an opera at the moment with a contemporary composer called Ian Wilson. He has Arts Council [of Ireland] funding for it. He has a singer, Elaine Mitchener, who comes from London for rehearsals, and when she came over she already knew all about us because she'd been working with David Toop and different London and European musicians. The sound world is a small world. Those that are at it a long time tend to know each other and they gain a reputation then at being caring and honest and good at what you do, and that spreads around.

M: And the audience is there in Cork as well: the audience has grown with the scene so that when you perform there is a really active appreciation.

D: Exactly, we have cultivated a listening audience. We performed three weeks ago in the Guest House with this Norwegian guy Tore H. Boe with an acoustic laptop and it was packed out. It was standing room only. People were pushing in the door! He was amazed that the audience was so good at listening.

M: Thinking of the early days working in small spaces with small resources, how important do you think is it to push performance and sound into the mainstream and into spaces like the Crawford Art Gallery and onto Lyric FM?

D: I think it's important in lots of ways in that it's taken that bit more seriously. People will pay money for it, and it's encouraging then for young people coming up as well because we always try to involve younger people.

M: In the last year or so there seems to be a new wave of focus on performance now in the visual art world. Even though performance has always been there, there seems to be a renewed focus. There are multiple symposia, multiple books, exhibitions, and essays. It seems the time has come now finally for performance, and you wonder does something shift then?

D: When you're at it as long as I am, you'll have seen a few of those! [*Laughing*].

I remember Alastair saying that one time, 'it goes in cycles'. The interest and the acknowledgement of it is cyclical. What I find interesting is people still regard it as a radical art form, it's one of those things that hasn't been embraced by the mainstream. I remember André telling me two or three years ago, last time we met, that he was at something and he got talking to a student who didn't know who he was, and she was telling him all about performance art and how radical and out there it was, and he was there lapping it up.

M: Well why do you think that is? I was reading something recently – it's not directly related – but it was to do with documentation and how we're now living in a society completely obsessed with documenting everything, and everything has to have a materiality to it. This includes the huge repository of the archive and yet performance, theatre and dance are in this kind of moment where the liveness of what they do means that the materiality is always vanishing, it's always just out of reach. So one of the things that people working in the field are constantly examining is how this kind of practice gets preserved so that it can studied and so on. But in a sense there's this practice (that in this culture of obsession with materiality) that's completely and always vanishing. It's always gone, it's just moved out of reach. I wonder if this is one of the reasons why we still consider performance to be this kind of radical art form?

D: Yeah, and if you talk to Alastair as well, there's almost two levels of performance art. There's the accepted institutional museum type of RoseLee Goldberg and Marina Abramović, and then there's the world where you're somehow black-market, that other world is the real world of performance art. It is the undercurrent world that has been there all the time. But it has gone through cycles; when Laurie Anderson had the hit *O Superman* we all thought we were going to be made! Also there was a huge interest from the punk movement in the whole Live Art aspect. I remember doing performances with Microdisney, and Five Go Down To The Sea in Cork. They'd have a whole punk night going on and they wanted performance artists in there doing Live Art as well. I remember Dave Clifford had a magazine called *Vox* in 1980, which was a hardcore punk scene publication which covered experimental music and performance art as well. So there were all those kind of crossover events happening in Cork and elsewhere.

M: Maybe there's a kind of social relevance that comes in cycles as well…

Listening to the recording of our conversation, I become aware of the sounds that I wasn't listening to at the time. Sounds were leaking into the room and onto the recording device that I had somehow edited out in the moment. I was so tuned to listening to Danny's voice and following the content of our conversation. Leaking in was the sound of gulls. Could that be right? They were so loud and so constant, I almost can't believe I didn't hear them at the time. What else did I edit out in the moment? What else did I subconsciously, selectively miss? The occasional sound of conversation mixed with laughter from other rooms. At one point a siren, synonymous with city centre space. How strange though, those gulls, so loud and ever present. They become most obvious in the gaps, in the pauses of our conversation. I quickly recall those moments where a flash of understanding happens and so much is said through expression and gesture that the need for words is rendered unnecessary. The device could not record these moments, so I am left with a quandary; I must also edit in some words in order to make sense through the written form. This process of editing, selecting, and omitting seems relevant to reveal somehow. To draw a relationship between this process and the act of recollection and remembering. This is just a trace of a conversation about memory, elements have been excluded, and added. But it captures, through this limited form, the essence and trajectory of that conversation, held in the offices of the National Visual Arts Library, Dublin, on 18 February 2014.

1. The Artist-led Archive is an archive of Irish artist-led organisations from the seventies to the present, curated by Megs Morley in 2006. The ALA is currently housed as part of the special collections of the National Library of Visual Art (NIVAL) Dublin. <www.theartistledarchive.com>.

2. Triskel Arts Centre is Cork's principal Arts Centre and was founded in 1978: <www.triskelartscentre.ie>.

3. *Performance* magazine was a UK based interdisciplinary journal and the key UK Live Art/performance magazine from the late 1970s to the early 1990s. <http://www.bris.ac.uk/theatrecollection/liveart/liveart_PMAG.html>.

4. The Eighth Amendment of the Constitution of Ireland introduced a constitutional ban on abortion by referendum in 1983.

5. Since its foundation in 1977, EVA International in Limerick has worked with some of the world's leading artists and curators. Formally an annual exhibition, since 2012 EVA International has become Ireland's Biennial of Contemporary Art. <www.eva.ie>.

6. Cork 800 was the anniversary celebration of 800 years of Cork's status as a chartered city in 1985.

7. Keening comes from the Irish/Gaelic term 'caoineadh' (to cry, to weep) and is a form of vocal lament associated with mourning that is traditional in Ireland.

8. Richard Martell, *Art Action 1958-1998* (Québec, Intervention Editions, 2001) is a compendium of 30 original papers presented during an international colloquium of artists and theorists on the development of performance art on the world scene.

9. The Cork Artists Collective is an independent non-profit artist-led organisation founded in 1985 managing two city central visual arts workspaces. <www.thecollective.ie>.

10. The Guesthouse is an artist-led initiative whose objective is to create a place for production, meeting, and cross-practice peer exchange, through a range of public events, activities and residencies, hosted in the context of a residential setting. <www.theguesthouse.ie>.

11. The National Sculpture Factory (NSF) is an organisation that provides and promotes a supportive and enabling environment for the making of art and the realisation of creative projects. <www.nationalsculpturefactory.com>.

12. *Electric Rain* was a Live Art, Music and Multimedia Event, based in Cork, Ireland; culminating in seven live-events, from 2003 to 2004.

13. Colette Lewis, Mick O'Shea, Aoife McGovern, Tom Tracey, Robby Collins, Monkey Studio and Eleanor Rivers.

14. Arts Trail was an artist led organisation founded in 1995 in Cork with an annual programme of exhibitions, talks, publications, and workshops.

15. *Sound Works* is the name given to the early sound events in Triskel and also to two festivals organised by Art Trail 2004-05.

16. INTERMEDIA was a festival organised in Triskel and elsewhere around the city in 1998.

17. Mobius (est. 1977), Boston USA is a non-profit, artist-run organisation, whose mission is to generate, shape, and test experimental art. <http://www.mobius.org>.

18. Asphasia Recordings was an artist run record label set up in 2005 with the aim of documenting, archiving, and releasing sound art recordings and related visual work.

19. *Farpoint Recordings* <www.farpointrecordings.com>.

POLYPHONIC RESONANCE:
Sound Art in Ireland

In August 2012, the sound art collective Strange Attractor presented a series of events in Boston, MA at Studio Soto and in New York City at Harvestworks.[1] The group, whose core members consist of Danny McCarthy, Mick O'Shea, Irene Murphy, Anthony Kelly, and David Stalling, began performing together in November 2010. Their debut took place at the Crawford Art Gallery in Cork. There, over the course of several months, they presented a series of live, improvisational events with a number of international guest artists, including David Toop and Mary Nunan, Stephen Vitiello, Alessandro Bosetti, Rhordi Davies, Steve Roden, Lee Patterson, and Jed Speare. It is during the Boston events that I first became introduced to Strange Attractor, and subsequently welcomed into a rich world of Irish sound art.

Opposite top: Vicky Langan, *In Order of Five Years*, 2012. Photo: Simone Della Fornace.
Opposite bottom: EL Putnam, *Livestock*, Market Studios, 2013. Photo: Lorcan Lawlor.

During a Strange Attractor event, a wordless discourse composed of sounds and images is cultivated and grows. The actions of one artist interact with those of others in this process of collaboration, or – more accurately – co-creation. There is a method to Strange Attractor's apparent improvisational madness. Just a few notes, some subtle sounds, and the winding down of conversations demarcate a start. Over time, other artists join in, contributing to a growing sonic landscape. At certain moments, Danny McCarthy slips silently away from his sound station to partake in performance actions, such as wrapping his head in the tape of audiocassettes and then sitting meditatively for a period of time.

Other times, Anthony Kelly moves quietly around the room, distributing small objects at others' stations, which can be appropriated or left at rest as static remnants of his contribution. Whenever a participant slips in or out of a performance, it's always an understated act, though the ambiance shifts depending on who is present and absent – actions that are reminiscent of the musician who slips off a traditional music session at the pub to grab a pint. David Stalling's sonic pulsations contribute a rhythmic undertone that is both comforting and grounding. Mick O'Shea and McCarthy's collected sound loops, both vocal and non-vocal, create feedback that introduces concrete moments into an abstract field of improvisation. The sounds that Kelly produces using found objects make the familiar foreign, as the crumpling of paper becomes an avalanche and marbles transform into sinking ships. In the midst of this apparent chaos, Irene Murphy distills actions into geometric forms that crystallise and grow, providing a sense of visual order to an otherwise cacophonous scene. These forms are reminiscent of O'Shea's molecular models, which increasingly creep into the space over the various performances. Of course, these descriptions are just slivers of the range of actions and sounds that each artist contributes. The combination of the visual and the aural fluctuate – sweeping waves that at times contradict, and at other moments coalesce into a beautiful sensation that subsides as fleetingly as it arrives. The performance ends as subtly as it begins – winding down into a slow crescendo of stillness as each artist waits patiently for the sounds to clear from the air.

The organic complexity of Strange Attractor means there is rarely a lull. Unlike other artists who have built their reputations on endurance by testing the limits of the human body, such as Marina Abramović and Chris Burden, Strange Attractor creates an opportunity to practice

'David Stalling's sonic pulsations contribute a rhythmic undertone that is both comforting and grounding. Mick O'Shea and McCarthy's collected sound loops, both vocal and non-vocal, create feedback that introduces concrete moments into an abstract field of improvisation.'

restraint; to listen and respond as opposed to dominating or promoting discomfort. Moments of contemplation welcome productive contributions, building an ephemeral architecture that provides a moment of respite; an invitation to be present and come together with others. Moving about the space and experiencing the performance from different angles allows for a range of perspectives and observations to collect and intermingle, like the sounds and energies being projected about the room.

Whenever I leave a Strange Attractor performance, I find myself more attuned to the sounds around me. Every step becomes a moment of meditation and an opportunity to create and respond. The durational endurance of each performance in conjunction with its ability to reiterate over a period of days allow Strange Attractor to unfold, creating layers of traces that wax and wane, are written over, erased, or left to stand as remnants of something that has been.

These artists employ distinctive approaches to their use of sound, which meld effectively into a polyphonic, visual, and aural experience for participants and the audience. In music, polyphony refers to when multiple melodies are played simultaneously. Russian philosopher Mikhail Bahktin highlights the significance of polyphony in his study of Fyodor Dostoevsky. He emphasises the importance of a subject-to-subject relation that is 'a plurality of independent and unmerged voices and consciousnesses, a genuine polyphony of fully valid voices'.[2] The resulting dialogic is a whole consisting of the interaction of several consciousnesses that are not merged, but maintain autonomy. At the same time, this whole is not a finished or unified entity, but it is a relationship of consciousness to consciousness. For Bakhtin, 'the essence of polyphony lies precisely in the fact that the voices remain independent and, as such, are combined in a higher order than in homophony.'[3] In music, homophony occurs when different parts of a score move in tandem, creating harmony. Polyphony,

> 'The ebbs and flows of Strange Attractor's aesthetic field provide a glimpse into the current Irish sound art scene while also providing a "keyhole" into how sound art has emerged and developed in Ireland.'

in contrast, embraces the independence of different sounds. As a result, in polyphony, meaning does emerge not from a single consciousness, but through the interaction of multiple voices. Bakhtin's description of the polyphonic provides insight to what occurs during a Strange Attractor event. The collective's title refers to a mathematical phrase, which according to the *Oxford English Dictionary*, is 'an attractor that is a fractal set, representing a situation in which the ultimate behaviour of a dynamic system is chaotic.' This chaos emerges from the polyphonic nature of Strange Attractor's artistic methods, though it is not an unpleasant experience. Instead, since the structures are so complex, it is possible for an audience member to drift in and out of the work, allowing for greater freedom and flexibility on behalf of the listener, who can focus on different aspects of a particular performance and still appreciate the work as a whole.

The ebbs and flows of Strange Attractor's aesthetic field provide a glimpse into the current Irish sound art scene while also providing a 'keyhole' into how sound art has emerged and developed in Ireland. Sonic pioneers from Ireland and abroad, including Danny McCarthy, interact with emerging talents, offering a collaborative opportunity that is rich in historical precedence and innovative experimentation. By not limiting the role of guest artists to the sonically inclined, Strange Attractor offers a multi-disciplinary, performance-based approach to the creation of aesthetic experiences, which in turn offers a microcosmic sampling of sound art in Ireland.

In general, greater attention is now being paid to the sonic qualities of art making. Douglas Kahn notes that the arts have never been mute, but it is only in the past few decades that sound has received critical attention in aesthetic discourse distinctive from music.[4] This transnational trend has gained a foothold in Ireland, where a number of world renowned sound artists have pioneered and popularised sonic practices, including Seán Ó hUigín, Fergus Kelly, and Tony Sheehan. Defining sound art is not clear cut or concise, as it draws inspiration from various kinds of artistic practice, blurring the boundaries between traditional genres and often being presented in a range of forms. Sound art takes the form of live music-like performances, gallery installations, conceptual allusions to noise or silence, auditory compliments to geographical tours, or pre-recorded albums. Its practitioners range from traditionally trained composers and performers to visual artists interested in expanding the sensory experience of art. Sound art is about the production of sounds as much as it is about the practice of listening and conceptual understanding. Sound art tends to resist traditional categorisation within music, the visual, and performing arts, though practitioners borrow heavily from other means of art making while emphasising a sonic experience. The notion of 'sound' in art refers to a range of concepts and ideas. It can designate prerecorded noises, musically produced tones, vocal inflections, or the act of listening. It can also refer to non-auditory events, or what Seth Kim-Cohen refers to as 'non-cochlear' sonic art – conceptual works that are about or allude to sound and listening, but do not necessarily consist of the production of actual noises.[5] In fact, what has come to be designated as 'sound art' has become so diverse that at times it seems the term is being used to loosely identify any work with a sonic component.

Numerous aesthetic scholars and art historians credit US composer John Cage with liberating sound and noise from the confines of traditional musical composition.[6] However, his work does not mark the beginning of sound's distinctive use as a medium. Working in the early twentieth century, Marcel Duchamp, Hugo Ball, the Dadaists, and Italian Futurist Luigi Russolo are also acknowledged for their sonic experimentations. The introduction of recording technology in the twentieth century along with electronic instruments, including the theremin and synthesisers, has opened up a whole new range of possibilities for sounds that could be produced and utilised by artists. In the 1970s, with the proliferation of consumer recording equipment, artists could more effectively capture and manipulate sounds, designating a growing popularity in the use of sound as medium. This coincides with increased access to video equipment, allowing for sound and moving image to gain a foothold in fine art gallery spaces. Additionally, the growing popularity of performance art, including the work of Fluxus, provided more opportunities for sound to enter artistic institutions. However, only in later years has sound come to be treated as a medium in its own right. 'Sound art' became considered a discrete type of artistic production during the 1980s.[7]

Above: Suzanne Walsh at Live@8, The Exchange, Dublin, 2011. Photo: Áine Phillips.

Right top: Dublin Lap Top Orchestra, Livestock, Market Studios, 2012. Photo: Lorcan Lawlor.

Right middle: Fergus Kelly performing at the Joinery in Dublin, 2013. Photo: EL Putnam.

Right bottom: Mick O'Shea, Strange Attractor at Studio Soto, Boston, 2012.
Photo courtesy of the artist.

Above: Danny McCarthy, *Tape Head (Erase)*, Studio Soto, Boston, 2012. Photo courtesy of the artist.

Left top: Softday perform John Cage's *4'33*, Limerick, 2012. Photo courtesy of the artists.

Left middle: Sean Taylor and Mikael Fernstorm, *Softday*, 2012. Photo courtesy of the artists.

Left bottom: Irene Murphy, Strange Attractor at Studio Soto, Boston, 2012. Photo courtesy of the artist.

Any attempt to present a concrete definition of what constitutes sound art must participate in a much larger debate that is beyond the scope of this analysis. For the purpose of this survey, the phrase 'sound art' is used to describe an artist's practice and works of art that utilise sound as medium or where sound functions as the primary component of a work. This broad description means that works may fall under other categories or genres, such as performance art, installation, and conceptual art. Also, some practices border on experimental music. However, the scope of this analysis is not so broad that every work with a sonic element can be considered sound art; rather, the works described in this survey are primarily sonic. The use of these specifications is intentionally related to how sound art has developed in Ireland.

Sound art emerged in Ireland concurrently with its growing popularity in other parts of the world. Just as Strange Attractor encapsulates a polyphonic event, sound art in Ireland incorporates a range of styles and techniques that do not always coalesce, but emerge as a conglomeration of many voices. Despite the distinctiveness of artists' methods, it is not uncommon for festivals and events to offer a range of sonic styles and techniques for the audience to engage with. While the artists' processes do not fall into specific categories, works tend to encompass a variety of trends that have become common in the Irish scene. Additionally, artists will not limit themselves to a particular technique, and it is quite common to see a single artist utilise a range of styles over her career. For example, Danny McCarthy can be considered one of the more prolific artists and organisers working with sound in Ireland. He has played a major role in introducing Ireland to a transnational network of the sonic arts through his personal artistic practice, collaborative endeavours, event organisation, invitation of foreign artists to Ireland, international travels, and collection and distribution of materials – such as sound art magazines and recordings – from around the world. McCarthy's work spans live performance and improvisation, sound mapping, conceptual projects, as well as the creation of indoor and outdoor sound installations.

Generally, sound art in Ireland can be divided into two major trends: sound performances, and artworks with a strong sonic component. The former can be sub-divided into an innumerable list of methods and techniques, but performances tend to incorporate composition and improvisation. Performances may be presented live or as recorded works. The latter trend is also quite broad, as artists create installations, map sonic geographies, and craft conceptual projects. This list is not meant

> '...artists find many ways to experiment with the sonic properties of objects. As long as something can make a sound, it may at some point be incorporated into a sound art performance.'

to be conclusive, but just provides a starting point for understanding the various kinds of sonic art production taking place in Ireland.

During sound performances, artists incorporate various tools, methods, and instruments for the production of sounds. From everyday objects fitted with contact microphones to synthesisers and invented instruments to looped field recordings and vocalisations, artists find many ways to experiment with the sonic properties of objects. As long as something can make a sound, it may at some point be incorporated into a sound art performance. This method of making sound art most closely resembles experimental music, and at times may be referred to as such, even though numerous practitioners come from a visual arts background as opposed to being musically trained. Some current artists in Ireland making sound art in this manner include: David Lacey, Harry Moore, Robin Parmar, Slavek Kwi, and *Softday* (Sean Taylor and Mikael Fernström).

One artist recognised nationally and internationally for his work is Fergus Kelly. Kelly's current sound practice centres on field recording, which he has been using since 1986 when he acquired his first personal recording device, a Walkman. He produces both live and recorded works, and in addition to field recordings, he utilises electronics, invented instruments, and processing techniques in order to compose soundscapes. According to Kelly, 'the work is about creating a space in which to connect with the sonic environment in a considered an meaningful way. [...] My work encourages focused listening and more active and engaged relationship with the sonic environment.'[8]

When performing live, Kelly emits an air of experimental precision in his process. His improvisational set up includes a mixing board, electroacoustic instruments, and a series of tools that range from handheld fans and milk foamers to traditional musical implements like cymbals and mallets. Despite the range of offerings on view, he tends to utilise only a few of these objects. This restraint makes Kelly come

'One time we played together, and I was doing a vocal thing, I was screaming so raw and intense and at the time I felt I was possibly overstepping the mark.'

across as an artist carefully in tune with the performance as it unfolds – instead of getting lost in an experimental jam, he maintains a sense of confidence in his compositional choices, while still leaving room for experimental play and volatility depending on the tools he chooses. This interplay between precision and play with the unknown is a distinctive characteristic of Kelly's work that can also be heard on his recorded pieces, such as *Congregation of Vapours* (2011), where electronic sounds and field recordings are integrated through a complex and lengthy editing process.

As noted previously, artists working with instrumentation and improvisation incorporate different styles and techniques. Paul Vogel utilises traditional musical instruments, like the clarinet, along with electronic sound samples on a laptop. Robin Parmar creates improvised and composed works incorporating field recordings. Paul Hegarty has earned recognition for his work with noise. Alluding to this eclectic blend of styles in his analysis of the sound art scene in Cork, Daniel Spicer (2011) quotes Vicky Langan, a 'punk/weirdo' improviser, who contrasts her work from Danny McCarthy and Mick O'Shea as containing a 'wildness' that the latter's process lacks. She states: 'One time we played together, and I was doing a vocal thing, I was screaming so raw and intense and at the time I felt I was possibly overstepping the mark.'[9] What is notable about this incident is not the observation of dissonance on behalf of Langan. It reveals a great trend found in sound art in Ireland – it is not uncommon to come across artists producing distinctively different sounds collaborating or presenting at the same event.

Other sound artists forgo exclusive reliance on mechanical and electronic instruments, and instead incorporate sounds produced by the human body, particularly the voice. Alanna O'Kelly's use of vocalisation is quite powerful, with her sound pieces incorporating chanting, calling, and keening (a traditional Irish wordless song of lament). Her sounds are intense, emerging from the depths of her body and tapping into a primal energy of the voice. During the 1980s, O'Kelly presented a series of experimental vocal works, including *Chant Down Greenham* (1985-86), which blend repetitive chants and sound of protests with wordless vocal expression. The vocalisation techniques are heavily influenced by the sounds of mourning. In an interview with Katy Deepwell, O'Kelly states:

> I saw women keening at Greenham, expressing grief in a way that is beyond crying. […] I knew I had to develop this work for myself. I will always remember that moment in my studio on Gardiner Street. I had this real bang tape recorder sitting on a chair. I went over and I crouched down beside it and I just let the sounds out of me. As I continued, they became very long and very deep, real belly sounds. They developed into a *caoin*. The silence in between was very intense, and it seemed to me a strong place from where the sounds could emerge, a critical space. It went right through the whole process of keening, of mourning, and became a celebration of life itself.[10]

In 1992, O'Kelly released a track on *Lament*, an album compiled by performance artist Nigel Rolfe. This album contains mostly the work of Irish traditional musicians as a memorial to the lives lost in the Troubles, the nationalist urban war that shook Belfast and the island for decades. O'Kelly's contribution – a single-breath scream that lasts 45 seconds – offers a disturbing interlude to the album. Instead of using words to convey the emotional depths of the Troubles, O'Kelly's raw and lingering guttural scream drives into the core of the listener, an echo of suffering and physical exhaustion that reverberates in the soul. Even as O'Kelly shifted to creating multi-media works during the 1990s, sound remained a prominent influence in her process.

Not all sound artists present their work in the form of live or recorded performances. Multi-media installation works that incorporate sound along with video, still imagery, or sculptural objects are also quite common. Just as there is a range of live improvisation and performance techniques, artists use sound in variety of ways when it comes to creating multi-media works. These works resemble what is commonly referred to as 'visual' art, but a heavy sonic component makes this identifier inadequate.

In addition to their live improvisational work, Anthony Kelly and David Stalling create sound and visual installations. Their work is commonly attuned to the geography of a space and location while considering the physical properties of light and sound. In 2008, they presented the installation *Sounding Arrival* at Art Trail in Cork. Occupying the

> 'Sounds and images shift between noise and silence, light and total darkness, in an unpredictable rhythm that keeps the spectator on edge. When the sound and image cut, a reverberant echo and traces of afterimage linger.'

refrigeration unit of the Southern Fruit Warehouse in the docklands, this minimally composed piece takes advantage of the unique properties of the room's architecture, particularly its twenty-second reverberation. In a corner of the totally darkened room, Kelly and Stalling place a stack of television screens simultaneously playing a video consisting of pulsating lights. An audio accompaniment comprised of electronically manipulated sounds fills the space in sync with the visual images, bouncing around the room's reflective, metallic surfaces. Sounds and images shift between noise and silence, light and total darkness, in an unpredictable rhythm that keeps the spectator on edge. When the sound and image cut, a reverberant echo and traces of afterimage linger. Spectators are not allowed to enter the space freely, but only a small group is admitted at a time and restricted to a far corner of the room. From this perspective, it is challenging to identify that the lights are being emitted from a stack of televisions, contributing to the nervous energy of the piece. Stalling and Kelly commonly create works that are site-specific, but *Sounding Arrival* is acoustically specific to its presentation space. What is striking about this installation is its dependence on the physical and spatial properties of light and sound and how these resonate in an environment. On the molecular level, sound is the physical disturbance of a medium resulting in the excitation of molecules. British scholars David Howard and Jamie Angus describe the properties of sound in the 'golf ball and spring model':

> [This model] consists of a series of masses, e.g., golf balls, connected together by springs. The golf balls represent the point masses of the molecules in a real material, and the springs represent the intermolecular forces between them. If the golf ball at the end is pushed toward the others then the spring linking it to the next golf ball will be compressed and will push at the next golf ball in the line, which will compress the next spring, and so on.[11]

The resulting motion is a longitudinal wave. Higher frequency sounds have shorter wavelengths, which cause them to be more directional. In contrast, lower frequencies have longer wavelengths that tend to spread out and are less predictable. US composer Alvin Lucier notes how each space 'has its own personality that tends to modify, position and move sounds by means of absorption, reflections, attenuations and other structurally related phenomenon.'[12] *Sounding Arrival* utilises the acoustic properties of the warehouse refrigeration unit with an extreme reverberation. While this environment is not ideal for listening to music, it enhances the work's distinctive sonic and visual qualities.

Irish composer Jennifer Walshe creates theatrical sound performances and installations that incorporate rich visual and conceptual play. She is renowned for her use of alter-egos while working, a tactic implemented in a number of projects that 're-write' Irish sound and art history. For example, in 2010, she initiated the project *Dordán*, which claims that minimalism in music began with a group of traditional Irish musicians during the 1950s. According to the story fabricated by Walshe, an Irish musicologist, Antoninne Ó Murchú, discovered a number of 'bizarre' recordings created in Cork in 1952 that are attributed to Pádraig Mac Giolla Mhuire. These recordings were to be released as an album by Raidió Teilifís Éireann (RTE) in 2010. This 'discovery,' which included sounds actually composed by Walshe and later performed by the Cork-based contemporary music group the Quiet Music Ensamble in 2013, are dominated by low, steady, droning sounds similar to the *uileann* pipes. However, pipes are never actually used in the music as, according to Walshe's history, Pádriac was so devastated by the premature death of his father Michael, a *uileann* pipe player, that 'he never played the pipes after the passing of his father. The structure of the pipes seemed to be in his blood, however, most significantly the instrument's focus on fixed drones.'[13] The Quiet Music Ensemble performance incorporates live instrumentation, spoken word, recorded sounds, performed gestures, and video projections that blend found footage, abstract poetic statements, descriptions of the music's meditative properties with a telling of the 'story' behind *Dordán*. In his review of the work, Toner Quinn states: 'For the thirty-five-minute performance, Irish culture is literally whatever we choose it to be.'[14] As with Walshe's other productions – including the large-scale conceptual exhibition project *Grúpat* (2008) and her invention of the 'Guinness Dadaists' (2012) (an Irish faction of Dadaism working in the early twentieth century) – great attention is paid to detail in this interdisciplinary performance that blends video, experimental music composition, and live action within a complex conceptual framework that also functions as a dialogic critique of Irish music history.

Using sound to geographically map a place has become increasingly popular in Ireland. Commonly referred to as 'sound walks', 'sound maps', or 'soundscapes', the use of sound in mapping can take on a variety of forms. These may include outdoor installations, guided audio tours, or archives of collected field recordings superimposed on a topographical map. In 2014, the pilot version of *LimerickSoundscapes* portal was officially launched. An interactive sound map of the city, this project is an ongoing collaboration between scholars and academics at University of Limerick, Mary Immaculate College, and Limerick School of Art and Design. Contributors include Drs Aileen Dillane, Colin Quigley, Martin Power, Eoin Devereux, Tony Langlois, and Mikael Fernström. The phrase 'soundscape' was coined by Canadian composer R. Murray Schafer, and is used to describe 'any acoustic field of study,' which may include a performance of composed music, a radio programme, or an urban, acoustic environment.[15] Accessible through the internet, the prototype of *LimerickSoundscapes'* growing archive consists of contributions from residents of the city who capture snippets of sound, music, and speech from around Limerick. Emphasis is placed on community involvement. The work of these volunteer collectors is coordinated by the *LimerickSoundscapes'* key members. In its current prototype form, the archive is located on a website (http://www.limericksoundscapes. ie/). The sounds range from mundane objects and activities to musical performances, including as 'Aerobics Class', 'Closing Time', 'Birds at the Wetlands', 'Music at the Milk Market', 'Muslim Prayer', and 'Television Shop'. When the title of a sound is clicked, a map marker is activated, displaying a pop up that contains more detail about the sound, the address and date it was recorded, and the date it was added to the archive, along with the option to listen to the sound. Tony Langlois of the Audio Research Centre at Mary Immaculate College describes how the purpose of this project 'is to create a sound archive of everyday life in Limerick City. Over time our work and leisure habits change, as do modes of transport and even the climate. As years pass, the soundmap will allow us to look back on our sonic past and enable future generations to listen to life in our time.'[16] This geographically mapped collection of field recordings provided by the city's inhabitants offers rich insight into the everyday life of Limerick and the urban centre's cultural topography.

Even though there are varied ways for sound art to be experienced, a notable quality about sound art in Ireland is the value placed on the

Opposite: Anthony Kelly and David Stalling, Live performance at The Joinery, 2012. Photo: Fergus Kelly.

'During the Intermedia exhibitions, it was not uncommon to witness barristers in suits and court clerks interacting with the sound installations. In the relational scenario of the event, there is an active process of sharing, which [...] informs individual and collective practices.'

live event. Performances can last anywhere between one and six hours, requiring patience on behalf of both participants and audience. These displays of endurance offer testament to the value of sound art in the Irish community. British writer Daniel Spicer observes these qualities in his description of *Sonic Vigil*, a 12 hour sound art performance that occurs annually in Cork: 'Such commitment from artists and listeners alike, says Mary McCarthy [director of the National Sculpture Factory], is an indicator of the centrality of art to the Irish identity.'[17] Danny McCarthy played a significant role in organising many of the early sound art events in Ireland that brought locals in contact with foreign practitioners. *Intermedia*, an annual festival organised by McCarthy and Tony Sheehan, exhibited sound art in conjunction with other experimental art forms, including installation, video, and performance. More recent music oriented festivals, including the *Dublin Electronic Arts Festival (DEAF)* and the *Hilltown New Music Festival*, have incorporated sound art alongside other forms of musical production. Galleries, such as the Crawford Gallery in Cork and The Joinery in Dublin, have presented sound art events. Notably, renowned practitioners from different parts of the globe participate in these events, introducing some of the key figures in sound art to the Irish cultural scene, including William Furlong and David Toop from the United Kingdom as well as US composer Alvin Lucier. As a result, significant transnational networks are established, which inform the practices of artists working in Ireland.

In general, events have played a major role in the development and growth in popularity of sound art in Ireland. Increased public funding for the arts during the late twentieth and early twenty-first centuries resulted in a proliferation of events throughout Ireland (with recent cuts to funding having the opposite effect). The use of the term 'event,' as opposed to concert or show, is intentional. Events function as gatherings for practitioners and listeners to share a common experience. Events are temporary – ephemeral and always passing – but they play a key role in the presentation and development of sound art. Considering that many Irish sound events, such as *Sonic Vigil* and *Soundings*, tend to be diverse in their artistic offerings, they provide opportunities for various methods, techniques, and perspectives of sound art to come together and merge, even if imperfectly. Additionally, the event is where the audience, sometimes purposely and other times accidentally, may encounter sound art for the first time. McCarthy describes how the Triskel Arts Centre is located above a popular restaurant for people working at the local court house.[18] During the *Intermedia* exhibitions, it was not uncommon to witness barristers in suits and court clerks interacting with the sound installations. In the relational scenario of the event, there is an active process of sharing, which, whether the participants are aware of this or not, informs individual and collective practices. The polyphonic nature of Irish sound art events prevents a homogeneity in style or techniques. As such, these events result in the collective creation of sound art in Ireland, as numerous individuals – artists, audience members, curators, and institutional representatives – jointly weave together a rich (and at times dissonant) cultural scene. Canadian scholar Brian Massumi describes how during an event there is a dynamic, temporary unity that is unique.[19] The participant experiences a world larger than its singular existence, which is perceived, felt, and interpreted in a state of co-occurrence. After an event culminates, this unity dissolves, but the impact of that event does not cease to exist. Participants continue onto other trajectories of existence, but the qualities of a particular event linger in the vestiges of memories and artifacts.

As such, the sounds resonate – they are reinforced and prolonged as they echo off the surface of the creative imagination. One method that encourages this process is the popularity of recording and distributing sound works. The creation and dissemination of high-quality digital recordings have extended the reach of sound art in Ireland from beyond the event, with numerous artists creating small recording labels to facilitate this process. According to US scholar Jonathan David Tankel, instead of treating recorded sound as a copy of a performance, it functions as a work 'based on a performance that is actualised when played back by or for listeners.'[20] New Zealand writer Caleb Kelly adds that as such, recorded sound is treated as more than just a means of documentation or a stand-in for the work of art.[21] Additionally, the import of sound art recordings from abroad has greatly influenced the work of some artists. Danny McCarthy recalls how he eagerly collected cassettes and records from sound artists from across the globe. After receiving these works through the post, he indulgently listened to them over and over again as he was never certain when newer works would arrive. During 1993 at the Triskel Arts Centre, McCarthy organised an exhibition based on recordings received through the mail. During this *Post Sound Art* event, 70 to 80 tapes from around the world were played for the audience, who could later re-visit a work by listening to it on one of the Walkman cassette players located in the gallery.[22]

In 2004, Anthony Kelly and David Stalling began running a label, later named Farpoint Recordings in 2007, dedicated to producing and distributing high-quality releases of sound art. In addition to paying careful attention to the qualities of the sounds themselves, great care is put into the creation of limited editions with unusual packaging. The intention is to create sound releases that can also be treated as art objects. According to Kelly and Stalling, the label functions as 'an artist-run creative project that seeks to publish works from the margins that intersect in some way with contemporary sound and audio-visual practices.'[23] Works released by the label include pieces by Irish sound artists, such as Linda O'Keefe, Claire Guerin, Karen Power, and Katie O'Looney. They have also released works produced in Ireland by foreign artists, such as *Dowsing* by US artist Stephen Vitiello, which originally took the form of a four channel sound installation presented at the National Sculpture Factory in Cork. Just as the distribution of recorded releases played a major role in the early development of sound art in Ireland, this technique continues to be used to disperse Irish sound art around the world.

Instead of being reducible to simple identifiable categories, sound art in Ireland is manifold. These variations can be detected at the numerous events dedicated to sound art, offering opportunities for creators and spectators to engage with this experimental and ever evolving medium. From the beginning, sound art in Ireland has participated in a transnational network of sonic artistic production, contributing to the rich differentiation of its practitioners. As such, it exists in a state of polyphonic resonance; a soundscape comprised of individual artistic identities that echo and reflect, functioning as symbiotic driving forces that perpetuate creative development in this conglomeration of a community.

1. Sections of this essay appear in E. Putnam, '... the transformative ability of Strange Attractor', in *A*. Kelly and E. Putnam (eds.) *Strange Attractor: Experiments in a Quinary Landscape and Other Fields* (Dublin: Farpoint Recordings 2014) pp. 52-55.

2. Mikhail Bakhtin, *Problems of Dostoevsky's Poetics* (Minneapolis: University Of Minnesota Press, 1984).

3. Ibid, p. 6.

4. Douglas Kahn, *Noise, Water, Meat: A History of Sound in the Arts* (Cambridge, MA: MIT Press, 1999).

5. Seth Kim-Cohen, *In the Blink of an Ear: Toward a Non-Cochlear Sonic Art* (New York and London: Continuum, 2009).

6. Caleb Kelly, 'Introduction: Sound in Art', in *Sound*, ed. Caleb Kelly (London and Cambridge, MA: The Whitechapel Gallery and MIT Press, 2011); Alan Licht, *Sound Art: Beyond Music, Between Categories* (New York: Rizzoli International Publications, 2007); Brandon LaBelle, *Background Noise: Perspectives on Sound Art (*New York and London: Continuum, 2007).

7. Kim-Cohen, *In the Blink of an Ear.*

8. Fergus Kelly, unpublished email correspondance with author, 23 March 2014.

9. Daniel Spicer, 'Global Ear Cork', *The Wire,* 331 (2011), p. 16.

10. Katy Deepwell, *Dialogues: Women Artists from Ireland* (London and New York: I.B. Tauris, 2005), p. 138.

11. David Howard and Jamie Angus, *Acoustics and Psychoscoutics,* (Oxford and Burlington: Focal Press, 2009), p. 3.

12. Alvin Lucier, 'Careful Listening is More Important than Making Sounds Happen: The Propogation of Sounds in Space', in *Reflections: Interviews, Scores, Writings,* ed. by Alvin Lucier (Cologne: MusikTexte, 1995), p. 430.

13. Jennifer Walshe, *Dordán,* 2010.

14. Toner Quinn, 'Where Noel Hill Meets Jennifer Walshe', *The Journal of Music,* 14 March 2014. <http://journalofmusic.com/focus/where-noel-hill-meets-jennifer-walshe>. [accessed 10 December 2014].

15. R. Murray Schafer, *The Soundscape: Our Sonic Environment and the Tuning of the World* (Rochester, Vermont: Destiny Books, 1993).

16. Jimmy Woulfe, 'Limerick soundscape records highs and lows of city life', *Irish Examiner,* 2014. [Online]. http://www.irishexaminer.com/ireland/limerick-soundscape-records-highs-and-lows-of-city-life-261003.html [accessed 27 March 2014].

17. Daniel Spicer, 'Global Ear Cork', p. 16.

18. Danny McCarthy, unpublished interview with EL Putnam, 25 March 2014.

19. Brian Massumi, *Semblance and Event: Activist Philosophy and the Occurrent Art* (Cambridge, MA and London, UK: MIT Press, 2011).

20. Jonathan David Tankel, 'The Practice of Recording Music: Remixing as Recoding', in *Journal of Communication,* 40 (1990), 34-46, (p. 36).

21. Kelly, 'Introduction: Sound in Art'.

22. McCarthy, Unpublished interview with EL Putnam, 25 March 2014.

23. Anthony Kelly and David Stalling, Profile: Farpoint Recordings 2007, *Farpoint Recordings* <http://farpointrecordings.com/profile/> [accessed 29 March 2014].

A TIMELINE OF SOUND ART IN IRELAND

1980

LIVE ART FESTIVAL,
CURATED BY DANNY MCCARTHY
TRISKEL ARTS CENTRE
CORK

PAUL VOGEL
CURATED BY
KEVIN FOX
DUBLIN

GUNTHER BERKUS
MIDLETON ARTS FEST
CURATED BY RAYMOND SEARSON
CORK

1985

MEL MERCIER
ROARATORIO - AN IRISH CIRCUS
ON FINNEGAN'S WAKE
CURATED BY JOHN CAGE
IRCAM PARIS

1981

SEAN TAYLOR
SENSE OF PLACE
TRISKEL ARTS CENTRE
CORK

*SOUND-
WORKS*
CURATED
BY DANNY
MCCARTHY
CORK

1986

MICK SHANAHAN, THE SELF
WITH ELEMENTAL EXTENSIONS
AND YAHWEH, GARTER LANE ARTS
CENTRE WATERFORD

INTERMEDIA
CURATED BY DANNY MCCARTHY
TRISKEL ARTS CENTRE
CORK

1990

FERGUS KELLY, TASK
5A ARTWORKS,
CURATED BY JOHN REDWICK
DUNLAOGHAIRE

1988

1991

DIARMUID MCDIARMUIDA
SIAMESE PIGEON
DUBLIN

1993

SEAN MAC ERLAINE
THE DA CLUB
DUBLIN

1998

IRENE MURPHY, ARTERIES
SENSE OF CORK
MIDSUMMER FESTIVAL
CORK

DAVID LACEY,
GARDEN OF DELIGHTS BOOKSHOP
DUBLIN

1997

BRIAN O'SHAUGHNESSY
RHIZOME
TRISKEL ARTS CENTRE
CORK

1999

PAUL HEGARTY
BODY WITHOUT ORGANS
CURATED BY JOHN YOUNGE
TEMPLE BAR GALLERIES DUBLIN

2001

KARL BURKE
SOUNDIN
TEMPLE BAR
DUBLIN

SVEN ANDERSON
MORNING ROOFTOP PERFORMANCE
BROADSTONE STUDIOS DUBLIN

2002

SLAVEK KWI
PROJECT
ARTS CENTRE
DUBLIN

DAVID STALLING
EAR ENSEMBLE
NEWBRIDGE ARTS CENTRE
NEWBRIDGE

SOUNDIN WITH KARL BURKE, HUGH O'NEILL,
DIARMUID MACDIARMADA, SLAVEK KWI, PAUL MURNAGHAN,
SVEN ANDERSON, SEOIDIN O'SULLIVAN, SEÁN MCCRUM,
FERGUS BYRNE, VARIOUS VENUES DUBLIN

2003

IMPROVISED SOUND EVENT,
CURATED BY DAVID LACEY, PAUL VOGEL
AND DENNIS MCNULTY, PRINTING
HOUSE, TRINITY COLLEGE DUBLIN

TONY LANGLOIS
VISONIC
UNIVERSITY OF ULSTER
COLERAINE

MICK O'SHEA
ART TRAIL
CORK ARTISTS COLLECTIVE
CORK

2004

DENNIS MCNULTY
VOLUME
CURATED BY MARIAN LOVETT
TEMPLE BAR GALLERY & STUDIOS
DUBLIN

*ARTTRAIL - SOUNDWORKS -
FOR THOSE WHO HAVE EARS*
CURATED BY JULIE FORRESTER,
VARIOUS VENUES
CORK

2005

ROBIN PARMAR
CONTROL TOWER SOUND
IMPACT THEATRE
LIMERICK

ED DEVANE
CURATED BY PAUL WATTS,
NEIL DONOVAN,
LAZYBIRD
DUBLIN

I-AND-E FESTIVAL [2005 – 2011]
CURATED BY DAVID LACEY,
PAUL VOGEL AND DENNIS MCNULTY,
TRINITY COLLEGE
DUBLIN

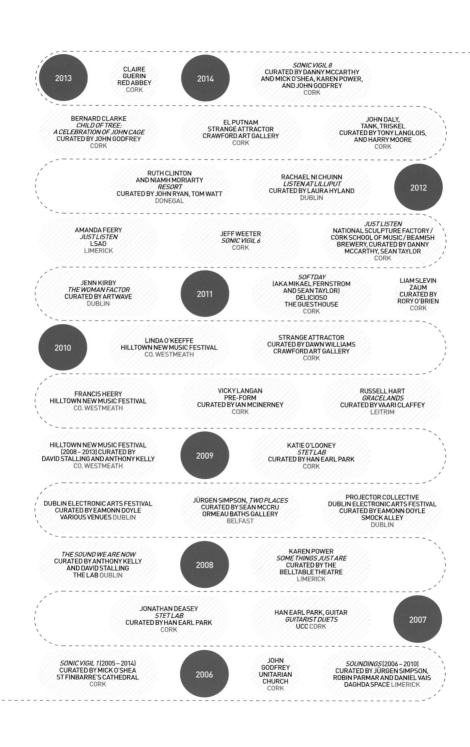

2013

CLAIRE
GUERIN
RED ABBEY
CORK

2014

SONIC VIGIL 8
CURATED BY DANNY MCCARTHY
AND MICK O'SHEA, KAREN POWER,
AND JOHN GODFREY
CORK

BERNARD CLARKE
CHILD OF TREE:
A CELEBRATION OF JOHN CAGE
CURATED BY JOHN GODFREY
CORK

EL PUTNAM
STRANGE ATTRACTOR
CRAWFORD ART GALLERY
CORK

JOHN DALY,
TANK, TRISKEL
CURATED BY TONY LANGLOIS,
AND HARRY MOORE
CORK

RUTH CLINTON
AND NIAMH MORIARTY
RESORT
CURATED BY JOHN RYAN, TOM WATT
DONEGAL

RACHAEL NI CHUINN
LISTEN AT LILLIPUT
CURATED BY LAURA HYLAND
DUBLIN

2012

AMANDA FEERY
JUST LISTEN
LSAD
LIMERICK

JEFF WEETER
SONIC VIGIL 6
CORK

JUST LISTEN
NATIONAL SCULPTURE FACTORY /
CORK SCHOOL OF MUSIC / BEAMISH
BREWERY, CURATED BY DANNY
MCCARTHY, SEAN TAYLOR
CORK

JENN KIRBY
THE WOMAN FACTOR
CURATED BY ARTWAVE
DUBLIN

2011

SOFTDAY
(AKA MIKAEL FERNSTROM
AND SEAN TAYLOR)
DELICIOSO
THE GUESTHOUSE
CORK

LIAM SLEVIN
ZAUM
CURATED BY
RORY O'BRIEN
CORK

2010

LINDA O'KEEFFE
HILLTOWN NEW MUSIC FESTIVAL
CO. WESTMEATH

STRANGE ATTRACTOR
CURATED BY DAWN WILLIAMS
CRAWFORD ART GALLERY
CORK

FRANCIS HEERY
HILLTOWN NEW MUSIC FESTIVAL
CO. WESTMEATH

VICKY LANGAN
PRE-FORM
CURATED BY IAN MCINERNEY
CORK

RUSSELL HART
GRACELANDS
CURATED BY VAARI CLAFFEY
LEITRIM

HILLTOWN NEW MUSIC FESTIVAL
(2008 – 2013) CURATED BY
DAVID STALLING AND ANTHONY KELLY
CO. WESTMEATH

2009

KATIE O'LOONEY
STET LAB
CURATED BY HAN EARL PARK
CORK

DUBLIN ELECTRONIC ARTS FESTIVAL
CURATED BY EAMONN DOYLE
VARIOUS VENUES DUBLIN

JÜRGEN SIMPSON, TWO PLACES
CURATED BY SEÁN MCCRU
ORMEAU BATHS GALLERY
BELFAST

PROJECTOR COLLECTIVE
DUBLIN ELECTRONIC ARTS FESTIVAL
CURATED BY EAMONN DOYLE
SMOCK ALLEY
DUBLIN

THE SOUND WE ARE NOW
CURATED BY ANTHONY KELLY
AND DAVID STALLING
THE LAB DUBLIN

2008

KAREN POWER
SOME THINGS JUST ARE
CURATED BY THE
BELLTABLE THEATRE
LIMERICK

JONATHAN DEASEY
STET LAB
CURATED BY HAN EARL PARK
CORK

HAN EARL PARK, GUITAR
GUITARIST DUETS
UCC CORK

2007

SONIC VIGIL 1 (2005 – 2014)
CURATED BY MICK O'SHEA
ST FINBARRE'S CATHEDRAL
CORK

2006

JOHN
GODFREY
UNITARIAN
CHURCH
CORK

SOUNDINGS (2006 – 2010)
CURATED BY JÜRGEN SIMPSON,
ROBIN PARMAR AND DANIEL VAIS
DAGHDA SPACE LIMERICK

HIGH PERFORMANCE

IT'S ALL I CAN THINK A
BOUT. IT'S ALL I CAN T
HINK ABOUT. IT'S ALL I
CAN THINK ABOUT. IT'S

ARTISTS & ISSUES

NEW YORK: ARTISTS CALL AGAINST U.S. INTERVENTION IN CENTRAL AMERICA

NANCY BUCHANAN & NICARAGUA ● KIM JONES & VIETNAM ● ROLANDO PENA & THE OIL GAME

★ **SPECIAL REPORT: PERFORMANCE IN ENGLAND AND IRELAND** ★

PLUS: VENTURA ON MOVIES ● PEPPE ON MARDI GRAS ● LOVELACE ON CAL ARTS ● VIDEO ● NEWS ● REVIEWS

ANTHONY SHEEHAN

SURVEY: IRELAND SOUTH OF THE BORDER
High Performance 1984
Issue 25

I was 21 years of age when I wrote this. It wasn't an academic essay – it was a subjective, topical piece for an issue of *High Performance*, the LA based Performance Art magazine. The Editors had accompanied the American performance artist Paul McCarthy on a tour of Ireland in 1983, met me in Cork, and asked me to write the article after seeing one of my own live pieces.

I think at the time someone was supposed to do a similar 'North of the Border' article, and I think Dublin was then to be covered separately again – it was 30 years ago so I'm not completely sure if those other articles happened, but I do remember the Editor liked the fact that I was such a young practitioner. There were really very few people in Ireland doing this kind of work, and Cork and Belfast were the two most active centres at that time, mainly because of the work and influence of Alastair MacLennan in Belfast, and Danny McCarthy in Cork.

It was an article about the scene written by a 21 year old as he saw it, and should be taken in that context. Looking back at it now there are things I wouldn't say (or any longer believe) but it's an honest account written by someone who was, at that time, one of the youngest performance artists in the country putting on work in professional spaces.

Opposite: *High Performance* magazine, 11.4 (1988), edited by Steven Durland, article by Anthony Sheehan. Photo courtesy Anthony Sheehan.

To discuss Irish Live Art in an American magazine poses certain problems. Irish Live Art is very isolated and largely uninfluenced by movements noticeable in American art.

Recently *High Performance* gave a lecture on American Live Art in Cork at the Triskel artspace. Talking to people afterwards I found that the main impressions were that, patterns of style and ideas were noticeable through the live work presented. A lot of artists seemed to share similar approaches, and the content of the work seemed to be based on a political framework, or at the very least contained political overtones. Perhaps that was the reason for the tendency of the reviews of the Belfast artist Alastair McLennan's recent performance in New York; despite Alastair's apolitical convictions, politics was read everywhere into his piece.

Irish performance art, as all Irish art, arises out of an isolation that is social and cultural. There is no 'fashion', no dominance of any particular idea or style. The live artists I shall deal with in more detail later have very different evolved styles, based on a personal expressive framework or on theoretical ideas. Politics is not a popular subject among Irish live artists, largely because they feel political Ireland is a joke.

Politics in Ireland, and the Irish political consciousness is, at most charitable, amateurish. Issues tend to be treated either with complacency or, where emotions are likely to get involved, with civil-war-like aggression. Political Ireland consists of a structure of conservatism inherited from the Catholic Church on one side, and an imitated liberalism of western countries on the other. These structures exist superimposed on one another. Liberal ideas have not yet replaced the old ideas, while at the same time older ideas are finding it harder to compete – a struggle perhaps common to any country 'coming of age', but Ireland is unique in that the division of ideology is very real. There is the Church and the State, the north and the south. The conservative tradition continually fights liberalism in a bid to avert what it sees as an entry into depravity. Liberalism claims modernization as its goal, but if the country is technically modernized, the attitudes of its people are not. Irish people live in a society with a complacency that can only be suspended when an issue is sufficiently over exaggerated so that the familiar caricature of 'fader against son' and 'bruder against bruder' becomes a feature of resolving the issue. The overall opinion of many artists is that this type of carry-on is best avoided, that the whole pendulum idea of progress is a waste of time.

DANNY McCARTHY uses his work to try to get through the no-man's land of Irish society by proposing pieces which objectify the situation in a graphic statement best summarized as 'think again'. For Danny McCarthy the impressions of Irish culture abroad and our impressions of ourselves are hopelessly boggled. He proposes that any discussion of Irish issues needs, first of all, a realization of the fundamental elements of that issue; by showing the basic simple reality of anything, the confusion will dissolve into tangibility.

The recent abortion referendum is an example. Here we had an issue that became a liberalist/conservatist civil war. For the Church, the proposal of an amendment which would constitutionally outlaw abortion allowed them (some would say forced them) to test the strength of their doctrinal influence on the people. (A previous amendment allowing the Church special privileges over legal issues was voted out.) In the heat of the 'debate' over this issue Danny did a performance titled *Referendum Addendum*.

> A bare tree is placed in the centre of the space. Tied onto the branches are doll's heads, which are packed with red ice. Already the ice has started to drip onto the plastic on the ground when the audience enters. Subject enters and begins to clean up the mess, which becomes more difficult. Tracing the shadow of the installation on the wall, he then breaks all the branches from the tree except the centre branch (phallic symbol).

Danny's message is simple – whatever happens in this amendment, we still have to clean up the mess. The piece approaches politics without being 'political'.

For *Three Days of Live Art* a performance festival in Belfast in November 1983, Danny did a piece titled *An Cliambh Solais* (Gaelic for *Sword of Light*). Danny uses the ancient blacksmith mythology to make statements relevant to the present. The divided Ireland, north and south, being the matter at hand, he set about constructing an installation, which was as follows:

> Two ropes are placed on the back wall of the area converging (V) in the centre. Candles are placed along these ropes. Two candelabra are placed inside this defined area, in between which is a pole. Danny lies on the ground in the area with a hammer and anvil hanging from his neck. Two swords, one green (Eire) one red (the North) are in each hand. Performing battle actions with the swords, subject then begins to forge a silver material over the sword of light, which is placed on the centre pole. The legend source: Ireland will unite when the swords of battle forge into the Sword of Light.

An environment is created where candles are placed on the ground, and a sound track of Gregorian chants are heard. A large sheet of white paper is hung on the wall. Subject stands against sheet, while slides of drawings, stained glass and white background slides are projected onto him. This proceeds for half an hour. Taking a chemical developer fluid he imprints his hands and face onto the sheet and steps away. The sheet is photographic paper, so an imprint of his whole body, plus the developer marks are left. Son the image will fade away.

A type of Turin Shroud perhaps, a technician's approach to the performance aesthetic: the performed artwork, which lasts only as long as the performance.

I think it would be fair to say that most live works in the Republic centres on Cork, thanks to the efforts of the Triskel Arts Centre. Art galleries have not done all they could do to aid the progress of Live Art. In 1981 the Third Eye in Scotland organised and sponsored a festival of Irish Live Art, which included Nigel Rolfe, Danny McCarthy, Alastair McLennan, and John Aiken. The Irish Arts Council has a love-hate relationship with galleries: and galleries with performers. The hate seems to predominate these days. Usually art galleries are reluctant when it comes to hosting performance events, and only by achieving establishment status can one show, let alone perform there.

Triskel is not stringent, a policy which has resulted in Cork's focus status for performance art. As a performer, I would not have been accommodated anywhere else. Considering I was not from art school and had not performed before, the Triskel accommodation policy is liberal by all standards.

Basically my interest was in writing. As time went on I found my ideas were not satisfying to me on paper, or as 'theatre', since I did not think in these terms. I have had difficulty translating literary devices to performance, and my pieces seemed, at the beginning, to veer into the violence of melodrama. My first performance, *Ambulance 5*, was an adaptation of a text based on a stream of consciousness of a dying accident victim. I created an environment of hospital-like colour and smell, in which my body was mummified on a table under blue spotlights. There were soundtracks, including a reading of the text. The piece was described as brisk, raw, and melodramatic.

A similar description was accorded to my more elaborate performance on schizophrenia titled *Imagine an Acrobat, Carefully Balanced on the End of a Match*. In order to dispense with the uncontrollable and undesirable melodrama, I worked out a quiet piece for Belfast titled Delirium and Age, visually contrasting youth (a child bouncing a ball in slow motion),

> 'My first performance... was an adaptation of a text based on a stream of consciousness of a dying accident victim. I created an environment of hospital-like colour and smell, in which my body was mummified on a table under blue spotlights.'

adolescence (disco music, disco slides) and old age. Illustrative of displacement, my action consisted of dragging myself out of the area using a cane. The soundtracks of the streets, of children and of a heartbeat during my exit provided a certain power and emotion. I'm not sure if I did dispense with melodrama, but two Belfast people remarked that the piece was 'very tense; it was what it is like to live in Belfast. Living here you never know when everything will just explode.' For me, this was a curious interpretation. There was no apparent intensity on this level during my other performances. I hazard the guess that whereas I felt the need to provide intensity in the parochial apathy of Cork, it was provided for me by the atmosphere of Belfast.

In general conclusion, my basis for working is to use raw technology to create environments in which the performer is either displaced or engulfed, and acts accordingly.

I would like to thank the following for assistance: Prof John Maguire, Department of Social Theory and Institutions, University College Cork. Mr. T.S. Linger, Computer Bureau, University College Cork. Triskel Arts Centre, Cork. All artists concerned. *High Performance* for taking a keen interest in Irish Live Work.

KATE ANTOSIK-PARSONS

THE DEVELOPMENT OF IRISH FEMINIST PERFORMANCE ART IN THE 1980s AND EARLY 1990s

The conservative political, economic, and social climate in Ireland during the 1980s inspired many women engaged with feminism to embrace the 'personal is political.' In particular, a number of referenda and events underscored women's bodies as a site upon which the struggle for sexual and bodily autonomy was waged. Women artists adopted performance art as a feminist strategy to question essentialist and monolithic constructions of the 'Irish woman', whilst responding to the political and social realities of women's lives.

This essay focuses on key performance practitioners such as Alanna O'Kelly, Pauline Cummins, and Mary Duffy examining the central issues that emerged from their feminist interventions, particularly around the representation of the body. The emphasis on the body in performance art as the primary means of expression presented these artists with an interesting challenge as they navigated identity and gender politics and grappled with the difficulties of representing the female body while subverting dominant patriarchal norms. I argue that by combining art practice with feminist activism, these artists partook in a type of embodied politics, that is provocative personal acts that exercise and resist power in local sites or through collective acts, resulting in the development of a culturally specific performance art movement in Ireland.

Opposite: Mary Duffy, *I grew up being grateful*, 1994. Photo courtesy of the artist.

IRISH FEMINISMS AND PERFORMANCE ART

The development of performance art as a medium of expression adopted by many Irish women artists working in the 1980s can be understood as a response to the conservative political and cultural climate. The status of women within Irish society came under intense scrutiny with the burgeoning second-wave Irish feminist movement in the 1970s. Women's perceived place under the political and religious ideologies that shaped the Irish nation was enshrined in Article 41.1.2 of the Irish Constitution (1937): 'In particular, the State recognizes that by her life within the home, woman gives to the State a support without which the common good cannot be achieved.' This patriarchal dictate that women best served the nation by focusing on their maternal responsibilities in the home inspired feminist groups as they agitated for equality, both in the workplace and in the home, by specifically targeting the removal of the marriage bar in the public sector, financial parity, equal access to education and importantly, the availability of contraception.[1]

As the 1970s drew to a close, feminist efforts shifted to the struggle for women's bodily and sexual autonomy. In 1979, the Dublin Rape Crisis Centre, a non-directive volunteer organisation, was established amidst efforts by groups like Women Against Violence Against Women to raise awareness about domestic and sexual abuse.[2] Though birth control was made legally available by the Health (Family Planning) Act (1979) for married couples, both doctor and pharmacist could refuse to provide it on grounds of conscionable objection. Abortion had long been prohibited in Ireland under Sections 58 and 59 of the *Offences Against the Person Act* (1861). However, the pro-life Eighth Amendment to the Irish Constitution (1983) asserted the right to life of the unborn child as being equal to the life of the mother, in effect making the legalisation of abortion impossible without a further Constitutional amendment. As a result non-directive pregnancy counselling services were halted and in 1986 a High Court injunction was enforced against providing information and assistance to women seeking to travel abroad for terminations.[3] Although abortion was legalised in the United Kingdom under the Abortion Act (1967) it was not permitted in Northern Ireland meaning that women in the north, like those in the Republic, were forced to travel to overseas to England and elsewhere for the procedure. When Irish voters returned to the polls in 1986 the referendum to lift the Constitutional ban on divorce was overwhelmingly defeated. Assessing the

'The surge in feminist cultural awareness around gender and sexual inequalities meant that women working with performance and time-based processes [...] grappled with certain issues around representing the body.'

impact of these events it can be asserted that feminist concerns on the island of Ireland at this time were distinct from their counterparts in the United Kingdom, Europe, and United States. For Irish feminists the body emerged as a lens through which the intersection of personal, political, theoretical, and practical concerns could be focused.

The surge in feminist cultural awareness around gender and sexual inequalities meant that women working with performance and time-based processes such as Pauline Cummins, Mary Duffy, Alanna O'Kelly, Frances Hegarty, Anne Tallentire, Anna O'Sullivan, and Maggie Magee grappled with certain issues around representing the body. Performance art afforded women artists a method of creating art that circumvented traditional fine arts practices like painting, drawing and sculpture that were historically determined by male artists. Performance art enabled both self-reflexivity and broader cultural awareness that fed into identity politics at the time and became a way for Irish women artists to engage with the body as a site of lived realities. Irish art critic Dorothy Walker noted that with the exception of Nigel Rolfe and Danny McCarthy, '[i]t is a noticeable aspect of contemporary Irish art that the most advanced work in the new media of performance and video is created by young women...'.[4] Many of the works created by the practitioners discussed in this essay created during this time were body based performances either live or to camera stem from the theoretical and conceptual concerns of performance art, particularly as they focused on the performance of subjectivities.

Pauline Cummins's artistic practice is intimately connected to her politics. The controversy surrounding a mural Cummins created in conjunction with the *Irish Exhibition of Living Art* (1984) installed at the National Maternity Hospital, Holles Street can be understood as a crucial moment in her performance practice. Interested in exploring issues around pregnancy and motherhood, Cummins completed the mural entitled *Celebration – The Beginning of Labour*, based on a previous work, depicted female figures holding a birthing mother aloft. The whimsical nude figures evoked the joyousness of the impending arrival. The mural was removed shortly after its completion by hospital authorities without the artist's consultation.[5] Reflecting on the installation of the mural, Cummins remarked: 'My experience of physically reproducing the painting in the courtyard of the hospital was very exciting, because people within the hospital would come and show their support even though others wanted to destroy it.'[6] This experiential aspect to the installation of the work can be understood in relation to how the body occupies space in performance, particularly in this highly gendered space of the maternity hospital. Cummins found that a related action of tying pink and blue ribbons onto the wrought iron railings outside the hospital similarly sparked a dialogue with interested parties as to the purpose of her efforts while aiding Cummins in her task. Both of these actions, which can be considered as Cummins's early encounters with the conceptual aspects of performance art enabled her to shift her practice from the confines of the studio and gallery grounded in traditional media created for passive spectators to performance and video work energised by the presence of active participants.[7] In a further extension of this transition and her desire to connect with 'real people', in 1986 Cummins became the first artist-in-residence to work with women inmates in Mount Joy prison.

For Mary Duffy it was the experience of her body as a 'political weapon' that provided the impetus for the shift in her practice towards performance. In the early 1980s Duffy, a disabled artist born without arms as result of thalidomide, an anti-nausea drug prescribed to women during pregnancy between 1959-61, was politically involved in the Women's Campaign for Disarmament that opposed the basing of cruise missiles at the Greenham Common Royal Air Force base in Berkshire, England. Her involvement was inspired when she saw graffiti in London in 1980 that read 'Nuclear War Means Thalidomide Forever.'[8] Yet the realisation of her body as a site of power did not happen until some time later. She describes:

> When I became involved in non-violent direct action at … Greenham Common in England, it usually meant using our bodies to barricade an exit or an entrance at the base, we would be forcibly removed by police lifting or dragging women by our limbs. When police grabbed my empty sleeves and pulled, my clothes came away

Opposite top: Alanna O'Kelly, *Echoes*, 1983. Photo courtesy of the artist.
Opposite bottom: Alanna O'Kelly, *Ómos*, video stills from The Crypt, St Mary's Abbey, Dublin. Part of the Performances at Project. Photo courtesy of the artist.

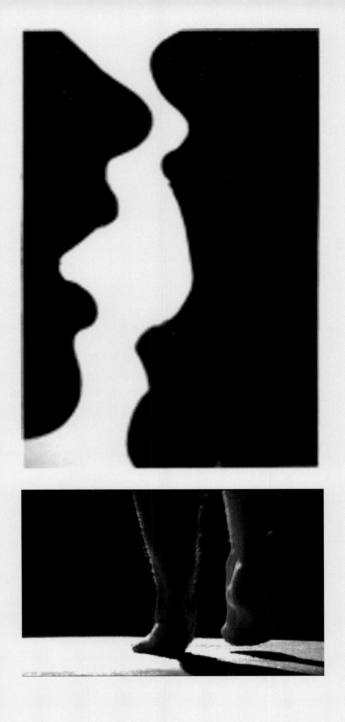

with them. They were then confronted with my half-naked body, with its uniqueness, its roundness and its threat.[9]

Though Duffy had not intended for her body to be used in this way, the anxiety producing provocation of its nakedness and disability became a way for her to connect the personal with the political. *Wishbone* (1983) a performative photograph in the Irish National Self-Portrait Collection (Limerick) indicates the potential of her body to function in this capacity. Duffy's body emerges from the darkness, illuminated by a sliver of light. The tilting angle of her head and raised leg form a strong diagonal yet the illusive quality to the image evokes the particular dynamics at work around identification and representation in Duffy's performances.

Alanna O'Kelly was similarly concerned with nuclear armament, inspiring her collaborative performance *Realignment* (1984) with Duffy performed at the *Mark Your Mark* Festival, Belfast (1984). Her first aural performances which incorporated keening were inspired by what she witnessed at Greenham Common entitled, *Sounds Around the Base*, when approximately 30,000 women gathered to raise their voices in protest to armament. O'Kelly heard a group of women calling out and crying in a way that reminded her of keening, or *caoineadh na mairbh*, the Irish funerary practice of crying for the dead. Describing her first experiments with the power of her own voice she recalled:

> I will always remember that moment in my studio on Gardiner Street. I had this real bangy old tape recorder sitting on a chair. I went over and crouched down beside it and I just let these sounds out of me. As I continued, they became very long and very deep, real belly sounds.[10]

The embodied nature of these first solitary experimentations with performance was primal and visceral. The physicality of bending her body, compressing her stomach and opening of her mouth as sound was forced outwards recall vomiting, but they also suggest that for O'Kelly, the body in performance is about embracing the abject. *Echoes* (1983) an early collaborative performance with Trish Haugh at the Douglas Hyde Gallery, consisted of O'Kelly and Haugh making sounds with the exhalation of breath into each other's mouths. This performance drew upon Inuit throat singing, a practice where two women facing each other make sounds into

'[...] we would be forcibly removed by police lifting or dragging women by our limbs. When police grabbed my empty sleeves and pulled, my clothes came away with them. They were then confronted with my half-naked body, with its uniqueness, its roundness and its threat.'

each other's mouths through inhalations and exhalations. As each took turns acting as a resonance box, the sound of their spent breath exiting the body and echoing in the other's drove the performance onwards. These physical performances later formed the basis for O'Kelly's now seminal work, *Chant Down Greenham* (1984-88)

Each of these artists experienced a moment when embodiment, or the experience of being present in their own bodies when placing themselves in a certain situation became of central importance to their artistic practice. In light of this there are several interconnections that can be drawn between the works of these three artists. Each artist aimed to highlight issues of bodily autonomy, that is the right to make decisions regarding one's health, reproductive health and sexuality. The landmark case *Gladys Ryan v the Attorney General* (1965) clarified that Article 40.3.1 and 2 of the Irish Constitution extends to the unenumerated right to bodily integrity. Bodily integrity is defined as 'the inviolability of the physical body' contending that the self-determination of human beings over their own bodies is a personal liberty and basic human right.

Questions of bodily autonomy surrounding women's experiences of childbirth were explored in Cummins's slide/tape piece entitled *Ann Kelly is a Midwife* (1986) shown at the Neighbourhood Open Workshops (NOW), Belfast. Cummins interviewed midwife Ann Kelly, who assisted her on the homebirths of her three children. The work commented on the increasingly medicalised management of birth in Ireland as images associated with hospital births like stirrups, doctors hidden behind masks, and needles interspersed with reassuring images of Ann's face, eyes, and hands. Ann spoke with quiet confidence about the potential empowerment of the birthing experience and the inherent capabilities of women's bodies. In 1997, controversy surrounded Ann's practice when An Bord Altranais, the

regulatory body for nursing professionals, sought a High Court injunction to halt her midwifery practice after receiving complaints against her by The Master of the National Maternity Hospital when Kelly presented a woman requiring assistance for a difficult labour to the delivery ward for admission.[11] Despite the concerns by hospital authorities that Kelly had underestimated the potential risks to baby and mother, the infant was delivered safely. The mother supported Kelly's management of her labour and even aided the midwife in locating legal representation. Though proceedings dragged out over two years Ann was eventually vindicated. Artworks like this raise questions about women's bodily rights during childbirth, and, perhaps unsurprisingly, remain worryingly relevant in the contemporary context as rates of caesarian deliveries in Ireland continue to soar. Moreover, in recent years the extent of physical and psychological suffering caused by symphysiotomies in Ireland has come to light. A controversial surgery that involved sawing the pubic bone to widen the pelvis during childbirth, symphysiotomies were carried out without consent on birthing women in Ireland between 1940s and the mid 1990s. In Ireland the Catholic Church, which ran most of the maternity hospitals, advocated the method as caesarian deliveries meant that women would have to avail of birth control to limit the amount of children they could bear. Women who underwent symphysiotomies suffered incontinence, difficulty walking and chronic pain. In this respect, a work like *Ann Kelly is a Midwife*, that subverted the unnecessary medicalisation of childbirth while celebrating and empowering women's birthing choices, highlights the desparity that still exists in Irish society.

The collaborative installation by Pauline Cummins and Louise Walsh, *Sounding the Depths* (1992) that contained a series of video projections, performative photographs, and sound installations was expressly concerned with bodily autonomy and sexual politics. In the first space, large composite images depicted the mouth of a woman with her lips tightly clenched, wringing hands and the two halves of a cockleshell being manipulated, edges grating against one another. In the second room, a large format projected video elaborated upon the shell/mouth/body images, imbuing them with activity. A mouth appeared, framed in a circle of light, reminiscent of the character Mouth from Samuel Beckett's *Not I* (1972). The tongue shifted slightly and the sounds of saliva were heard. A composite image of the mouth projected onto the torso appeared forming a face with breasts for eyes. The sound of the breath was slightly drawn; a shallow but

Opposite top: Alanna O'Kelly, *Realignment*, 1983. Photo courtesy of the artist.
Opposite bottom: *Extracts performance*, Paris, 2012. Photo courtesy of the artist.

warm, gasping 'ha.' The mouth was highlighted by a directed light source, like a flashlight, that shone into its opening. This emphasis implied the expected submersion of the viewer. The mouth opened wide to form a perfectly round circle, allowing the tissue of the soft palate and throat to be exposed, suggesting the act of swallowing. In the final room were several large four by six foot cibachrome colour photographs depicting the mouth superimposed on a female torso. The size of the mouth projected onto the body was akin to a visual consumption of the body. Although the mouth is the site of spoken language, in this work the vocalisations of this body communicated through breath, saliva, grating shells, and the jarring sound of grinding teeth, were potential non-verbal threats. When alive, the shell of the cockle, a bivalve mollusc is shut tightly, though it may be prised opened. The symbolism of the open cockle in this work is inspired by the empowerment of speaking from the depths of the body.

Sounding the Depths attempts to comprehend the fusion of the psychological and physical body. There was a tension established between surfaces and textures throughout the installation. The shells and composite images of teeth and torso alluded to the vagina dentata, a myth about a toothed vagina that reiterated fears about castration anxiety. The projection of the mouth dominates the body because it is of equal size to the torso. The movements of the shells and mouth highlighted a desire to sever the cultural expectations placed on the body, reiterated during a video sequence where a pair of hands, cradled one on top of the other, were outstretched and cupped like those waiting to receive Holy Communion. Next, the mouth slightly opened, in a movement reminiscent of the utterance of 'The Body of Christ' when the Eucharistic sacrament is offered from priest to communicant. Unlike the transubstantiated male body of Christ, the female body offered in the work was not easily consumed.

Sounding the Depths set up a dialogic tension between the performance of female bodies, as recorded and projected throughout the installation, and the experience of viewers' bodies as they as moved sequentially through three separate rooms. For the artists this was conceived of in relation to the idea of the gaze. Cummins remarked 'as the woman gazes down into herself there is no gaze that concerns her except for her own. The "male gaze"[...] grazes on the surface of the body. This work is concerned with a depth that cannot be possessed by passing consumption.'[12] This self-gazing in manifested in the 'head down' position adopted by the artists as they observed the projection

'[...] female sexuality in this work fluctuated between celebratory and threatening, the very idea of representing the naked female body, in such startling realism, was tremendously provocative given the restrictions on women's bodies during this time period.'

of the image upon their bodies. However, in relation to the viewer, who was literally inserted into the heart of the work, the act of gazing, defined as looking intently, appeared to be eclipsed by the embodied responses to the work. Irish art critic Bruce Arnold remarked: 'But the voice sound, the liquid dripping, the gleam of mucus, all have a compelling, nearly hypnotic force to them.'[13] Artist Jaki Irvine noted that the work, contextualized in strictly woman-centred terms, employed strategies that were understood to be fraught with issues about identification:

> The female viewer is encouraged to embark on a similar process of self discovery. The political strategy adopted here is a familiar one in terms of feminist artistic practices [...] Yet despite the fact that a sense of community and solidarity between women is a necessary prerequisite for women grouping together to effect political change, it is still a strategy which is inherently problematic.[14]

Likewise, art historian Hilary Robinson notes one of the most challenging aspects was premised upon the expectation of bodily relationality: 'Some women to whom I spoke on the night of the private view found it challenging, or even frightening, to be in a situation which, they felt, expected them to identify with images representing the possibility of inhabiting a body deeply sexed and the site of enunciation.'[15] Though female sexuality in this work fluctuated between celebratory and threatening, the very idea of representing the naked female body, in such startling realism, was tremendously provocative given the restrictions on women's bodies during this time period.

Crucially, the anxiety raised by the unbounded body in *Sounding the Depths* forced the viewer to confront the perceived boundaries between self and Other. By engaging with the cultural representations of Irish women and sexuality in the 1980s and 1990s *Sounding the Depths* threatens normative representations.[16] In the wake of the debates about sexual autonomy in Ireland, *Sounding the Depths* discouraged celebratory identification by destabilising the viewer's experience of self, providing a highly visceral understanding of how the margins of the body engage with the politically charged debates about women's bodies. In this particular work the performative, sensory, and embodied experiences of the viewer, as one of many bodies within this bodily performance, suggests that the subject-object relationship is carried throughout the work, implicating the viewer in the making of the work's meaning.

Embodiment in Alanna O'Kelly's works, expressed either through sound or physical presence, is of central importance. A number of her works like *Chant Down Greenham* (1984-88), *No Colouring Can Deepen the Darkness of Truth* (1992), *Ómós* (1995), *A'Beathú* (1996), and the *Burial of Patrick Ireland* (2009) employ keening, or *caoineadh na mairbh*, the marginalised oral tradition of crying for the dead that she reclaimed in order to articulate the importance of the past in the present.[17] O'Kelly's *Omós* was performed the crypt of St. Mary's Abbey, Dublin. The audience was guided from the Project Arts Centre to the location and handed the following statement upon entering the cold, darkened crypt:

> I am twelve years old
> I run, barefoot, dressed in an old coat
> I see two gentlemen, traveling in a coach
> On the road from Leenane to Westport
> I run beside their coach
> I don't ask for anything
> I keep pace with them
> They tell me over and over that they will
> Give me nothing
> I do not ask for anything
> I keep my silence
> They shake their heads, ignore me, debate
> And argue, wonder at my perseverance
> I keep pace with their wheels
> I do not speak
> I do not look at them
> They give me a fourpenny piece
> I take it
> I turn on my heels and run.[18]

O'Kelly's performance strictly focuses on the actions of the girl and the practice of 'running.' Barefoot and dressed in black, the artist crouched down in the centre of the floor, lit solely by a low spotlight. O'Kelly began to keen facing the floor and turned her head to project the notes to different points of the vaulted ceiling. Standing up, she began to keep pace on the spot with only her feet and ankles lit by the spotlight.[19] As her actions intensified the viewers became aware of the texture and quality to her breath. A spotlight highlighted the contrast between the cold concrete floor and the feet as they lightly tapped the ground. Maintaining an ever-quickening pace, O'Kelly ran continuously in place for 30 minutes.

O'Kelly subverts the distant historical event of the Famine by reinserting the 'personal' back into the past, innovatively setting up the opposition between the subjectivity of a female Famine victim against the patriarchal authority of the establishment. In the original story recorded in the travel journal Rev. William Sidney Godolphin Osborne, a Famine observer, two male travellers watch as a poor adolescent girl stricken with hunger keeps pace alongside their carriage. *Omós* capitulates the hierarchy of the male observers in relation to the impoverished girl through the use of the first person 'I', subsequently privileging the subjectivity of the girl. In *Omós* O'Kelly works with and against the forces of various sounds, articulating a tension between silence and sound that reasserts female subjectivity. O'Kelly's re-written text reiterates the girl's silence, 'I don't ask for anything', 'I do not ask for anything', I keep my silence', 'I do not speak.' In Osborne's version, it is the exhibition of weakness from the girl, which appears as a cough, an involuntary exhalation of air that causes his companion to take pity and throw coins towards her. Yet in *Omós*, the girl does not seek alms, her actions call for recognition of her dignity. The inability to 'speak' highlights the dynamics of the colonial and the gendered relationship, yet in *Omós*, as in Chant Down Greenham, claiming the right to speak is circumnavigated by non-lingual sounds. The breath functions as the ultimate symbol of life, without it, one cannot live. The spotlight on the feet provides a visual affirmation of her presence, yet they symbolically tread a fine line between life and death. In *Omós* the feet of the artist function as a surrogate for the mother who demands respect for her child. In doing so, the body and the breath articulate a recognition of the past.

The title of the work, *Ómós*, is Irish for respect. As an acronym OMOS stands for 'Our Mother of Sorrows', also known as 'Mater Dolorosa.' The image of the suffering mother is common in Western religious art and has been represented in different types of iconography, including the pietà. This

'O'Kelly's re-running of the girl's arduous journey expresses solidarity not only with calls for women's reproductive rights, but with the journeys overseas women in Ireland make everyday to exercise their right to bodily autonomy.'

connection to the grieving mother is also implied in the original location for this performance, in the crypt of St. Mary's Abbey, Dublin.[20] The potential connection to the Virgin Mary is striking, given that until the decline of Marianism in the late 1950s, a special emphasis was placed on the reverence of the Virgin in Ireland. The period in which this performance was produced, at the end of the twentieth century, was a time when the struggle for sexual autonomy exposed unrealistic cultural representations of maternity in Irish society. In this regard this powerful performance recalls the plight of the 14 year old at the centre of the 'X case' (1992). In December 1991, a girl became pregnant as a result of rape by a family acquaintance who had been sexually abusing her for over two years. The girl and her parents sought to travel to the UK to obtain an abortion and in doing so informed the gardai of their plans should a fetal tissue sample be required as proof in the pending case against her abuser. What subsequently followed provoked wide-scale outrage, as the Attorney General successfully sought a High Court injunction that barred her from travelling to do so. Though overturned by an appeal to the Supreme Court, this particular case remains a lightening rod for advocates for reproductive choice in Ireland. In response, O'Kelly's re-running of the girl's arduous journey expresses solidarity not only with calls for women's reproductive rights, but with the journeys overseas women in Ireland make everyday to exercise their right to bodily autonomy.

Mary Duffy's performative photographic works provided a different perspective on the right to bodily autonomy. Ann Millett-Gallant places Duffy's work alongside Petra Kuppers, Carrie Sandahl, Cheryl Marie Wade, and Sally Banes, other disabled women artists whose work exists at the intersections of the feminist art movement, contemporary performance, and disability rights.[21] In the eight panelled photographic work *Cutting the Ties that Bind* (1987) a sequence of images, reminiscent of the motion studies of British photographer Eadweard Muybridge, Duffy's body emerges from underneath white drapery that recalls classical Greek statues. As her disabled body is revealed from beneath the shroud it challenges normative associations of beauty. *I Grew Up Being Grateful* (1994) was a work created for the *Inside-Out* Arts Council travelling exhibition that sought to explore what it means to transition from childhood to adolescence to adulthood. As a child Duffy was made to wear large, prosthetic arms in an effort to render her body 'normative.' Duffy mentally and physically suffered the negative effects of these non-functional 'arms.' In *I Grew Up Being Grateful* a child's solemn face hidden in partial shadow peers out at the viewer. Her small face appears weighted down by the bulk concealed beneath her jumper, presumably her prosthetic limbs. Text from an earlier exhibition describes Duffy's childhood: 'After all that your gas powered arms are rejected, they are heavy, they hiss, and when your cylinders of gas run empty, from the heavy pack on my back, you've condemned me to walk about with arms outstretched, like as if I've just been crucified.' Arising in dynamic curvilinear lines from the top of her head is a juxtaposed image of her bent legs. They appear not once but twice. The doubling of this part of her body suggests their dual function as both arms and legs. In the upper right hand corner a blurred image is that of the artist rising from a seated position. The double exposure of the photograph articulates a tension between stilling and animating her body. The title of the work likewise tries to complicate the idea of 'grateful', referring to expectations that as a disabled child, Duffy was obliged to feel a debt of gratitude that her situation was not worse. Conversely, to be 'grateful' as an Irish woman meant being submissive, accepting one's lot in life. This aspect of the work highlights the intense pressures of conformity that Irish women faced and acknowledges the risks to those who did not. Read in this way, Duffy's performative photograph can be understood as an embodied refusal for Irish women, both corporeally and ideologically, to be fixed into place.

In her performances and photographs, light and shadow are the defining factors that suggest the tension between presence and absence in these images. Tom Duddy observed: 'The one who is composed, who is formed and shaped, who is exposed to the light, is herself. She causes images to happen by being actively present in them.'[22] In a sense Duffy is sculpting her own body, making the viewer aware of how she inhabits space and the 'negative space' around her body. As a traditional compositional tool 'negative space' is a term that refers to the empty space around a two-dimensional or three-dimensional object. Yet in Duffy's performances her body is more than an object, she is the subject that inhabits the picture plane imbuing it with life. Therefore the light and shadow that so skilfully

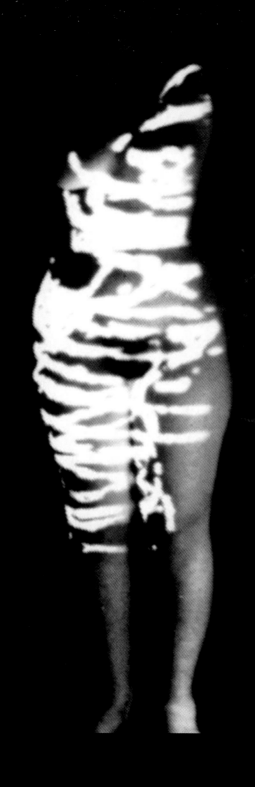

conceals and reveals her body questions the viewer's anticipation of the whole and fragmented self.

Though Duffy has garnered considerable international criticism in the past 15 years indicating the depth of her engagement and the power of her performances around disability arts, her performances have received scant historical attention in terms of Irish art. In the slide/tape work *Asking for It* (1986), two bodies appear, Duffy's and that of either friend or lover, they touch and press together in an embrace. The voiceover addresses the difficulties Duffy faced around touching and being touched. 'You tell me that you like to hug trees, you feel that you appreciate it. Sometimes I feel like a tree when you hug me, warm radiating and rooted. Other times I feel like a telegraph pole, straight, unbending and wired.'[23] Yet the title of the work also alludes to the social mores of Irish society that was quick to stigmatise women who expressed their sexuality in overt ways. The right to autonomy is also alluded to in the work *Pride and Prejudice* (1989), two photographic panels that employed written and visual format to highlight 'the problems of a sexual identity when the body is disabled.'[24] A reviewer of the *Sexuality and Gender: Irish Art of the Nineteen Eighties* (1990) was critical of the exhibition of these panels in the show without the accompanying video work: 'Without seeing the full video of which these two panels are but a part, the Duffy piece is itself disabled.'[25] Though the comment is aimed at the difficulty artists often face when distilling performance and time-based work through photographic images, the lack of awareness in suggesting that Duffy's work is 'disabled' by the format in which it is presented in suggests the double marginalisation that disabled women artists, like Duffy, faced in Irish society.

Women performance artists like Cummins, Duffy, and O'Kelly shifted beyond a preoccupation with the formal language of art to interrogate how political engagement, theoretical concerns, and contemporary art revolves around women's bodies. The body as primary material extended beyond the earlier concerns of feminist performance artists as the representation of the body assumed double importance in Irish culture. When Pauline Cummins asserted: 'as a woman my body was my country' she pointed to the enduring legacy of Irish nationhood projected onto the bodies of Irish women.[26] In doing so she emphasised ownership of her own body and attempted to subvert the pervasive patriarchal representations of women. Reflecting on the media frenzy surrounding the Kerry Babies Tribunal (1984), an unsolved murder case in which a young mother, Joanne Hayes, was accused of double

Opposite: Mary Duffy, *Stories of a Body*, 1990. Photo courtesy of the artist.

'The aim of many women was to reclaim the power to create their own images, and what consequently arises in feminist performance art is a tension between the lingual and the embodied. In Irish performance this assumed a new significance as women struggled to find their voices in a culture that had previously silenced them.'

infanticide, Cummins explained: 'it struck me very forcibly that her "image" was constructed not only by the media – but also through the very language of the law, the court system, the judge's attitudes. Language is non-visual, but nonetheless creates highly significant images.'[27] The aim of many women was to reclaim the power to create their own images, and what consequently arises in feminist performance art is a tension between the lingual and the embodied. In Irish performance this assumed a new significance as women struggled to find their voices in a culture that had previously silenced them.

Nowhere is this more evident than in the autobiographical performances of Cummins, O'Kelly, and Duffy. The presence of a strong oral culture in Ireland perhaps partially grounds the explanation as to why these artists fused contemporary performance and storytelling, though it is important to note that other feminist performances artists like Rachel Rosenthal and Karen Finlay had also adopted this format. In relation to storytelling, German literary critic Walter Benjamin states: 'The storyteller takes what he tells from experience – his own or that reported by others. And he in turn makes it the experience of those who are listening to his tale.'[28] In storytelling, the latent potential of the narrative enables the active participation of the audience to interpret the embedded meaning.[29] Furthermore storytelling encourages this active participation by providing a framework through which specific collective and individual identities are located.[30] It also enables another means for the personal to become political in feminist performance. As Adrian Kear and Deborah Steinberg suggest: 'Narration [...] both enables and embeds the performative constitution of collective and individual identities; it provides a structuring dialectic mediating the imaginary and the material.'[31]

In the intimate *One Day…In Time (Extracts from Una O'Kelly's Diary November 1981-1988)* performed at the Orchard Gallery in near total darkness, O'Kelly read selected passages from her mother's diary, spanning the public and private divide. Accompanied by pre-recorded sounds of a clock and a typewriter she read out:

> Loughie went back to Aran and seemed a bit lonely leaving. No matter what you do for your children in this world, you can't save them sorrow. I expect it would be better if when they grew up you severed all connections with them and took no interest at all in their doings, at least they'd be less sad at the final parting. The troubles in the North are escalating. The Reverent Robert Bradford was assassinated and several (Ulster Defence Regiment) supposedly innocent people have been gunned down. The Irish Republican Army (IRA) are on the rampage, and now the Unionists are beginning to strike back […].[32]

The act of reading a personal diary in a performance fuses the normally separate public and private. The performance further accentuates how O'Kelly's artistic practice articulates memory by juxtaposing different temporalities. The act of reading her mother's diaries allowed O'Kelly to reflect personally on contemporary issues. She recalls, 'I was interested in her politics, her reading of the daily news issues, her feelings about Northern Irish people as a southern Irish woman.'[33] This highlights the artist's awareness of the situation in Northern Ireland as a locus through which to examine her own Irish identity. The date selected from the diary, 1981, was a significant year in the Republican movement in Northern Ireland. During this year, IRA prisoner Bobby Sands was elected as a Member of Parliament in a by-election for Fermanagh and South Tyrone, while on hunger strike to reinstate special status as political prisoners.[34] Shortly thereafter Sands died, calling international attention to the stand-off between Margaret Thatcher's government and the interned IRA members. The strike was eventually called off in October 1981, but not before a total of ten men had died as a result of self-imposed starvation. Certainly, the turbulent events of 1981 in Northern Ireland resonated with the then current events in 1988, particularly the highly publicised killing of three IRA members in Gibraltar. Given that the location of this performance was in the Orchard Gallery in Derry City, one of the most contested cities during the Troubles in Northern Ireland, the references to these political events assume a double importance.

This shifting between public and private highlights the political and social position of women during the 1980s. The sound of the typewriter references Una O'Kelly's journalistic background and underscores the public concerns of journalism and the private concerns of mothering. The sound of the clock, indicating the passage of time, serves as a reminder of the distance from the events contained in the diary and of the distance between the artist and her mother. This performance occurred several years after the death of the artist's mother and can be understood as an attempt by O'Kelly to establish a connection with her mother based on memory. Similarly, Frances Hegarty's *Turas* (1995) also seeks to re-establish a connection with the maternal figure through the artist's attempts to regain her lost Irish language. Oral history is often used to reconstruct the personal lives of individuals, relying on the accounts of the individual to emphasise what events were important in their particular narratives.[35] Documents such as diaries and letters are rich sources for women's history, often times the only existing evidence of personal and familial lives.[36] This performance suggests the possibility of retrospectively constructing a personal narrative based on the act of reading private family history. Belarie Zatzman terms this as a 'shadow narrative', one that is constructed in the liminal spaces of subtext and locates itself between histories and the spaces mediated by imagination.[37] The connection between self and Other, or in this case, self and mother is one that the artist seeks to establish in the 'liminal spaces of subtext' literally located in the absences and silences of the diary.

A performed image created in relation to *One Day…In Time* captures the importance of subtext in understanding the potential power of these memories. O'Kelly is photographed on one side of an acetate reaching out to the written page, lightly touching the surface with the tips of her fingers. The camera focuses on the physical connection of O'Kelly with the words, while the image of the artist is somewhat out of focus. This serves to blur the artist's face, giving the impression that it is perhaps the artist or her mother that appears through the page. When reading the acetate, it is apparent that O'Kelly also sees the viewer from a veiled perspective. The page acts as a prism to transmit memory, refracting it in different ways to artist and viewer. From the artist's perspective, the writing is projected onto the distant figures of the audience, metaphorically symbolising the transformation of private concerns into the realm of the collective. As the writing is reversed for the viewer, one is totally dependent on the artist to recall and tell her mother's story. From the position of the viewer, the writing becomes inscribed on O'Kelly's body.

Importantly, the artist's hand touching the page serves as a type of bodily communication. 'The body, however, recognizes and receives communication directly from other bodies, allowing posture, gesture, and imagery to develop as alternative means of transmitting knowledge and feeling of various states of being.'[38] A bodily connection is established through the stilled movement of the outstretched hand whereby the viewer intimately connects with the body of the performer.

Pauline Cummins's *Unearthed* (1988-91) is another performance that explored different aspects of the socio-political situation in Ireland. For Cummins the early physical performances of the 1970s that embraced 'horror, blood, feathers, animals' found in the works of Viennese Actionists were not particularly appealing. Instead she sought to locate her performances in the existing oral tradition in Ireland.[39] She begins by locating her performance in the personal: 'Irish? I'm not Irish... well I'm not really Irish. You see my mother is English.' Cummins questions her own identity and prompts the audience to consider what it means to be 'Irish.' She recalls, 'But I liked having an English mother. She always had great insights into Irish things. She was very funny and she'd point out many contradictions about our society. She was usually right.' Cummins relates several personal childhood recollections that suggest differences between the artist and her mother while projected slide images change intermittently on a screen. It is when she asserts 'Politics never seemed to matter until Derry happened', referencing the killing of thirteen civilians known as 'Bloody Sunday' that the performances transitions from the personal to the political. At one point Cummins lightheartedly asks 'Do you want to hear a joke? What's a head job in Ireland?' She responds 'a hood over the head and a bullet through it.' Repeating her answer again more slowly for emphasis, the change in pace and tone allows the gravity of this 'joke' to sink in for the viewer. An image of her face painted white appears next to where she stands. Her hands, painted black, rise to the side of her face conveying agony and grief. This emotive image is in contrast to her carefully composed live appearance.

In 1983 Cummins began working on the underlying concept of *Unearthed* as is evidenced from the *Unearthed: Working Drawings* (1983) included in *Irish Exhibition of Living Artists*. These early drawings depict a body partially uncovered from a grave dug in a turf bog. The sketches detail that the skeletal remains are of fired clay and porcelain and wrapped in old bandages, clearly referencing the phenomenon of bog bodies, mummified

> 'Nigel Rolfe inserted his naked body into a turf furrow where he lay completely still for several hours, questioning the relationship between the human body and nature.'

human remains discovered in peat bogs that are preserved through chemical processes. As of 1987 over 80 bog bodies had been uncovered in Ireland since 1750, most date from the late medieval to the modern age, but some have been identified as human sacrifices from the Iron Age.[40]

Bogs have fascinated artists least not because as Karin Sanders writes they are deeply uncanny, 'neither water, nor land, bogs are liminal spaces, thresholds between surfaces and depths, ambiguous sites of origin.'[41] *In Bog Action (Aktion im Moor)* (1971) Joseph Beuys ran into a peat bog, allowing his body to sink deeper and deeper into the muck. As his body vanished from sight only his trademark fedora floated on the surface of the bog symbolising his desire to return to nature.[42] In the performance *Ledge* (1981), Nigel Rolfe inserted his naked body into a turf furrow where he lay completely still for several hours, questioning the relationship between the human body and nature. *Unearthed* may also have another frame of reference, Ana Mendieta's *Silueta* (1973-80) series, yet while the body in Mendieta's performances explore the tension between female visibility and material traces the bodies in *Unearthed* emerge rather than recede. Combined with Cummins's voice over: 'I live with these half dead, half alive people, waiting for the cease-fire, longing to be released with them, from this eternal waiting' they take on an ominous tone. Perhaps the most potent images of this performance are a series of raku-fired masks. These masks reference death masks but their appearance, with hallowed eyes and contorted twisted mouths, does not suggest a placid pallor of death, but the grim agony of being bound in this conflict for an eternity. Juxtaposed with the image of Cummins screaming, the symbolic and real bodies communicate the complexities of Irish identities. It is possible to see how the concerns of *Unearthed* resonate in contemporary performance, specifically in works like Amanda Coogan's *Medea* (2001) and *How to Explain the Sea to an Uneaten Potato* (2008).

Opposite: Mary Duffy, *Cutting the Ties that Bind*, 1988. Photo courtesy of the artist.

Left: Pauline Cummins, *Unearthed*, 1988-91, Projects UK commission.
Right: Pauline Cummins, *Holy Ground*, Wicklow 2000.
Photos courtesy of the artists.

Top: Pauline Cummins and Louise Walsh, *Sounding the Depths*, 1992, detail of collaborative video and photographic installation, collection of the Irish Museum of Modern Art.
Bottom: Pauline Cummins and Sandra Johnston, *Holy Ground*, Wicklow, 1999.
Photos courtesy of the artists.

'The white projected light was sketchy in appearance [...] It emphasised her torso and visually obscured the surface of her body. She recalled memories of hurt and humiliation under the medicalised gaze that stripped Duffy of her subjectivity as a child.'

Mary Duffy's *Stories of a Body* (1991), first performed at the Belltable Gallery, Limerick, adopted the medium of storytelling to interrogate bodily difference. A slide image of stones was projected onto a square pillar in the centre of the darkened gallery. It cross-faded into an image of more stones.[43] The projection slowly dissolved to form a spiral. Then Duffy appeared naked, standing beside the pillar. Her body was illuminated by the projections.[44] The white projected light was sketchy in appearance, reminiscent of scribbled pencil-markings. It emphasised her torso and visually obscured the surface of her body. She recalled memories of hurt and humiliation under the medicalised gaze that stripped Duffy of her subjectivity as a child:

> I stand here like I've stood here many times before so that you can assess the damage. You have words to describe me, and although I cannot give them a voice, I know all of them. But to acknowledge that I can see you, how you discuss me, like a textbook, stick pins in me to ascertain whether I can feel, ask me to perform, is more than I am willing to do. And all the time you are getting about the business of assessing the damage. I built a wall around me. I can't even remember when I began, I don't even know if it had a beginning.[45]

The catalyst for this performance was a visit to a General Practitioner in 1990. The doctor broadly assumed that Duffy harboured animosity towards medical professionals. This experience caused the artist to reflect on how she felt disempowered as a child from the constant medical scrutinisation.

The exchange between artist and viewer is important in understanding how the use of the body in this work can reconceptualise perceptions of bodies. The representation of Duffy's body drew upon a troubling figure that provoked and challenged perceptions about the divide between normative and non-normative bodies. *Stories of a Body* was not only about reclaiming the artist's subjectivity, but also challenging the viewer. As her body confronted audience expectations, it became a site of exchange. Duffy herself has voiced the ambiguous position she occupies: 'Even among my own community of disabled people I felt that my experience was reflected through another perspective, this time a disabilist perspective – I am one of those able disabled people – the non-wobbling, non-dribbling, well-educated types – in short a "walkie-talkie".[46] It may then be understood that her body inhabits the perceived divide between ability and disability, which in this performance the divide was articulated through the gaze. In moments when the artist remained still, the viewer's gaze actively surveyed her, meanwhile when her body was in motion she disrupted the viewer's gaze by asserting a confrontational look of her own. In observing the shifting role of the viewer in this performance, it is clear that early on, one is encouraged to actively identify with the medical gaze that attempts to harness and control her unruly body. This allowed the spectator to indulge the forbidden desire to have unfettered visual access to her naked body. The realisation that the viewer could transgress the boundaries of a polite gaze while becoming the object of the artist's gaze, in turn, questions the seemingly objective nature of the gaze.

An awareness of this interplay leads to an intense consideration of the viewer's own subjective experience. The work is transformed into a hierarchal exchange between perceived ability and disability, objectivity and subjectivity. In this performance, '[d]isability [...] is a disruption in the visual, auditory or perceptual field as it refers to the power of the gaze.'[47] In *Stories of a Body*, the hierarchy between ability and disability capitulates as the audience listens without intervening while in narrating her experience Duffy claims her right to speak. Though Duffy's work is centered firmly in the personal, it translates to the political, not only in the context of disabilities rights, but allowed for disability to be read as a metaphor for the cultural expectations placed on women's bodies in Ireland. When presented in this embodied manner, Duffy challenged the internalised self-scrutiny that imposed unobtainable models of Irish womanhood, enabling viewers to contemplate the possibilities and alternatives for Irish women.

FEMINIST PRAXIS

Though these artists manifested and sustained ongoing dialogues between performance art, feminism, and Irish society, their practices encompassed another crucial aspect worthy of critical reflection. Irish artists engaged with feminism were inspired by the critiques of international women artists, critics and activists that sought to highlight how the power of pervading ideologies operated to exclude and marginalise women in visual art on the basis of gender. American art historian Linda Nochlin argued that patriarchal ideologies of power assert themselves over women disguised as assumptions about gender difference, contending that: 'Ideology manifests itself as much as by what is unspoken – unthinkable, unrepresentable – as by what is articulated in a work of art.'[48] Nochlin cautioned that symbolic power is invisible and 'can be exercised only with the complicity of those who fail to recognise either that they submit to it or that they exercise it.'[49] One of the ways in which feminists sought to expose and destabilise this symbolic power was through feminist activism in addition to their attacks on representation. Commenting on efforts of Irish feminists, Margrit Shildrick states: 'For feminists, there has always been the example of some very strong women to look back on, but also a sense in which the repressions that have assailed Ireland over many centuries have taken their toll on the social and political promotion of women in particular.'[50] Moreover, Shildrick argues that for these feminists, theory and practice occupy a symbiotic relationship.[51] Although Fionna Barber argued that Irish modernist artists like Mainie Jellett and Evie Hone were the 'active bearers of culture', the notion of women's agency in relation to art production in Ireland was never more relevant, nor more urgent, than it was during the 1980s and early 1990s as these women sought to assert claims over their own bodies. Therefore, describing feminist performance as 'praxis' is wholly appropriate when considering how women merged the visual, verbal, auditory, and embodied practice with their activism.

The establishment of three collaborative networking groups, Irish Women Artists Link (IWAL, London, 1986), the Women Artists Action Group (WAAG, Dublin, 1987), and the Northern Irish Women Artists Group (NIWAG, Belfast, 1987) coincided with the efforts that artists were making in their individual practices. Though not all of these artists were working in performance or time-based practices, these groups played important roles in promoting the idea of feminist praxis and supporting women artists working in performance. Networking as women artists helped to establish slide libraries (WAAG Slide Library or Women's Visual Arts Slide Library, Goldsmiths College) that served as important repositories of visual record of artists whose works might not be preserved in public collections and exhibition catalogues. These groups enabled women artists to bypass traditional gallery structures, which at the time were unequivocally male-dominated, by offering access to alternative spaces. In the absence of a contemporary art museum, practices like performance, installation, and video practices were similarly reliant on alternative spaces.

Spanning nearly five years, with membership including artists, critics, curators, art historians, and educators, WAAG was perhaps one of the most effective of the three organisations. The goals outlined in WAAG's constitution included expanding the dominant aesthetic to encompass all forms of creative expression; educating the general public about women's contributions to the Arts; ensuring the inclusion of women in the history of art; to promote a viable system that provides an opportunity for realistic economic survival in the Arts, including financial parity and equal access to grants, funding, and employment for women.[52] In 1988 WAAG joined the International Association of Women Artists (IAWA); allying themselves with feminist groups in other countries enabled the group to cross boundaries by sharing common aims and increasing limited resources by pursuing joint objectives.[53] Cummins, Duffy, and O'Kelly were all involved with WAAG to varying degrees, and it is possible to understand how groups like WAAG supported the praxis these artists sought to develop.[54] These feminist groups ran several performance workshops for specialist and non-specialist audiences, meaning that women from different backgrounds could utilise performance as a means of expression. In 1988, WAAG held a two-day performance workshop, organised by O'Kelly, with Frances Hegarty and Anne Seagrave.[55] O'Kelly ran a performance workshop in Derry (1988) and another in Dublin in 1989 entitled *Sounding Out – Sexuality, Voice and Power.* Through their various activities, organisations like WAAG, IWAG, and NIWAG critiqued the institutionalised exclusion of women artists from important exhibitions and attempted to engage feminist praxis on a practical level.[56]

Cummins, Duffy, and O'Kelly had a number of documented interactions with feminist artists from the United States and the United Kingdom. In 1987, they presented their work at a panel organised by May Stevens for the Women's Caucus for Art at the College Art Association Annual Conference entitled *The Politics of Identity: Entering, Changing and Being Changed.* Their work was situated alongside that of Adrian Piper and Cecilia Vicuña, two performance artists known for their feminist interventions into identity and otherness. Disseminating their work in this fashion, amongst artists, critics, historians, in an international setting ensured valuable opportunities for cross-cultural dialogues amongst feminists artists working in different locations. Both Stevens and Helen Chadwick participated in a seminar held by WAAG in Derry (June 1988) where, along with Moira Roth, they discussed different approaches to feminist art, essentially laying the groundwork for establishing connections between work in Ireland and

'Performance art in Ireland, as elsewhere, offers possibilities for engaging in meaningful dialogues: as a process that provokes exchanges about ideas of privilege and power, as an empowering embodied practice and as legitimising critique that unites art and feminist activism.'

abroad.[57] Stevens's influence on O'Kelly is evident on a conceptual level, yet it is clear that she has also been inspired by O'Kelly's work, demonstrating that Irish women artists were engaged in cross-cultural dialogues with other feminist artists. When Stevens's husband, the artist Rudolf Baranik died she commenced a project of spreading his ashes in bodies of water. She travelled to Ireland where she performed the action in Connemara with O'Kelly and her family.[58] This action recalls the private performance O'Kelly undertook at this same location upon the death of her mother for *Dancing with My Shadow* (1988), indicating further interconnections between feminist performances in Ireland and abroad.

CONCLUSION

Though performance art emphasises specific and unique temporal conditions attached to being present in the moment, the assessment of the works in this essay suggest important wider connections with the socio-political climate at the time of their creation. For artists working at the intersections of feminism and performance, these artistic interventions fused the personal and the political. Hilary Robinson, paraphrasing art historian Griselda Pollock, asserts that 'a central task for feminists in Ireland (including artists and art historians) is to critique the concept "Irish woman", not just as a way of writing about the lives of actual women, but as an institutionalised ideological practice of representation in and of the culture.'[59] While Irish cultural nationalists in the early twentieth century appropriated the bodies of women as ciphers for the nation, second-wave Irish feminists challenged these long-standing tropes by rendering visible women's lived realities. In this sense, the performance works of O'Kelly, Cummins, and Duffy were transgressive because they focused on the body, provocatively advocating the subjectivity of the individual against the authority of the establishment. If in Irish society women's bodies are sites of conflict, women performance artists that activated abject and unruly bodies, or that represented fragmented bodies as a means of countering wholeness that can be controlled, evaded patriarchal authority. On a separate but related point, viewing these historical works from a contemporary perspective allows one to critically engage with the political, economic, and social issues embedded in Irish society. In contemporary Ireland, where the right to reproductive freedom is barred; where a woman's death occurs at a maternity hospital because she was refused a life saving abortion; where the national broadcaster, RTÉ censors a gay rights activist for labelling the vitriolic writings of opponents to same-sex marriage as homophobic; where a terminally ill woman is denied the right to die; where direct provisions for asylum seekers are exposed as grimly inadequate, it is alarmingly clear that bodies and the rights of those bodies continue to remain a pressing concern.[60] Performance art in Ireland, as elsewhere, offers possibilities for engaging in meaningful dialogues: as a process that provokes exchanges about ideas of privilege and power, as an empowering embodied practice, and as legitimising critique that unites art and feminist activism.

1. Linda Connolly and Tina O'Toole, *Documenting Irish Feminisms: The Second Wave* (Dublin: Woodfield Press, 2005), p. 27.

2. June Levine, 'The Women's Movement in the Republic of Ireland, 1968-1980', in *The Field Day Anthology of Irish Writers: Irish Women's Writings and Traditions*, ed. by Angela Bourke, (New York: New York University Press, 2002), pp. 177-228 (p. 187).

3. Lisa Smyth, *Abortion and Nation: The Politics of Reproduction in Contemporary Ireland* (United Kingdom: Ashgate, 2005), p. 10.

4. Dorothy Walker, 'Looking Back', in *The GPA Irish Arts Review Yearbook* (1988), pp. 26-30 (p. 26).

5. This mural was mentioned in an RTE programme, *I Live Here* (1989).

6. Katy Deepwell, (ed.) 'Pauline Cummins interview', *Dialogues: Women Artists from Ireland* (London: I. B. Tauris, 2005), pp. 33-43, p. 39.

7. Elizabeth Beaucamp, 'Performance Artists End Up with Audience in the Palms of Their Hands', *The Edmonton Journal*, 16 November 1991.

8. Mary Duffy, Unpublished email to the author, 15 February 2011.

9. Mary Duffy, 'Disability, Differentness, Identity', *Circa*, 34 (1987), 30-31 (p. 30).

10. Katy Deepwell, (ed.) 'Alanna O'Kelly interview', *Dialogues: Women Artists from Ireland* (London: I. B. Tauris, 2005), pp. 138-148, p.138.

11. Carol Coulter, 'A Happy Ending for a Midwife's Tale', *Irish Times*, 22 May 1999, p. 8.

12. Alston Conley and Mary Armstrong, 'An Interview with Pauline Cummins and Louise Walsh', in *Re/Dressing Cathleen: Contemporary Works from Irish Women Artists*, ed. by Alston Conley and Mary Armstrong (Boston: McMullen Museum of Art, Boston College, 1997), pp. 118-9, (p. 119).

13. Bruce Arnold, 'Art', *Irish Independent*, 11 May 1992.

14. Jaki Irvine, 'Review: Sounding the Depths, Irish Museum of Modern Art, Dublin, 1 April - 9 May 1992', *Circa* 62 (1992), p. 66.

15. Hilary Robinson, 'Disruptive Women Artists: An Irigarayan Reading of Irish Visual Culture', in *Irish Studies Review* (2000), 57-72 (p. 62).

16. In an earlier slide/tape and sound installation, *Inis t'Oirr/ Aran Dance* (1985), Cummins explored female sexuality and the gendering of craft using the nude male body.

17. Other artists have also been inspired by the power of keening. Anna O'Sullivan had a work included in *Divisions, Crossroads, Turns of Mind: Some New Irish Art* curated by Lucy Lippard and more recently Áine Phillips incorporated aspects of keening into her performance *Love Lies Bleeding* (2004).

18. Alanna O'Kelly, *Ómós Statement*, National Irish Visual Artists Library (NIVAL) File.

19. Luke Clancy, 'Live Art: O'Kelly/McClennan/Byrne/McAleer Project Arts Centre', *Irish Times*, February 16 1995, p. 14.

20. Amanda Coogan later used this site for *Yellow: Re-Performed* (2010).

21. Ann Millett-Gallant, *The Disabled Body in Contemporary Art* (New York: Palgrave Macmillan 2010), p. 38.

22. Tom Duddy, 'Mary Duffy, Belltable Arts Centre, Limerick 20 November-15 December 90', *Circa* 56 (1991), 39-40 (p. 39).

23. Ibid., p. 40.

24. Mike Catto, 'Sexuality and Gender, Douglas Hyde Gallery 23 October-17 November 90', *Circa* 55 (1990), 38-39, (p. 39).

25. Ibid.

26. Pauline Cummins and Louise Walsh, *Sounding the Depths: A Collaborative Installation* (Dublin: Irish Museum of Modern Art, 1992), p. 6.

27. Ailbhe Smyth, Pauline Cummins, Beverley Jones and Pat Murphy, 'Image Making, Image Breaking', *Circa* 32 (1987), 13-19, (p. 14).

28. Walter Benjamin, *Illuminations* (Boston: Houghton Mifflin Harcourt, 1968), p. 87.

29. Ibid., p. 88.

30. Adrian Kear and Deborah Lynn Steinberg, 'Ghost Writing', in *Mourning Diana: Nation, Culture and the Performance of Grief*, ed. by Adrian Kear and Deborah Lynn Steinberg (London: Routledge, 2002), pp. 1-14 (p. 9).

31. Ibid.

32. Moira Roth, 'Live Art in Derry,' *High Performance*, 11.1 (1988), p. 58.

33. Ann Wilson Lloyd, *Alanna O'Kelly* (Contemporanea, 1991), p. 52.

34. Tim Pat Coogan, *The IRA*, (New York: Palgrave 2002), p. 500.

35. Bridget Brereton, 'Gendered Testimonies: Autobiographies, Diaries and Letters by Women

as Sources for Caribbean History', *Feminist Review* 59 (1998), 143-63 (p. 144).

36. Ibid., p. 145.

37. Belarie Zatzman, 'The Monologue Projects: Drama as a Form of Witnessing,' in *How Theatre Educates: Convergences and Counterpoints with Artists, Scholars and Advocates*, ed. by David Booth and Kathleen Gallagher (Toronto: University of Toronto Press, 2003), p. 36. (pp. 35-55)

38. Rebecca Sachs Norris, 'Embodiment and Community', *Western Folklore* 60.2-3 (2001), 111-24 (p. 117).

39. Elizabeth Beaucamp, 'Performance Artists End Up with Audience in the Palms of Their Hands', *The Edmonton Journal*, 16 November 1991.

40. Raghnall Ó Floinn, 'Irish Bog Bodies', *Archaeology Ireland*, 2.3 (1988), p. 95.

41. Karin Sanders, *Bodies in the Bog and the Archaeological Imagination* (Chicago: University of Chicago Press, 2012), p. 7.

42. Thomas McEvilley, *The Triumph of Anti-Art: Conceptual and Performance Art in the Formation of Post-Modernism* (New York: McPherson and Company, 2005), p. 264.

43. Luke Clancy, 'Duffy/Patrickson/Donaghy Project Arts Centre', *Irish Times* February 15 1995, p.12.

44. Pauline Cummins, 'Mary Duffy: Onder Ons Gezegd', *Ruimte* 8 (1991), 26-31, (p. 30).

45. Text from Installation, Rochdale Art Gallery, 1990 in Sally Dawson, 'Women's Movements: Feminism, Censorship and Performance Art', in *New Feminist Art Criticism*, ed. by Katy Deepwell, (Manchester: Manchester University Press, 1995), p. 113.

46. *Mary Duffy*, artist's website, <www.maryduffy.ie>.

47. Lennard J.Davis, *Enforcing Normalcy: Disability, Deafness and the Body* (New York: Verso, 1995), p. 129.

48. Linda Nochlin, *Women, Art and Power and Other Essays* (London: Thames and Hudson Ltd. 1989), p. 2.

49. Ibid.

50. Margrit Shildrick, 'Introduction: Emergent Strands or Theory on Edge?' in *Theory on the Edge*, ed. by Noreen Giffney and Margrit Shildrick (London: Palgrave MacMillian, 2013), pp. 1-9, (p. 1).

51. Ibid, p. 2.

52. WAAG Files, 'Women Artists Action Group Draft Constitution', 15 October 1988, p. 1. NIVAL Files.

53. Breeda Mooney, 'On the Record', *Circa* 59 (1991), p. 50.

54. Pauline Cummins and performance artist Anne Tallentire were respectively founding members of WAAG and IWAL.

55. WAAG Files, Performance Workshop, 1988, NIVAL Files.

56. Fionna Barber and Geraldine Reilly, 'Could do Better… the Hyde and Women's Art', *Circa*, 58 (1991), p. 37.

57. Stevens's *Special Project One plus or Minus One* was installed in the Orchard Gallery, Derry in 1988.

58. Patricia Hills, *May Stevens* (Petaluma: Pomengrante Communications, 2005), p. 61.

59. Hilary Robinson, 'Disruptive Women Artists: An Irigarayan Reading of Irish Visual Culture', *Irish Studies Review* 8.1 (2000), 57-72 (p. 58).

60. The tragic death of Savita Halappanavar (28 October 2012) occurred when she presented at the National University Hospital, Galway with a miscarriage. She was 17 weeks pregnant at the time and requested a termination. This request was denied and she subsequently developed septicemia and died of multiple organ failure. See Kitty Holland and Paul Cullen, 'Woman "denied a termination" dies in hospital', *Irish Times*, 14 November 2012.

Gay Rights activist Rory O'Neill, also known by his drag persona Panti Bliss, was a guest on the Brendan O'Connor *Saturday Night Show*. His interview was later censored on the RTE Player so it would not be available to viewers online. See Michael O'Regan, 'Calls for Rabbitte to give details of reported RTE payment to Iona Institute', *Irish Times*, 13 January 2014, p. 10.

Marie Fleming was a woman who took her case to the High Court, that she be allowed the right to euthanasia, which is currently illegal in Ireland. See 'Marie Fleming loses Supreme Court appeal challenging ban on assisted suicide', *RTE News* 29 April 2013, <http://www.rte.ie/news/2013/0429/387096-marie-fleming-to-hear-supreme-court-appeal-ruling/> [accessed 9 February 2014].

Under Irish law asylum seekers are unable to work, or receive education or social welfare. They are typically housed in direct provisions facilities while their cases await adjudication for refugee status. For information on direct provisions to asylum seekers see: Carl O'Brien, 'State fears reform of system will attract asylum seekers', *Irish Times*, 28 October 2013, p. 1.

HELENA WALSH

DEVELOPING DIALOGUES:
Live Art and Femininity
in Post-Conflict Ireland

Over the last three decades a strong force of women artists, from or living in Ireland and making Live Art, have gained national and international acclaim. This chapter reviews select performances from a broad range the most provocative contemporary female live artists related to the Irish region. The live artists discussed in this chapter, I suggest, enable a countering of cultural constructions of femininity in an Irish context by troubling what Rebecca Schneider, in her book *The Explicit Body in Performance* (1997), calls the 'dreamscape of modern identity.'[1]

Opposite: *LABOUR*, London, 2012. Photo: Marco Berardi.

'The artists in *LABOUR* [...] make evident the draconian patriarchal ideologies that continually inform the rigid policing of female sexuality in an Irish cultural context.'

I see these live artists as productively interrogating the 'identity effects, bodily markings, historical legacies' that Schneider asserts 'repeat as noisome ghosts, marking and re-marking' and bearing 'reality effects' within 'the social dreamscapes' that constitute our Symbolic Order.[2] 'Even in combat boots,' Schneider notes, 'feminine form is hounded by the historical legacy of sex-discrimination in everyday social practice, by the history and control of woman's 'appropriate' imaging, and by the effects which that appropriation (The Modern Woman, the Cult of True Womanhood, the House Wife) has on women's lives.'[3] In directly courting the constructions and inscriptions of the female body that Schneider asserts ghost 'feminist counter-constructions,'[4] the live artists discussed in this chapter, I argue, make evident the gendered historical conventions that continually contain female sexuality and open up the possibilities for the development of more empowered identifications.

I firstly outline the significant shifts that occurred throughout the 1990s within the 'post-conflict' Irish region that I see as relevant to the work of contemporary live artists. I offer an explanation of the term 'post-conflict' for those unfamiliar with Irish history, as well as outlining the specific ways I am using this term within this essay. In particular, I outline cultural histories related to the gendering of labour and the containment of female sexuality that entered public discourse during the 1990s. Exploring these issues further I discuss performances by a number of artists in relation to cultural constructions of femininity. This discussion foregrounds my subsequent reflection on *LABOUR* – a touring group durational exhibition of Live Art focused on issues of gender and labour in an Irish context that I both participated in and co-curated with Amanda Coogan and Chrissie Cadman in 2012. *LABOUR* featured 11 female artists native to or resident within Northern and Southern Ireland. It toured three sites of geo-political relevance and occurred in sites related to work. *LABOUR* was produced by Benjamin Sebastian, the co-director of]performance s p a c e[and the first live exhibition occurred in this space on 9 February 2012. On the 25 February *LABOUR* travelled to Void Gallery in Derry/Londonderry and the final exhibition took place on the 10 March in The Lab, Dublin.[5] In each durational exhibition the participating artists performed simultaneously for eight consecutive hours, in reflection of an average working day. Engaging the processes of repetition and duration to perform traditional gendered labour, alongside the use of archaic aesthetics, the artists in *LABOUR*, I argue, make evident the draconian patriarchal ideologies that continually inform the rigid policing of female sexuality in an Irish cultural context. Charting the progression of the performances across the three successive sites, I outline the importance of the live communal dialogues which emerged between the artists in enabling the development of expressions that work against the limiting of women's political agency in the 'post-conflict' Irish region.

LIVE ART AND THE POST-CONFLICT IRISH REGION

The term 'post-conflict' refers to the period following the implementation of the Northern Irish Peace Process in response to the sectarian conflict in the North, commonly called 'The Troubles', that escalated from the late 1960s. Initiated with the signing of the Anglo-Irish Agreement in 1985, the Peace Process coincided with the Republic of Ireland's unprecedented economic growth throughout the 1990s, a period referred to as the 'Celtic Tiger' era. Of course, I realise it would be naïve to claim the Northern Irish region at peace in light of continuing sectarian tensions in recent years,[6] or equally hail the Republic of Ireland's economic triumphs given its economic collapse and acceptance of economic bailouts from the European Union (EU) and the International Monetary Fund (IMF) in 2010. Indeed, the fragile global economic climate, within which the Irish Republic's economic collapse and acceptance of EU and IMF bailouts is wrought with instability, offered an apt backdrop to *LABOUR*.

Rather, I use the term 'post-conflict' here to demarcate the significant shifts during the 1990s that came with the modernising ethos of the Celtic Tiger and the signalling of an end to the violence of The Troubles. These shifts brought about a loosening of the oppositional and defiant narratives of the past maintained by British-unionist-Protestants and Irish-nationalist-Catholics following the revolt of British Rule during the 1916

Rising and the subsequent partition of Ireland with the establishment of the Irish Free State in 1922. In the 1990s the past was opened up to broader exploration.[7] The neoliberal ethos of the Celtic Tiger loosened somewhat the significant power the Catholic clergy assumed over state affairs in Southern Ireland throughout the twentieth century. The decriminalisation of homosexuality and lifting of restrictions on the availability of contraception in 1993, alongside the legalisation of divorce in 1995, demonstrate the socially liberating influence of the Celtic Tiger.

Significantly, the systematic clerical sexual abuse of children in state-sanctioned Catholic Industrial and Reformatory Schools throughout the history of the independent Irish state entered public discourse in the 1990s. The emergence of long-silenced traumatic histories into the public domain at this time sobered the newly affluent Irish government, preoccupied as it was at the time with triumphantly parading its 'rags to riches' success story and finding ever more ways of marketing Irishness and Irish nostalgia to global audiences. Alongside the abuses in residential schools, the detention of women in a punitive regime of slave labour – in for-profit industrial laundries within the Republic's Magdalen Laundries – gained attention.[8] This led to the closure of the last of these Catholic convents in 1996. Following the intervention of the United Nations Committee Against Torture (UNCAT), the Irish state's long-standing denial of complicity in sustaining these punitive systems of gendered degradation was refuted with the publication of The McAleese Report in 2013.[9] However, the abusive nature of these institutions was downplayed within the report, most notably through the exclusion of 796 pages of survivor testimonies compiled by the campaign group Justice for Magdalenes.[10] The refusal by the female Catholic congregations that ran the Magdalen Laundries to contribute to redress for women surviving incarceration in these institutions heightens these denials. These issues are also relevant to Northern Ireland, for example, Amnesty International and UNCAT have called on the Northern Irish Executive to investigate the operations of the Magdalen Laundries in the north.[11] Equally, inquiries into abuse in children's homes and the juvenile justice system in Northern Ireland between 1922 and 1995 began in January 2014, as part of the Inquiry into Historical Institutional Abuse in Northern Ireland.

Opposite top: Chrissie Cadman, *LABOUR*, London, 2012. Photo: Marco Berardi.
Opposite bottom left: Amanda Coogan, *LABOUR*, London, 2012. Photo: by Marco Berardi.
Opposite bottom right: Elvira Santamaria Torres, *LABOUR*, 2012. Photo: Jordan Hutchins.

The increased adoption of the processes of repetition and duration within post-conflict Live Art, I suggest, is crucially bound up in the revelations of the past 30 years. Indeed, numerous female live artists have used these processes to examine the histories of the Magdalen Laundries, as I noted in my contribution to *Brutal Silences: Live Art and Irish Culture* (2011); a study guide commissioned by the Live Art Development Agency, co-authored by Ann Maria Healy and myself.[12] The use of temporal processes to interrogate cultural histories is relevant to Amelia Jones observations of temporality. She states:

> Temporality leads to a critical tension and an acknowledgement of histories – and the bodies that made and inhabited the past – as well as the relationality of our own sense of identification, in this body today, with these materialised versions of human creative action from the past.[13]

The exploration in post-conflict Live Art of 'the bodies that made and inhabited the past' is concerned, I argue, with productively broadening or complicating cultural histories and national identities in the Irish region.

Importantly, in repetitiously interrogating cultural histories in the wake of globalisation, female live artists highlight that despite the seeming modernity of our contemporary world, women's bodies remain restrained by a set of considerably out-dated patriarchal norms. Indeed, the restrictive abortion laws in the Irish region outline the ongoing restraints placed on women's bodies. Notably, the total protection of foetal life in the Republic's 1983 abortion amendment, Lisa Smith asserts, was centred on marking Ireland as a 'morally distinct nation-state' in the face of 'impending globalisation.'[14] Equally, while England, Scotland and Wales clarified the circumstances in which abortion is permissible under the Abortion Act 1967, Northern Ireland remained exempt from this legislation. As Ruth Fletcher notes, this demonstrates that 'the control of women's fertility is symbolically and materially important to several different species of nationalism in the region: Irish postcolonial conservatism, Irish anti-colonial republicanism and British unionism.'[15] Or, as Fionola Meredith, referencing the abortion laws in the Irish region, puts it, 'policing the Border pales into insignificance when it comes to policing women's bodies.'[16]

'Enlarged upon the body, the mouths make it appear as though the body had been opened up or split, while the teeth of the open mouths make monstrous and threatening the female form.'

CHALLENGING CULTURAL
CONSTRUCTIONS OF FEMININITY

In deploying their bodies within their work many female artists operate against the rigid containment of female sexuality. For example, in 1992, a collaborative installation by Pauline Cummins and Louise Walsh entitled *Sounding the Depths* was exhibited in the Irish Museum of Modern Art, Dublin. In a video piece that constituted part of this installation the artists projected imagery of their mouths onto their naked torsos. Enlarged upon the body, the mouths make it appear as though the body had been opened up or split, while the teeth of the open mouths make monstrous and threatening the female form. Jaki Irvine notes that the mythical imagery of the toothed vagina, 'the vagina dentata,' is suggested through this imagery, 'registering a simultaneous fascination and dread of sexuality associated with the female body.'[17] The opening up of the female body in *Sounding the Depths* is also relevant to Jones's observations around Sigmund Freud's theories of castration anxiety. Jones draws attention to the gendered binaries within Freud's theorising of fetishism in relation to the figural boy's fear of castration where through 'the establishment of this representational body as a phantasmagorical replacement for the woman's lost or absent penis (the boy fears castration by the father).'[18] The 'end result' of this, Jones points out, is a 'seemingly endless tendency in patriarchy to project women's bodies as fetishes to palliate this anxiety.'[19] However, as Jones notes, 'the important constructing here is that it is definitely not her genitals but her body as a sealed and so unthreatening, objectified thing that is represented.'[20]

The patriarchal representation of the female body 'as a sealed and so unthreatening, objectified thing' is significant to the social construction of femininity in the Irish region founded upon the figuring of an emblematic relationship between the female body and the nation. Nations, Sally R. Munt asserts, are 'often depicted as a vital body, with a heart, lungs, mind, and extremities, concomitant with the fantasy of the bounded sealed body' and can be deemed 'healthy or diseased.'[21] Opening her rich semi-autobiographical account, *Mother Ireland* (1976), Edna O'Brien asserts 'Ireland has always been a woman, a cave, a cow, a Rosaleen, a sow, a bride, a harlot, and of course, the gaunt Hag of Beare.'[22] As the title of her book presupposes, O'Brien takes aim at one of nationalism's most revered icons, the proverbial Mother Ireland. For Munt, the 'rhetoric of Mother Ireland needing her sons to rescue her from (sexual) bondage has a long and potent genealogy,' bound to Ireland's colonial past.[23] Indeed, the image of the dry-breasted Mother Ireland unable to nurture her offspring (the nation) enabled the unspeakable horrors of the Great Irish Famine (1845-51) to be expressed and was central to fuelling the 1916 Rising. However, following the establishment of the Irish Free State the combined submissive serenity of the self-sacrificing and nurturing Mother Ireland and the passive sexuality of the virginal Catholic Madonna spearheaded the increased moral regulation of Irishwomen. Maria Luddy notes, the 'politicisation of sexual behaviour had been a feature of Irish nationalism from the late nineteenth century, evident most strongly in the equation of the British garrison with a source of moral and physical contagion for Irishwomen.'[24] Yet, with the British garrison gone explanations for the increase rather than plummeting of sexual immorality, Luddy asserts, gave way to the conclusion 'that the real threat to chastity and sexual morality resided in the bodies of women. Thus moral regulation, by Church and state, attempted to impose standards of idealised conduct, particularly on women, that would return the nation to purity.'[25]

The performance *Wet Cup* (2000) by UK-based Irish artist, Kira O'Reilly, can, perhaps, be read as relevant to the moral policing of female sexuality.[26] The performance deployed historical medical practices that are based on the purification of toxins through drawing blood from the body. In *Wet Cup*, an assistant placed numerous heated glass cups on O'Reilly's body with ordered repetition. Subsequently the assistant made incisions in the flesh demarcated by the multiple rounded glass vessels. When the cups were placed back on top of these incisions O'Reilly's blood seeped into them. Gianna Bouchard notes that O'Reilly's use of medical practices 'address female subjectivity, memory, the materiality of the body and its traces.'[27] Clearly broader readings can be related to O'Reilly's

Opposite: Kira O'Reilly, *Wet Cup*, 2001. Photo courtesy of the artist.

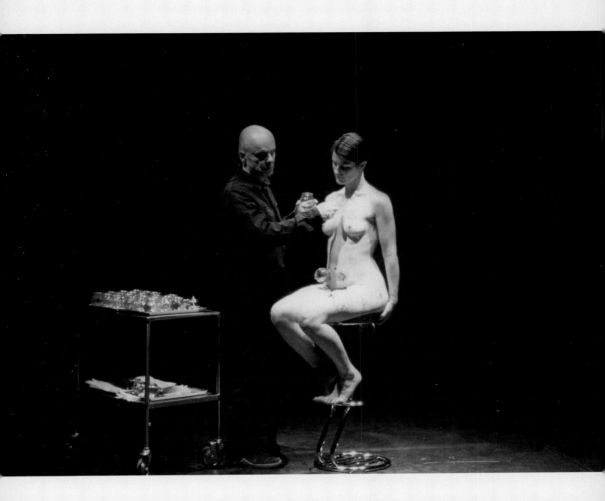

'At one stage with her head in the bucket, she makes rapid, yet tense and restrained, movements with her arms and legs. At another point she momentarily holds the tap to her crotch, parodying phallic imagery.'

performance. However, in using purifying practices on her female body, O'Reilly raises consideration of the archaic patriarchal ideologies relevant to the specificity of an Irish context. For example, those ideologies that situate 'the real threat to chastity and sexual morality' as residing 'in the bodies of women' referred to by Luddy.[28] Yet, in breaching of the boundaries of the body, causing the body to leak, the performance equally operates against 'the fantasy of the bounded sealed body,' outlined by Munt.[29]

Anne Seagrave, another influential artist in Ireland and internationally, also resists the fetishising of the female body in her durational performance *Jamais Vu*, which premiered at the Granary Theatre, Cork as part of *Bodily Functions* in 2005.[30] With her skin whitened, Seagrave performed this piece naked apart from a rectangular piece of mirror covering her breasts. In the performance she utilised a number of objects, including an old-fashioned tin bucket and a tap from a sink basin, allowing reference to the everyday, domesticity and cleanliness and thus, perhaps, patriarchal ideologies that locate female sexuality as a threat to morality. Seagrave repetitiously performed a series of intensely physical and rigidly choreographed actions. At one stage with her head in the bucket, she makes rapid, yet tense and restrained, movements with her arms and legs. At another point she momentarily holds the tap to her crotch, parodying phallic imagery. Importantly, with the rectangular mirror strapped to breasts, reflecting the gaze back towards the viewer, while at the same time displaying her genitals, in other words, the unsealed female body, Seagrave actively resisted the fetishising of the female body.

In a performance that constitutes part of *Violent* (2010-13), Sinéad O'Donnell also draws attention to the restraining of women's political agency, while simultaneously offering a retort to patriarchal norms.[31] O'Donnell performed with a tall tower of white dinner plates. Exceeding her height, the stack of plates wavered precariously as O'Donnell strained to steady it by hugging and pressing her body against it. Throughout the performance a soundtrack played, in which the word 'violent' was repeated alternatively by male and female voices. After a period of time, O'Donnell stepped back and let go of the tower of plates, and on pushing them forward, they crashed on the floor with an explosive bang.

Now based in Belfast, O'Donnell is originally from Dublin and her performance, I suggest, speaks of the restraints placed on women both north and south of the border. For instance, the references to domesticity within O'Donnell's sustained struggle to steady an excessive amount of dinner plates enables contemplation of the legislative confinement of women to the home and duties of procreation in the southern Irish state post partition. Led by the dictates of Catholic doctrine, the newly established southern state introduced a number of regressive laws, which restricted women's political and reproductive autonomy. For instance, the Criminal Law Amendment Act (1935) implemented a complete ban on contraception, including the importation or advertisement of contraceptive methods. In the same year The Conditions of Employment Bill (1935), advocated that men should be favoured over women in the work place. Article 41 of the 1937 Irish Constitution (Bunreacht na hÉireann) notoriously acknowledged the state's prioritising of hetero-normative family values and women's 'special' place in the home. This oft-quoted article states 'the State recognises that by her life within the home, woman gives to the State a support without which the common good cannot be achieved.'[32] The Civil Service Act (1956), commonly referred to as the 'marriage bar,' required that women working in the Civil Service resigned on marriage. This act, Frances Gardiner observes, crowned 'almost four decades of increasingly authoritarian legislation, which curbed women's self-determination to the extent that political involvement was severely curtailed, if not actually impossible, for most women, save as political wife, sister or mother.'[33]

This curtailing of women's working rights and political involvement was repealed following the Republic of Ireland's joining of the European Union in 1973 and the revival of the feminist movement during the 1970s. Nonetheless, slave labour camps for women remained in operation until 1996, while the prioritising of motherhood in rigid anti-abortion laws in the Republic is a continuation of the systematic repression of women foregrounded in the 1937 Constitution. O'Donnell's performance, I suggest, questions the endurance of archaic patriarchal ideologies that associate a set of idealized feminine traits with Irish womanhood, equating womanhood with motherhood and resigning women to the duties of the homestead. Equally, the repetition of the word 'violent' in the performance brings to mind issues concerning domestic violence and conflict. This, I suggest, is relevant to Lisa Fizpatrick's exploration of the representation of sexual and domestic violence on the Northern Irish stage and 'the ways in which the political and civil conflict in Northern Ireland' influences 'attitudes to interpersonal violence and, in particular violence against women.'[34] Drawing on the use of the phrase 'an armed patriarchy' in studies that consider domestic and sexual violence against women in Northern Ireland, Fitzpatrick outlines that in 2006 a 'significantly higher proportion of rapes were committed at gunpoint in Northern Ireland, compared to the rest of the UK and Ireland.'[35] Notably, Fitzpatrick highlights 'an intertextual engagement with foundation stories of colonial conflict, in which woman and land are elided and gender violence becomes part of a narrative about national identity and self-determination.'[36] In defiantly sending the phallic tower of plates crashing towards the floor, O'Donnell, however, issues a staunch retort to patriarchal violence in the home.

LABOUR: DEVELOPING DIALOGUES

Turning to a discussion of *LABOUR* now, I outline the performances in this exhibition as enabling a broadening of discourses around issues of gender and labour in the Irish region. Excavations of the past occurred as the participating artists responded to the different histories of the sites the exhibitions toured. Responding to these sites, the performances highlighted the often historically negated labours of women. However, *LABOUR* equally enabled a contemplation of the continued inequities and invisibility experienced by labouring women today.

In countering the invisibility of women's work, *LABOUR*, I argue, gave body to the material effects of the devaluing of women's affective and immaterial labour. Discussing labouring practices that do not generate material products but produce, organise and alter emotional experience, Shannon Jackson uses the term 'the immaterial turn' to refer the shift

'[...] in repetitiously performing labour traditionally assigned to women, the artists in *LABOUR* resisted reiterating symbolic patriarch power relations that fetishise female bodies as an object of male desire.'

towards post-Fordist systems of production in Western economies during the 1970s, when 'labor became more service oriented and engaged in the production and exchange of affect.'[37] Post-Fordism is characterised by a move away from production line manufacturing systems, synonymous with automobile manufacturer Henry Ford, which produced in case of demand towards 'Toyotaist' models. Led by advances in information technologies Toyotaist models manufacture flexibility in response to communication with customers and markets. The decentralisation of the workforce and the outsourcing of material labour abroad, enabled by the advancement of global communication networks, is a significant feature of post-Fordist economies of production. Equally, relevant here, as Jackson highlights, is the 'so-called "knowledge economy,"' in which immaterial products circulate 'as information, software, and other forms of "cognitive" innovation.'[38] Notably, Jackson asserts 'affective labor has long been "women's work." And – akin to other performance laborers – gendered workers have experienced such work as deeply "material," whatever its immaterial effects.'[39]

Reaching back into the past, the artists in *LABOUR* repetitiously performed histories unresolved in the present. In doing so, *LABOUR*, I suggest, allowed a questioning of 'modernity's failed utopianism' by initiating a 'politics of delay,' to borrow Laura Mulvey's words, from the introduction of the second edition of her seminal text *Visual and Other Pleasures*, published in 2009.[40] This is equally relevant to Jones's pointing towards how feminism has slowed down and durationally complicated 'the fixing of meaning by exposing the bodies and investments inevitably playing a role in any interpretation.'[41] Also relevant to *LABOUR*, in *Capital* (1867) Marx asserts the 'fetishism of commodities has its origin' in 'the peculiar social character of the labour that produces them.'[42] Importantly, in repetitiously performing labour traditionally assigned to women, the artists in *LABOUR* resisted reiterating symbolic patriarchal power relations that fetishise female bodies as an object of male desire. In particular, I pose the communal dialogues that developed between the various works in *LABOUR* as significant to heightening the subversive potential of both the individual performances and the collective environment.

In outlining the multiplicity of approaches to the eight-hour duration within the individual performances in *LABOUR*, I emphasise the collective dialogues that developed between the artists through the use of sound, image making, and action. These dialogues, as I will detail, emerged cautiously, yet steadily strengthened across the successive sites. The development of the works in *LABOUR* in response to communal dialogues and the movement across sites, is perhaps relevant to what Jones terms as a 'queer feminist durationality;' a process of thinking unresolved the nature of identification that takes into account relational interpretations that constitute how we see and relate to art.[43] She argues that 'engaging the durational is clearly a way of revivifying aesthetics: of taking it away from its classical forms of fixing the object within the purview of a judgmental, specialist gaze by opening up the work to the process of interpretation and meaning making.'[44] Queerness is implicated in the durational, she suggests, as it 'indicates the impossibility of a subject or meaning staying still, in one determinable place' and allows the potential of unsettling the visual field 'by opening out the durationality of our desiring relationship to particular aspects of the world.'[45] Feminism, she concludes 'must become queer and durational – it must acknowledge not only the temporality and processual nature of identifying but also the intersectional quality of how and what we identify in ourselves and others.'[46] Jones asserts the 'cunt in cunt art' can enact 'queer feminist durationality,' noting that 'in spite of 40 years of feminist anti-essentialist critique, the cunt won't disappear' and 'explodes the frames of critical analysis.'[47]

Of course, as one amongst the participating artists, it would be impossible for me to account for the totality of the dialogues between the participating artists, not least because in the midst of an eight-hour durational performance there is a loss of time, but because I offer partial and subjective experience. However, in highlighting some of the dialogues sparked in *LABOUR* as the exhibition progressed across the successive sites, I outline the production of an energized live environment within which mundane, oppressive and repetitive acts became imbued with a transformative and destabilising power.

LONDON: SEX IN A COLD CLIMATE

Notably, many of the participating artists in *LABOUR* are members of collectives engaged in group durational performance. Chrissie Cadman and Anne Quail are both members of Northern Irish group Bbeyond, which was established in 2001. Belfast-based, Mexican-born, Elvira Santamaria Torres has also performed with Bbeyond and is a member of Black Market International.[48] Pauline Cummins, Michelle Browne, Frances Mezzetti, and formerly Amanda Coogan, are members of Performance Collective, a Dublin-based group of live artists founded in 2007 invested in developing an 'understanding of where individual practice meets the collective act.'[49] Also, one of the contributions to *LABOUR* was collaborative. Frances Mezzetti and Pauline Cummins were specifically commissioned to perform their work, *Walking in the Way*. After undertaking research in the local community based on observing the ways men spend their time, the artists transformed themselves into convincing male personas and performed in the local community. In London, Mezzetti and Cummins were struck by the overwhelming impact the 2012 Olympics had on the local community, heightened by the close proximity of the Olympic stadium to]performance s p a c e[. Over the 'working day,' Mezzetti took the role of director and instructed Cummins to mark Olympic circles at various sites, such as outside Hackney Town Hall and in a snow-covered park. Mezzetti and Cummins were trailed by a team of photographers who covertly recorded their activities. At intervals during the day these images were projected in the space where the other nine artists were performing. In the final hours Mezzetti and Cummins came to the performance site, remaining in their guises and interacted with the other performers.

Located in a former plumbing factory of an industrial estate in East London, an area synonymous with migrant labour,]performance s p a c e[offered an appropriate site for the first exhibition, allowing consideration of the relevance of the UK's proximity to the Irish region. The positioning of a harp, the prominent emblem of the Irish nation, by the door of]performance s p a c e[offered an apt portal for audience entering the London exhibition. The harp, however, was unstrung. It constituted part of Áine O'Dwyer's work, which confronted the systematic abuse of children in Ireland's Industrial and Reformatory Schools, as detailed in The Ryan Report (2009). Wearing bright red knickers and an altar boy's gown that was far too small for her adult body, O'Dwyer fused child-like innocence with disturbing sexual undertones as she rocked up and down on a purpose built white rocker. In London, O'Dwyer combined this rocking with her transformation behind a curtain from the obedient 'altar-child' into a conformist vision of ideal Irish womanhood. Emerging from behind the curtain in a flowing green and gold gown at intervals throughout the performance O'Dwyer undertook the process of re-stringing the harp, at times, plucking at the newly inserted harp wires to provide a minimal score.

Many works in the first exhibition explored the Magdalen Laundries. Áine Phillips most forcefully bought the histories of these institutions to the space in her performance *Redress: Emotional Labour*. Phillips's approach to the eight-hour duration was to break her performance up into three distinct parts or 'images.' The first image constructed by Phillips found her walking around the space focused on the black ink stains seeping though her white trousers and top with credible dismay, as if she were rotting from inside out. As she moved around the space, recordings of the testimonies of women surviving these institutions, collated by the artist Evelyn Glynn, played. Audience members had to lean close to Phillips's body to hear these recordings, which came from a mini-speaker stitched into her clothing. Of course, the playing of these testimonies in the space was significant at the time. The women of the Magdalen Laundries had yet to receive a state apology. Yet it gains an equally potent significance, given the negation of 796 pages of survivor testimony from the McAleese Report, published almost a year later. In the second part Phillips, still with the recording, wears Irish dancing shoes given to her by an award-winning dancer; the soles of the shoes are encrusted with broken glass. Disabled by these shoes, Phillips crawls around the space stopping at intervals to place her hand on the feet of audience members. In the final segment, responding to the testimony of a Magdalen survivor that states 'these stories are now, coming out in parts, as though stuck in a web,'[50] Phillips, without the recording, struggles to move around the space trapped inside a giant fishing net.

Michelle Browne's contribution, *The Grace of God*, while based on her grandmother's trade as a dressmaker, also referenced the Magdalen Laundries. Browne noted 'many women during my grandmother's lifetime were putting needle to thread in Magdalene Laundries as an act of penance, forced labour for the sins of the female: vanity, "a love of dress," display of sexuality or being an unmarried mother.'[51] From a boom of coarse navy fabric Browne made pinafore uniforms for little girls on which she inscribed the words 'The Fallen' with chalk, thus referencing biblical stories – from Eve's fall from grace to Mary Magdalene – that place emphasis on the female body as the site of temptation, threat to moral purity and eternal salvation. Reminiscent of those still worn in primary schools in Ireland, Browne's uniforms highlighted the ongoing regulation of the female body. As commentary in the *Irish Times* in April 2012 pointed out, 'ninety per cent of State-funded primary schools are still controlled by the Catholic Church, despite the church's loss of authority and influence in the wake of child abuse scandals.'[52]

Amanda Coogan's costume, comprised of numerous white, full-length, high-street winter jackets bought in Primark (Penneys), allowed reference to the mass-production of clothing and out-sourcing of labour to underdeveloped countries synonymous with high-street retailers. While this contrasted with Browne's material labour and old-fashioned production line, together these performances bridged links between the slavery experienced by the women in the Magdalen Laundries and the continuous exploitation of women workers globally. Coogan's staining of her coats with a steady stream of blue dye that bubbled from her mouth was in rhyme with Phillips's stained clothes. However, in contrast to Phillips embodiment of subjugation, Coogan's presence on the central staircase in]performance s p a c e[, was invested with authority. Her pose and heavy robes were reminiscent of a religious figure about to descend from an altar to deliver a sermon. However, all that came from her mouth was deep blue dye, blemishing the pristine whiteness of her robes, aptly highlighting the hypocrisy within the Catholic Church's assumption of moral authority and its own 'fall from grace' in the wake of the abuse scandals.

A more subtle reference to the Magdalen Laundries was found in the title of Anne Quail's work, *The Good She*. Quail told me that this title was a pun on The Good Shepherd, one of the religious orders that ran the Magdalene Laundries. Quail's actions, cradling her bundle of tea bags as if it were all that she owned in the world, were deeply melancholic. Her sometimes-stilted singing of *The Mountains of Mourne*, the well-known ballad by Percy French that captures the growing disillusionment of a nineteenth-century Irish emigrant with the promise of prosperity in London, added to the sense of forlornness she embodied. Referencing this song, Ann Rossiter notes that 'Irish women in nineteenth century Britain, much as their sisters in the twentieth century, remain largely hidden from history' as the ethnicity of migrants in Britain had not been 'systematically recorded.'[53] Interestingly, the maintaining of access for Irish workers to the British labour market as Ireland strove to break ties with the Commonwealth so as to become a Republic in 1949 coincided with what Kathleen Paul terms 'a strange piece of legislation,' namely the 1948 British Nationality Act.[54] According to this act, Paul notes there were 'three types of people in the world: British citizens, aliens and Irish citizens.'[55] Whilst this act afforded Irish citizens the privileges of British citizenship without becoming a British subject, it also, as Paul notes, highlights UK policy makers' 'deeming of "race" rather than skin colour to be an unmodifiable and genetic characteristic.'[56] Rolling around the space hugging a bundle of teabags, Quail in her purple Victorian dress referenced the loneliness and invisibility of the domestic service migrant labourer. Her stitching of teabags to the end of her dress and to the skin of her hands complemented Browne's sewing activities. Together these performances spoke of the gendering of labour roles in the post-war period when, as Paul outlines, women were assigned jobs within the textiles industry, nursing, and domestic service.[57]

In titling her performance for London, *Mutt – mutter - mother - máthair – mutter – mutt*, Chrissie Cadman was clearly focused on the work of mothers. Cadman's playful alignment of the English word mother with its Gaelic counterpart 'máthair' aptly brings to light the split identifications still resonant in her native city, Derry/Londonderry. Equally, the word 'mutter' means mother in the German language. Yet, in English it denotes a form of quiet and indistinct speech. In her conflation of the

Opposite top left: Anne Quail, *The Good She*, *LABOUR*.
Photo: Jordan Hutchins. Opposite top right: *LABOUR* poster, 2012.
Opposite bottom: Ann Maria Healy, *I Do Not Feel Ashamed*,
LABOUR, Dublin, 2012. Photo courtesy of the artist.

word mother with 'mutter' – and the more derogatory 'mutt' – a term used to refer to a non-pedigree dog Cadman plays with the invisibility and lack of recognition afforded maternal labour. Sat in a bath of ice, amongst the cloths she both writes on and scrubs with washing powder, Cadman's numbed body spoke of the toil of women, long overlooked or frozen out of dominant discourses. Ann Maria Healy also mediated on mothering roles. Healy sat rigidly at a table set with two stones and a neat, spotlighted, circular pile of wheat grain. She wore a short orange dress, which complemented the warm hues of the wheat. Throughout her performance in London the pile of wheat remained untouched and Healy instead ground the stones. She asserts the wheat and wheat grinding in her performance 'looks back at the Roman Goddess Ceres who was the goddess of agriculture, fertility and motherly relationships.'[58] In combining this reference with an adaptation of Meredith Brooks's well-known song *Bitch* (1997), Healy merged the archaic with the contemporary. The lyrics of Brooks's song, like the wordplay in Cadman's title, highlights the multiple positions occupied by women and derogatory terms used to vilify them. Brooks sings as follows:

> I'm a bitch, I'm a lover
> I'm a child, I'm a mother
> I'm a sinner, I'm a saint
> I do not feel ashamed

The initiation of my own contribution to *LABOUR* also considered the past in order to reflect on the present. In particular, I sought to explore notions of purity that situate penance as a condition of female sexual pleasure and their relationship to the ongoing territorial control of women's bodies through the remaining bans on abortion. Up to 5,000 women a year from the Republic of Ireland, alongside up to 1,500 women form the North, travel to the UK to access abortion services. I was inspired by June Goulding's memoir *The Light in the Window*,[59] which details the year she spent working as a professional mid-wife in the Sisters of the Sacred Heart of Jesus and Mary 'mother and baby home' in Bessboro, Co. Cork. Opened in 1922, the same year as the Irish Free State was established, this institution became a model for other such homes where 'first offenders' – women who fell pregnant outside of wedlock for the first time – were admitted. Following birth women nursed their babies until they were forced to give them up. As the McAleese Report outlines, women were also transferred from these homes to the Magdalen

> **'I operated in a space demarcated by a circular bed of soil. 40 or more condoms filled with washing powder, a reference to the Magdalen Laundries and ideologies of moral purity, were placed in the centre of the soil.'**

Laundries. Outlining the punitive nature of these institutions, Goulding recalls that the women in Bessboro were constantly taunted with one question by the head of the religious order charged with their care: 'was the five minutes' pleasure worth all this?'[60]

In the performance I made militant and sexual the Virgin Mary's serenity and chasteness. I wore a blue dress embossed with gold and a gold-sprayed balaclava, which had numerous knitting needles spiked through its top resembling, perhaps, a crown of thorns or the halos often depicted on the heads of religious figures. Ten baby bottles containing my menstrual blood, collected over a six-month period, were attached to an army belt, which circling my waist looked like a bullet belt. Numerous bottlebrushes and an army pouch containing Catholic Holy Communion were attached to another belt. Throughout the performance I operated in a space demarcated by a circular bed of soil. 40 or more condoms filled with washing powder, a reference to the Magdalen Laundries and ideologies of moral purity, were placed in the centre of the soil. Interwoven so as to form a circle of coiled phalluses these laundry-filled condoms were synonymous with the snakes depicted in representations of the Virgin Mary. Speaking of this imagery in her book, *Alone of All her Sex: The Myth and the Cult of the Virgin Mary,* (1976) Marina Warner notes that 'various cultures all over the globe […] tell tales of women bitten or penetrated by snakes – an experience that brings on menstruation.'[61] She highlights that the alignment of snakes with notions of immortality, wisdom and rebirth has been erased within Christianity due to the persistent association of snakes with evil. Speaking of Eve's consumption of the forbidden fruit in the Garden of Eden, Warner notes, the 'penalty of eating the fruit of knowledge offered by the snake was partly the curse of menstruation; and the implication of the Immaculate Conception, whereby Mary conquers the serpent, is that she is spared it.'[62]

During the performance I play with this imagery and offer a retort to Christianity's outlining of menstruating female bodies as inherently wicked and menstruation itself as a form of punishment. For instance, at intervals I rolled the balaclava down over my face and placed one of the condoms inside my vagina. On taking one of the knitting needles from my head I pierced the condom by pushing the needle repetitively in and out of the simulated penis as it extended from my vagina until the white washing powder sprayed out onto the soil. I then stood the used knitting needle upright in the soil on the covered spot like a triumphant explorer mapping out and pitching a claim to new territory. In penetrating my vagina with the 'snake' I offer a retort to the Virgin Mary's seeming purity. While with my parodying of a man pissing and, in turn, my territorial marking of the soil, I made apparent the patriarchal ideologies at play within the symbolism of the Virgin Mary. Offering a further violation of the ideologies of purity proliferated by the dichotomy of virginity and motherhood within the Immaculate Conception, in the London performance I spelt out the phrase 'was the five minutes' pleasure worth all this?' on top of the circular bed of soil with Catholic Holy Communion. I formed the letters of the words by placing the round wafers on top of the soil, subsequently soaking the wafers with menstrual blood from the bottles.

Given the harsh and chilly atmosphere, caused by the irreparable failure of the heating system in]performance s p a c e[, there was not much pleasure on display in London. Those who trudged through the snow to attend this first exhibition were met with soaked, stained, soiled, and shivering bodies locked into restrained, repetitive actions. As the unstrung harp that greeted audience members hinted, *LABOUR* in London was about as far from the romantic and idyllic visions of Irish culture promoted by the Irish Tourist Board as one could get. Rather, this first instalment of *LABOUR* brings to mind the phrase, Sex in a Cold Climate, the title of one of the first exposés to emerge on the Magdalen Laundries.[63] The only relief to the grating, oppressive atmosphere came via Elvira Santamaria Torres's helium filled constructions. Over the course of the eight-hours Torres set afloat black and white plastic bags in the space. The upturned red roses and cherries she attached to these floating bags had a playful sculptural beauty. At the Long Table with Lois Weaver, held the day after the first exhibition, Torres observed that her use of roses is a tribute to the feminist icon and Marxist revolutionary Rosa Luxemburg

Opposite top: Chrissie Cadman and Áine Philllips, *LABOUR*, Dublin, 2012. Photo: Sally Anne Kelly.
Opposite bottom: Frances Mezzetti, *LABOUR*, Dublin, 2012. Photo: Michael Holly.

and that the cherries 'were also to do with women,'[64] perhaps relevant to Jeannette Winterson's book *Sexing the Cherry* (1989) or the slang use of the word 'cherry' to describe a woman's virginity. The programme of public forums with artists, audiences, and scholars that accompanied the live exhibitions, I suggest, contributed to the development of the communal dialogues in the *LABOUR* exhibitions.[65]

And, despite the severe atmosphere set in London, points of connection and communal dialogues began to emerge. This primarily happened through sound. The peaks and troughs in the communal energy sparked occasions of loud connectivity through escalating sounds, and at other times, instances of collective silence. Healy, at intervals, would match loudly the words 'Bitch,' 'Mother,' 'Child,' 'Lover' to her grinding of the stones. At times, her repeating of the words 'Child Lover' in quicker succession made more sinister the sexual undertones inherent in O'Dwyer's rocking as her red encased bottom and forced smile alternatively flew up in the air. Using her body to vigorously rock the bath, tying thick metal chains to it and dragging it across the floor in a show of threatening strength, violently beating sodden cloths across the metal shutters of the space, Cadman became a force to reckon with. The rocking of O'Dwyer's horse began to chime with Cadman's shaking bath, as my plunging of a bottlebrush into an emptied baby bottle found rhythm with Healy's grinding of stones. Coogan's scrubbing of her jackets on the steps of the stairs joined this symphony of sounds, as did Torres's whistling. These symphonies often rose slowly, gathering a steady, restrained pace before suddenly dissipating into an almost deafening silence. Torres's calm counting in Spanish, 'uno, dos tres,' at one point during this silence, added a notation that caught the audience by surprise, immersed in this industrious sound-scape summoning Irish culture. This use of language offered a potent reminder to the audience that what was occurring before them related to broader contexts.

DERRY / LONDONDERRY: BRIDGING DIVIDES

LABOUR progressed to Void Gallery, Derry/Londonderry, strengthening these communal dialogues. Void Gallery, previously one of the numerous shirt factories located within and on the outskirts of the city, predominantly employed women, who in many cases were the main breadwinners in their families. An extension of the flax and linen industry, shirt factories were present in the city from the 1850s. Demonstrative of what Jackson calls the 'immaterial turn'[66] in the 1970s, this industry began to fall into decline in the latter half of the twentieth century as such labour was outsourced abroad.[67] Yet, the heritage of this industry remains potent as Maoliosa Boyle, Manager and Curator at the Void Gallery, observes: 'most families have had a mother, sister, aunt or grandmother who worked in one of the 25 factories in and around Derry's city centre.'[68]

The division of the artists across two rooms in this gallery promoted greater movement amongst the artists. One room housed Browne, Coogan and Quail, alongside O'Dwyer's rocking horse and Phillips's fishing net. Healy, Torres, Cadman, and myself took up residency in the other. In particular, Phillips and O'Dwyer moved frequently between the two rooms. Phillips often crawled past me with the stories of the oppressed emitting from the speaker stitched into her clothing. Similarly, O'Dwyer, like an overgrown child still under the spell of religious doctrine and eager to please, came close and stopped by me for a time, with her hands joined in prayer and her faithful smile beaming. At these moments, I sometimes looked down on them without emotion or tilted my head away nonchalantly. My serenity hardened. I made the odd foray into the room next-door. Balaclava down, armed with a bottle and brush, I marched, sometimes manically, through the space while simultaneously winding around the brush inside the bottle in a cyclical fashion. My machine-like movements chimed well, at times, with O' Dwyer's monotonous rocking. At other times I interrupted the more meditative atmosphere of the room, in which Browne diligently stitched, her boom of navy fabric and her production line finding new meaning in this site. Like an over-dressed shop mannequin Coogan stood statuesque and elevated on the raised base of a pillar; her multiple high-street jackets had an inherent connection to this building given the mass outsourcing of the shirt industry abroad. Dressed in black and seated at a table Quail engaged in the slow de-threading of her purple dress. Storming in, twisting my brush around my bottle as if powering a wind-up toy or perhaps, my mechanical marching, I felt like an aggressive line-manager coming to oversee the workforce and push their production. Meanwhile, Browne stood atop the table with the boom of fabric protruding from between her legs like a giant cock, Quail rubbed dismembered tea-bags into her face with her eyes held shut and Coogan streamed bubbling blue spit. This room, while quiet, had an equally disturbing air.

LABOUR, Derry, Londonderry, 2012. Photo: Jordan Hutchins.

'Past and present, inside and outside, strength and subjugation, 'men' and women, met and merged in individual performances and collective interactions.'

In the opposite room, there was a much more raucous and intense energy. Healy based herself on the floor amidst a massive pile of wheat, at times diving into it and flinging it across the floor. Thus the pile of wheat, neat and circular in London, developed a disorderly effect. Placing two much larger stones between her legs as she knelt down, made Healy's coarse grinding more aggressive, primal, and sexual. Mirroring Healy's positioning of the stones, sitting on the soil, I held a baby-bottle to my crotch and plunged the bottlebrush in and out of it, parodying male masturbation. Cadman, furiously blew bubbles, rocking unnervingly in the bath, not unlike a volcano about to explode. We assembled an orchestra of unsettling sounds, a guttural rallying cry that reverberated around the gallery and into the room next door. The intensity in this room grew as Torres covered her head in the long strip of red fabric she had earlier trailed around the gallery. From this fabric, a line of helium filled black and white plastic bags flowed. Suddenly, I found myself marching, led by Torres. She paced round the room in circles and the row of balloons followed diligently behind her red-covered head like a bodiless army.

Sat unashamedly on my heap of soil, strewn with condoms, empty bottles, teats and upright needles and drenched in a mixture of blood and milk, with one foot cocked in the air and my high-heeled shoe dangling suggestively from my big toe, I flirted with Fran Mezzetti and Pauline Cummins when they arrived. Both were looking dapper, following their new haircuts in a local barbershop. Ironically, in their male guises they became the first women to have their hair cut in this particular barbers, a mainstay of the city. As Cummins held an umbrella over her head and I pondered whether it was raining outside, Mezzetti took from a brown paper bag a number of neatly folded men's shirts. After attaching these shirts to one another, she slowly dragged them in a trail across the floor. As I watched the crisp clean shirts journey through the space and pick up the traces of soil, suds, and pieces of grain, I thought how funny: the 'men' have come 'home' to clean up one hell of a dirty day's labour.

DUBLIN: PERFORMING HOLES

The external and internal activities of Mezzetti and Cummins as women in the guise of 'men' playfully trouble the gendering of labour and the boundaries between inside and outside. Yet in the full 24 hours we performed together, there was a constant collage of colliding paradoxes. Past and present, inside and outside, strength and subjugation, 'men' and women, met and merged in individual performances and collective interactions. Indeed, as *LABOUR* toured to Dublin, a rather ironic dialogue developed. While women in the north filed into factories, often performing the role of breadwinner, women in the south were increasingly entrapped in the home as a result of state legislation. The location of The Lab in the heart of 'the Monto,' Dublin's historic prostitution district, and in close proximity to the Magdalen Laundries on Sean MacDermott Street, aptly draws on the curtailing of women's liberties in the post-independence south. There were fervent efforts to clean up 'the Monto' in the years following the establishment of the Southern Irish Free State. Referencing the notorious 'madams' who ran the brothels, the Director of The Lab, Sheena Barrett, describes 'the Monto' as a 'place where women have endured and shown immense courage despite hardship, exploitation and inhumanity often at the hands of women.'[69] Indeed, the exploitation of women by women outlines a parallel between the Magdalen Laundries and brothels.

The insertion of female bodies inside the glass walled building of The Lab brought to mind the history of prostitution and exploitation associated with this location. Anne Quail and myself inhabited the upstairs mezzanine of The Lab. The other artists worked on the ground floor below us. Torres took up residency in a separate room as she required complete darkness for her performance. Chrissie Cadman, dressed in silky red bloomers and vest, worked on the pavement outside the main gallery windows. There were absent bodies too. Pauline Cummins was in Istanbul due to an artistic venture scheduled prior to *LABOUR*. Nonetheless, she went *Walking in the Way* in Istanbul the day before the live exhibition and sent images of her activities, thus bringing another layer of context to the space. Demonstrating the precarity of artistic labour, Áine O'Dwyer had had an accident and suffered a concussion just before the exhibition. Given the repetitive rocking involved in her performance, she was unable to participate as planned. Gone was the faithful child, but present at the exhibition in her civilian clothes, O'Dwyer at times set her rocker in motion with a slap of her hands. Both her presence and her absence were felt as the haunting sound reverberated.

Amanda Coogan invested greater movement in her performance, trailing up and down by the windows and swinging the train of jackets around her body. At times, flat on her back, her legs held in the air in symmetry with the excess of arms dangling from her jackets, she looked like an upturned centipede. Yet Coogan displayed an almost monstrous femininity, as she lay on her back with the jacket fronts lining her body and running down between her spread legs. The jackets' rounded necks punctured her body with a row of holed orifices, not unlike a line of large unsealed cunts. The open holes in Coogan's jackets contrasted with Browne's pursed lips, tightly furled around a row of spikey pins. However, these pins protruded from her mouth like sharp pointed teeth. Browne nonetheless offered an image arousing fears of castration anxiety. The results of Browne's material labour now hung from the ceiling above her head. 'The Fallen' had, thus, arisen.

Healy ground with yet larger stones. At times, she curled over, her head resting on stones set amid piles of grain, almost foetal like. At other times, she lay down on her back with a stone resting on her belly. Looking down from the mezzanine, it appeared she had been hit by a meteorite fallen from space, pierced through her midriff and pinned to the floor. However, bawling out 'ashamed' with the weight of the rock bearing down on her womb, critiqued a culture that restrains women's reproductive rights. Healy had a feminine fierceness, accentuated when she marked her face with the dust generated from her grinding of the stones, which she dampened by licking in an almost animalistic fashion.

In her darkened room, Torres soaked paper in a bucket of water. The trickling sounds of the water brought a mysterious element to the room. She then embedded long pieces of white string in the soggy paper and threw it upwards. It stuck to the ceiling and the strings dangled down to the floor. These strings were illuminated by ultra violet light bulbs. Torres dressed in black was not fully visible to the audience. Using her invisibility she played with these strings to make a surreal moving sculpture of shadows and light. Torres told me afterwards that at one stage, on arranging the strings in a circular shape, a child curled up on the floor inside this circle of light as if, she said, 'it was a womb.' Outside on the street in her rosy red attire, Cadman also used a bucket of water. She

Opposite top: Michelle Browne, *LABOUR*, Derry, Londonderry, 2012.
Opposite bottom: Pauline Cummins and Frances Mezzetti, *Walking in the Way*, *LABOUR*, Derry, Londonderry, 2012. Photos: Jordan Hutchins.

> **'Pressing her whole body against the window, she compressed her painted lips against the glass to leave round mouth marks, spraying the windowpane with blood-red bullet holes.'**

vigorously scrubbed the pavement and tied love messages to the pillars with red string. Her energetic activities were, thus, at once violent and affectionate. At times she drew the outlines of the scene unfolding inside on the windowpane with bright red lipstick, freeze-framing actions, as if to make a time-based record in lipstick traces. Pressing her whole body against the window, she compressed her painted lips against the glass to leave round mouth marks, spraying the windowpane with blood-red bullet holes. Frances Mezzetti, in the guise of a male Dublin City Council worker, referencing the authority that runs The Lab, aided Cadman to clean up the streets and tidied the space as if she were a man attempting to assert dominance by ordering the endlessly unfolding mess. Holding string in her hands over the balcony of the mezzanine, she moved her arms up and down, as if she were a puppeteer, responsible for moving the bodies below.

In my big dirty bed of soil on the mezzanine overlooking the 'working girls,' my Madonna was transformed into a 'madam.' Cadman scrubbed the street with washing powder below me. Sitting upon my soil, I occupied my time suggestively toying with my detergent filled condoms. Stretching, pulling and stiffening them, I placed each one under scrutiny. I polished them with my skirt, or arranged them into piles in accordance to their size and stiffness. Critically playing with patriarchal conventions, emphasised an empowered choice. Disappointingly small or floppy ones were discarded, thrown over my shoulders or at the audience with a roll of my eyes to signal my disapproval. The firmest ones were selected for insertion into my vagina, only to be violently destroyed shortly thereafter. I spat soggy altar bread at the audience, which I chewed in my mouth before catapulting it towards them from between my lips, rounded together like a canon barrel. At certain points, Mezzetti came into the upstairs space and attempted to sweep and tidy my mass of soil with a broom. As she did, I continued to toy with my cocks or stuff my mouth with altar bread pulled from a plastic bag, like I was eating crisps. Hugely content on my dirty plot of earth, my cunt openly displayed, Mezzetti's attempt to render me 'tidy and clean' was thus a futile task.

In the same space, Anne Quail made incredibly slow movements around the space, each melting into the next in a dreamlike fashion. At times she was tied to the railings of the mezzanine with the remaining fabric of her purple dress. With the dismembered shoulder of her purple dress hanging over her face she continued to shred what remained of it, thread by thread. Blinded and bound, her vulnerability contrasted with my overtly defiant sexual behaviour. Quail's bondage by cloth connected to Phillips's stained clothes as she shuffled around the space. With the memories of the Magdalen Laundries emitting from her body, Phillips ensured the unresolved trauma experienced by women remained present. Indeed, pressing her black-stained body against the frame of the downstairs window, glaring out on the world, Phillips endowed stained womanhood with a heightened visibility, making the shameful stigmatising of women in Irish culture irrevocably apparent. With Phillips's reference to the Magdalen Laundries and mine to the madam, the histories embedded in our midst came to light. Importantly, *LABOUR* did not shy away from the weight of oppression experienced by women historically nor the injustices continually experienced by women. Rather, it held these oppressions present, persistently referencing the excessive, often-hidden, labours undertaken by women, and their material effects, while simultaneously developing empowered, productive, and indeed pleasurable feminist discourses.

1. Rebecca Schneider, *The Explicit Body in Performance* (London and New York: Routledge, 1997), p. 44.

2. Ibid.

3. Ibid.

4. Ibid.

5. The input of Maoliosa Boyle, Manager and Curator at the Void Gallery, and Sheena Barrett, Director of The Lab was hugely valuable. Lois Keidan, the director of the Live Art Development Agency (LADA), London was consistently supportive of *LABOUR* from its initial conceptualisation. *LABOUR* was supported by The Arts Council of Ireland (Dublin exhibition), Derry City Council, University of Ulster, The Graduate School of Creative Arts and Media, Dublin and Queen Mary University of London. A number of assistants generously helped in the smooth running and documentation of the live exhibitions, while an array of businesses in each location provided various props, materials, and equipment as support in kind.

6. For examples, the announcement in July 2012 that three dissident republican groups were to merge and reclaim the banner of the IRA, and the riots sparked during loyalist protests in December 2012 following the decision to stop flying the Union Jack flag above Belfast City Hall all year round, highlight continuing sectarian tensions in Northern Ireland.

7. For example, a number of films based on contentious events in Irish history were made during this period. These include Ken Loach's *The Wind that Shakes the Barley* (2006) based on the long-silenced Irish Civil War (1922-23) resultant from the partition of Ireland or those focused on the 1981 hunger strikes in the H-Block Prison during the Troubles, such as Steve McQueen's *Hunger* (2008).

8. There are two spellings used in reference to these institutions: Magdalen and Magdalene. I use the former but quote the latter in certain cases.

9. The McAleese Report, chaired by Senator Martin McAleese is titled in full as 'Report of the Inter-Departmental Committee to Establish the Facts of State Involvement with the Magdalen Laundries.' The report was published 5 February, 2013. It can be accessed on the official website of the Department of Justice and Equality <http://www.justice.ie/en/JELR/Pages/MagdalenRpt2013> [accessed 10 December 2014].

10. Justice For Magdalenes, 'State Involvement in the Magdalene Laundries: JFM's Principal Submissions to the Inter-Departmental Committie to establish the Facts of State Involvement with the Magdalene Laundries', 16 February 2013.

11. Amnesty International UK, official website, 'Amnesty Welcomes United Nations recommendation to NI Executive to investigate Magdalene Laundry and Clerical Abuse', 3 June 2013 <http://www.amnesty.org.uk/news_details.asp?NewsID=20805> [accessed 11 June 2013].

12. Ann Maria Healy and Helena Walsh, 'Brutal Silences: Live Art and Irish Culture' (2011) A Study Room Guide for the Study Room of the Live Art Development Agency, London <http://www.thisisliveart.co.uk/resources/catalogue/brutal-silences-a-live-art-development-agestudy-room-guide-on-live-art-> [accessed 5 March 2014] This Study Room Guide was exhibited in]performance s p a c e[for a week after the first instalment of *LABOUR*.

13. Amelia Jones, *Seeing Differently: A History and Theory of Identification and the Visual Arts* (London and New York: Routledge, 2012), p. 6.

14. Lisa Smyth, *Abortion and Nation: The Politics of Reproduction in Contemporary Ireland* (Britain and Burlington: Ashgate Publishing Limited, 2005), p. 2.

15. Ruth Fletcher, 'Post-colonial Fragments: Representations of Abortion in Irish Law and Politics', *Journal of Law and Society*, 28.4 (2001), 568-89, (p. 572).

16. Fionola Meredith, 'North's politicians revert to type on abortion', *The Irish Times*, 18 October 2012 <http://www.irishtimes.com/newspaper/opinion/2012/1018/1224325412766.html > [accessed 18 November 2012].

17. Jaki Irvine, 'Sounding the Depths, Irish Museum of Modern Art, Dublin, 1 April - 9 May 1992', *Circa*, 62 (1992), 64-66, (p. 65).

18. Jones, *Seeing Differently,* p. 80.

19. Ibid.

20. Ibid.

21. Sally R. Munt, *Queer Attachments: The Cultural Politics of Shame* (Hampshire: Ashgate, 2007), p. 63.

22. Edna O'Brien, *Mother Ireland* (Middlesex: Penguin Books, 1976), p. 11.

23. Munt, *Queer Attachments*, p. 64.

24. Maria Luddy, *Prostitution and Irish Society: 1800–1940* (Cambridge and New York: Cambridge University Press, 2007), p. 195.

25. Luddy, *Prostitution and Irish Society,* p. 195.

26. Kira O'Reilly, 'Blog', *Kira O'Reilly* <http://www.kiraoreilly.com/blog/> [accessed 3 March 2014].

27. Gianna Bouchard, 'Skin Deep: Female Flesh in UK Live Art since 1999', in *Contemporary Theatre Review,* 22.1 (2012), 94-105 (p. 101).

28. Luddy, *Prostitution and Irish Society,* p. 195.

29. Munt, *Queer Attachments*, p. 63.

30. Anne Seagrave, *Jamais Vu*, Cork 2005 Archive, Cork City Council. <http://www.cork2005.ie/programme/strands/architecture/bodilyfunctions/jamaisvu.shtml> [accessed 4 March 2013].

31. Sinéad O'Donnell, 'Violent performance series 2010-2013,' *Sinéad O'Donnell* < http://www.sineadodonnell.com/projects/sinead/violent-performance-series-2010-2013 > [accessed 3 March 2014]. I witnessed this performance at the National Review of Live Art, Glasgow (2007).

32. Department of the Taoiseach, *Bunreacht na hÉireann / Constitution of Ireland*, <http://www.taoiseach.gov.ie/eng/index.asp?docID=243> [accessed 15 September 2012].

33. Frances Gardiner, 'Political Interest and Participation of Irish Women 1922-1992: The Unfinished Revolution', in *Irish Women's Studies Reader*, ed. by Ailbhe Smyth (Dublin: Attic Press, 1993), pp. 45-78 (p. 51).

34. Lisa Fitzpatrick, 'Performing Gender, Performing Violence on the Northern Irish Stage: "Spittin" Blood in a Belfast Sink,' in *Contemporary Theatre Review*, 23.3 (2013) 302-13 (p. 302).

35. Fitzpatrick, 'Performing Gender, Performing Violence on the Northern Irish Stage', p. 303-4.

36. Ibid., p. 304.

37. Shannon Jackson, 'Just-In-Time: Performance and the Aesthetics of Precarity', *TDR: The Drama Review*, 56.4 (2012), 10-31 (p. 12).

38. Ibid., p. 13.

39. Ibid., p. 24-5.

40. Laura Mulvey, *Visual and Other Pleasures* (Basingstoke: Palgrave Macmillan, 2009 [1989]), p. 182. p. xxv.

41. Jones, *Seeing Differently*, p. 174.

42. Ibid., p. 79.

43. Ibid., p. 6.

44. Ibid., p. 174. Emphasis in original.

45. Ibid., p. 174 -175. Emphasis in original.

46. Ibid., p. 177.

47. Ibid., p. 180.

48. Black Market International is a collective of international performance practitioners, founded in 1985.

49. *Performance Collective*, artist website <http://www.theperformancecollective.com/> [accessed 24 Febraury 2013].

50. Áine Phillips, *Redress: Emotional Labour,* statement *LABOUR* exh. cat. Amanda Coogan and Sheena Barrett, eds. (Dublin: The Lab, 2012). A pdf version of the catalogue can be downloaded from the official website of The Lab <http://dublincity.ie/main-menu-services-recreation-culture-arts-office-lab-previous-exhibitions/labour> [accessed 10 December 2014].

51. Michelle Browne, *The Grace of God*, statement *LABOUR* exh. cat.

52. School Patronage', *The Irish Times* (11 April 2012). <http://www.irishtimes.com/newspaper/opinion/2012/0411/1224314607471.html> [accessed 10 June 2012].

53. Ann Rossiter, 'In Search of Mary's Past: Placing Nineteenth Century Irish immigrant Women in British Feminist History', in *Women, Migration and Empire*, ed. by Joan Grant (Stafford: Trentham Books, 1996), pp. 1-29 (p. 2).

54. Kathleen Paul, 'A Case of Mistaken Identity: The Irish in Postwar Britain', *International Labor and Working-Class History*, 49 (1996), 116-42 (p. 116).

55. Ibid.

56. Ibid.

57. Ibid., p. 117.

58. Ann Maria Healy, *I Do Not Feel Ashamed*, statement *LABOUR* exh. cat.

59. June Goulding, *The Light in the Window* (London: Ebury Press, 2005).

60. Goulding, *The Light in the Window,* p. 143.

61. Marina Warner, *Alone of All her Sex: The Myth and the Cult of the Virgin Mary* (London: Pan Books, 1985 [1976]), p. 268.

62. Ibid.

63. *Sex in a Cold Climate*, dir. by Steve Humphries (Testimony Films for Channel Four Witness Series, 1998).

64. Torres, in Long Table discussion, Queen Mary University of London, 10 February 2012. (My transcription). The Long Table is an experimental approach to public forums devised by Lois Weaver that stylizes the informality of a dinner table atmosphere to generate engagement and participation, discussion and debate.

65. The events that accompanied *LABOUR* included the aforementioned Long Table in London, a pre-exhibition discussion with local artists and *LABOUR* artists in Derry/ Londonderry organised by Chrissie Cadman and a day-long symposium in Dublin curated by Sheena Barrett, Director of The Lab, and Amanda Coogan, also held the day before the live exhibition.

66. Jackson, 'Just-In-Time', p. 12.

67. Culture Northern Ireland, 'The Shirt Industry: The Textile Industry in Derry' *Culture Northern Ireland* 12 December 2008 < http://www.culturenorthernireland.org/article/451/the-shirt-industry > [accessed June 2012].

68. Maoliosa Boyle, statement, *LABOUR* exh. cat.

69. Sheena Barrett, statement, *LABOUR* exh. cat.

MICHELLE BROWNE

PERFORMANCE ART IN IRELAND THE NEW MILLENNIUM

Since 2000 there has been a huge upsurge of interest in the practice and presentation of performance in the south of Ireland. The first decade of the twenty-first century has seen artists build on the strong work made in Irish performance during the previous 30 years while creating and embracing new and greater opportunities to experience live embodied performance practices across the country. There has been a surge of younger artists dedicating their art practice to investigations of the body, action, space, time, and gender. This essay will look at the many platforms that have developed for performance since 2000. I will discuss the ways in which performance has been presented, as artists explored the potential of established and more improvised spaces to exhibit their work. Furthermore, some of the key concerns for artists in this period will be examined, drawing out relationships and synergies between practices.

Opposite: Fergus Byrne with participant Cindy Cummings, *May I Draw Your Eye*, *Between you Me and the Four Walls*, Project Arts Centre, Dublin, 2013. Photo: Joseph Carr.

'The actual physical embodied act of viewing performance in the live moment is as important as the live presence of the performer: as the actual effect and consequence of experiencing performance opens up new aspects of its meaning and its function.'

In the catalogue to her exhibition *Falling Into People's Mouths* at the Bonington Gallery at Nottingham Trent University, Anne Seagrave is quoted as saying that in the 1990s 'it was very different making performance work in Ireland, as there isn't the same set-up or support for venues doing Live Art so we were trying to make things for and create our own spaces.'[1] During the early 2000s support was still relatively small, but by 2005 there was a noticeable rise in independent platforms around the country to fill the perceived gap in presentation of performance art practices. In the lead up to this period, Seagrave was instrumental along with Oscar McLennan in curating and producing a series of performance and multimedia events at Arthouse (now Filmbase) in Temple Bar during the 1990s and early 2000s, until the venue closed its doors in 2002. Arthouse also hosted *Appearances*, a collaborative project with six artists working in performance and multimedia. Pauline Cummins, Frances Mezzetti, and Sandra Johnston were key participants in the live embodied works produced at that time and their participation led to further collaborations between the artists throughout the 2000s. In Limerick the *Real Art Project* was active in developing platforms for live performance and sound art through the work of artists such as Sean Taylor, Amanda Dunsmore, Aileen Lambert, and Emma Johnston. The Triskel in Cork was also a hub of activity through events like *Intermedia* curated by Tony Sheehan in 2001.

Seagrave, McLennan, Dunsmore, and Taylor exhibited and performed at international festivals around Europe and their experience was brought to bear on a younger generation of artists practicing and studying in the late 1990s. Many of the key figures of performance in the 1990s were teaching in colleges around the country and the impact this had on the number of artists turning to performance within their own practice was considerable. Pauline Cummins, Nigel Rolfe, and Alanna O'Kelly taught in Dublin, Gerard Leslie in Galway, Áine Phillips in the Burren College, Amanda Dunsmore and Sean Taylor in Limerick, and Hilary Gilligan in Sligo. Further into the 2000s younger artists like Amanda Coogan, Barry, Dominic Thorpe, and

I led workshops at third level institutions as the inclusion of performance training at art colleges steadily increased throughout the decade. Performance master classes also became a key component of Firestation Artists Studios's professional development programme from 2007, with workshops by Alastair MacLennan, Brian Connolly, Sandra Johnston, and Boston based Marilyn Arsem proving hugely important in the development of the practices of many artists in Ireland.

Similarly the rising economic wealth of the country between 1996 and 2007 translated into more funded projects from The Arts Council of Ireland and through city and county councils. A period of growing optimism pervaded, characterised by a will to support more challenging and experimental practices. This was augmented by the fact that many public art programmes were moving more and more towards the ephemeral, the temporary, and the performative.

Tulca Season of Visual Art in Galway began as a distinct entity in 2002, and from 2005 onward had a dedicated performance strand, *Tulca Live,* in its programme. This strand was curated by Áine Phillips between 2005 and 2007. Following this performance was integrated into the overall curation of the festival, as one of a number of performance exhibitions receiving funding to promote and foster live practice. *Excursions,* in Limerick, was initiated by Limerick City Council arts officer Sheila Deegan to fill the gap left by the disbanding of the *Real Art Project* in 2002. *Excursions* ran from 2005 to 2009 and proved an important vehicle for younger artists from Limerick School of Art and Design and others such as Alex Conway, Aileen Lambert, Áine O'Dwyer, Lisa Marie Johnson, and myself to present live work. *Excursions* also made links with international practitioners such as Anthony Howell and Lone Twin.

In Cork, Tony McLeane-Fay began the *Bodily Functions* series which ran from 2005 to 2007 presenting work by Nigel Rolfe, Alistair MacLennan, Áine Phillips, Amanda Coogan, Aideen Barry, and Kira O'Reilly alongside international practitioners like Franko B and Ron Athey, while creating greater links with the Live Art Development Agency (LADA) in London through talks and seminars. LADA was a great support to Irish artists in this period, helping to compensate for a lack of infrastructure and scholarly research around the art form in this country.

This rising visibility of performance in Ireland was especially important for younger artists, who lacked a coherent written or visible Irish history of the art form. The significance of witnessing the direct experience of live performance is immeasurably beneficial in gaining understanding and impact from its affect. Peggy Phelan writes in her influential book *Unmarked*:

> Performance implicates the real through the presence of living bodies [...] It must involve a full seeing of the Other's absence (the ambitious part), a seeing which also entails the acknowledgement of the Other's presence (the humbling part). [...] Performance honours the idea that a limited number of people in a specific time/space frame can have an experience of value which leaves no visible traces afterwards.[2]

The actual physical embodied act of viewing performance in the live moment is as important as the live presence of the performer: as the actual effect and consequence of experiencing performance opens up new aspects of its meaning and its function.

In Dublin a number of events and platforms for live work developed in this period which also enabled this live experience. *Offside Live I & II,* at Dublin City Gallery The Hugh Lane, were curated by Fergus Byrne and Pallas Projects (Mark Cullen and Brian Duggan) to present live performance and experimental sound works. In 2006 I began *Out of Site*, a series of performances in public space that ran from 2006 to 2008 in Dublin. *Out of Site* presented the work of over 40 national and international artists over this period and engaged with the changing nature of the city as urban regeneration and building development were on the rise and the economic crash was looming. The interest in curating these works stemmed from a desire to make visible our relationship to public space, how we share public space and how we produce society through the interaction of bodies in these spaces. The American art historian and critic Amelia Jones notes that:

> The body, as the work of Marxist urban theorist Henri Lefebvre suggests, is the means by which we produce ourselves as social beings, by which we produce 'social space'...The body... has more and more aggressively surfaced during this period as a locus of the self and the site where the public domain meets the private, where the social is negotiated, produced and made sense of.[3]

The locating of embodied practices into the fabric of the city questioned our sense of belonging or ownership of those spaces and places in the city. As part of *Out of Site* Sandra Johnston, Susanne Bosch (an artist from Germany who was based in Belfast between 2006 and 2012) and Marilyn Arsem (USA based performance artist) explored the arena of property sale right at the cusp of the economic crash, seeing a move from the instant sale of housing to panic at the realisation that the bottom was going to drop out of an over inflated

'This sense of possession, of ownership of a domain by virtue of one's sex is clearly visible as they blend into their surroundings. No comment is passed. There are no side-glances. Even when the actions take on a more surreal character...'

property market. Frances Mezzetti developed a site-specific work for York Street, where she grew up in Dublin's city centre, which dealt with the gradual erosion of the historical fabric of this part of the city through redevelopment. Working with bricks reclaimed from the site, Mezzetti built up a series of actions on York Street and wheeled them in a wheel barrow to Stephen's Green where she engaged her audience in stories of the street.

Mezzetti was continuing on from her long exploration of sites and histories throughout this decade, with earlier works such as the *Appearances* project with Cummins and Johnston. As Moira Roth noted in the text for *Appearances* 'I often felt that I was a witness to their witnessing of history.'[4] Cummins and Mezzetti have worked closely for the last 15 years. In 2009 they began a series of investigations into the performance of gender in public space through a project called *Walking in the Way*. The collaboration draws out their individual interests in the social, political, and historical aspects of site and how the site as source can expose the characteristics of social relations in a particular location. *Walking in the Way* has been performed in Dublin, Belfast, Edinburgh, London, Derry, Madrid, and Istanbul. In each site the artists carry out meticulous research into the area to identify specific actions and locations from which to work. They dress as men in order to infiltrate the world of men. They were not hiding and were therefore not in disguise, but instead they embodied men, donning men's clothes, applying facial hair, and exploring their own relationship to maleness. This allowed them to investigate their gendered position in public space. From simple acts like leaning on a bin in the street, standing around and loitering in the city, the artists were finding actions, behaviours, and gestures that allowed them to understand positions which they, as women, were unable to access. This sense of possession, of ownership of a domain by virtue of one's sex is clearly visible as they blend into their surroundings. No comment is passed. There are no side-glances. Even when the actions take on a more surreal character, there is still a sense of belonging, of permission to carry out strange activities and rituals like marking out boundaries in chalk (Dublin), carrying large oversized objects (Seville), doing a traditional Irish dance in the middle of

She describes this approach as 'longitudinal durational performance presented as living installation in the gallery.'[11] Her works operate in a clear linage with Abramović, with duration and often endurance forming significant aspects of her practice. In 2009 Coogan was included in *Marina Abramović Presents* at Manchester International Festival at the Whitworth Art Gallery (Alistair MacLennan and Kira O'Reilly also took part). The walls were stripped bare of the usual paintings and the exhibition took over the entire gallery, with four-hour performances by 14 artists, each day over 17 days. Coogan performed *The Fall*, which had previously been presented at The Kevin Kavanagh gallery in Dublin. A large bed-like platform was placed in the grand stairwell of the gallery and over the course of the four-hour duration each day Coogan leaped from the banister of the staircase down onto a yellow bed below. Time became a real factor as the physicality of the action took its toll on her body; she was endurance and resilience personified. While Alastair MacLennan, a highly influential presence in Irish performance known for his durational performances, slowly and methodically worked with a host of materials including shoes, tree branches, and fish. MacLennan speaks of duration 'in the sense of becoming aware of being there second by second by second, so that time becomes palpable. It makes us focus on what it is that we are living through.'[12] Coogan's durational work makes us aware of the mortality of the body and of the unpredictability in each effort to jump. Coogan's gestures, postures, and staging in this work revealed her signature referencing of art historical pieces, such as Yves Klein's *Leap into the Void*, with more subtle references to Joseph Beuys through the use of the hooked cane, Eugene Delacroix's *Victory Leading The People (28 July 1830)* and religious icon painting.

Following her inclusion in this experimental performance exhibition, Coogan embarked on a series of works in the same vein, which explored the potential for performance presentation and representation within institutional and gallery structures, while also examining alternative sites and vehicles for her work. In 2010 she presented *Yellow-reperformed* as part of the Dublin Theatre Festival where she invited five performers, both visual artists and performers working within a theatre context, to perform her work over the course of six nights (Coogan was the sixth performer). Each night a different woman inhabited Saint Mary's Abbey in Dublin, once used by Alanna O'Kelly for her seminal performance *Ómós*, in the 1990s. Each performer was given a script or score, outlining the main actions, gestures, and shapes of the piece. The work investigates the presence of the performer, how different bodies can inhabit the same piece. There is much written about the contemporary prevalence for reenactment of works. Amelia Jones questions this interest, its relationship to the art market and its need to commodify.[13] Coogan however is more interested in the role of the performer within the work and how the physical body and presence of the performer can alter or change our perception of the performance. The most striking differences for me were those between Olwen Fouéré and the emerging performers Ann Maria Healy and Victoria McCormack.

Fouéré is a veteran performer who works mainly in theatre. She has a powerful presence and strong, resilient appearance. During her performance there was at no point a sense that she would break, despite the grueling requirements; incessantly scrubbing fabric while sitting atop a large metal bin filled with cold soapy water. There was less a sense of endurance but rather more controlled virtuosity in this performance. Fouéré was like a workhorse, the sense of training in her craft coming through as she tackled the job at hand. Ann Maria Healy and Victoria McCormack betrayed a frailty and a vulnerability that was missing in Fouéré's performance. Healy at points looked swamped by the meters of yellow fabric and visibly shaken by the cold. In some way her performance was closer to real life in that at times you could see her struggle to go on. It felt less like a rehearsed piece and more like a true grappling with action, time and presence. As Helen Carey highlights in the curator's essay:

> Lighting, set dressing, sound and staging, with audience management and Front of House staff, all the vocabulary hint at a theatricality compounded when one knows that the methodologies of Coogan's 'script' is modeled on the Beckett pared down approach. Coogan in this activity is acutely aware of the traditions she mixes and messes; this Irish theatricality is infused into the work. She also messes the categories of performer, and asks the performers to find themselves in the work but quietly insists there is a YELLOW shape.[14]

In *Yellow-reperformed* Coogan is tackling the intersections between the forms of theatre and performance art, investigating the intrinsic presence of the performer. *Yellow-reperformed* ultimately appeared like a theatre or a stage set. Although the performers inhabited the piece they did not transform it in any new or radical way and the sense of rehearsal was palpable. As with Beckett's highly choreographed pieces that are recreated faithfully to the scripts; there was no space for 'elements of chaos with the unknown and unpredicted erupting dynamically through [the] live artworks.'[15] This work continued to have a further life as an art film, made in collaboration with filmmaker Paddy Cahill. As the audience watched the live performances Cahill was present in the space, almost as another performer, documenting meticulously the duration of each event.[16] The film is presented as a multi-screen piece of each artist performing the piece simultaneously. The film was subsequently

'[Fergus Byrne's] study of Butoh and martial arts are key to his understanding of the workings of the body and he sees these practices as enabling an extension of the limits of his body. Stylistically they inform a focus on slow precise movements.'

presented as part of the Dublin Film Festival 2012, offering yet another forum in which to present Coogan's investigations into performance.

Coogan was also instrumental in the presentation of *Right Here Right Now* at Kilmainham Gaol in 2010 (along with Dominic Thorpe and Niamh Murphy) and *LABOUR* in 2012 (with Chrissie Cadman and Helena Walsh). In both events a number of artists performed simultaneously over a long duration. She curated *Accumulator* at Visual in Carlow, an exhibition of performance where six artists performed for six hours, each on a different weekend, building on the action and detritus of the one before. This emphasis on duration is a clear directive from Coogan and she has thus greatly influenced the kind of performance art experienced in Ireland during this period.

Somewhat of a counterpoint to this, a number of platforms emerged across Dublin city that allowed for the presentation of shorter, more instantaneous works of performance. *Livestock* was formed in 2009 by Eleanor Lawlor and Frances Fay as a regular artist-led event and is an initiative of The Market Studios, Dublin. *Livestock* was conceived to support and promote artists presenting experimental performance based work, incorporating diverse performance and sound-based works with an emphasis on cross-disciplinarity. *Livestock* has hosted works by a variety of performance practitioners including Katherine Nolan, Eleanor Lawlor, Ciara Scanlon, Catherine Barragry, Fergus Byrne, and many others. In 2009 Lynette Moran initiated *Live Collision* which is keenly influenced by trends in Live Art practice in the UK. Moran's curatorial platform looks at experimental theatre, digital media, and its impact on live performance and she has been instrumental is bringing some of the most exciting artists working internationally in these forms to audience in Ireland.

Dominic Thorpe and Ciara McKeon initiated *Unit 1* in 2010, to facilitate the creation of live performance work, providing audiences with the opportunity to see new work on a regular basis. *Unit 1* has made important links with *Bbeyond* in Northern Ireland, and both organisations have collaborated to present the work of significant international practitioners alongside emerging artists. McKeon has also been involved in curating larger scale performance events and in 2012 she curated *4:3:12* at Block T in Smithfield, Dublin, presenting the work of 29 national and international performance artists including Sinéad and Hugh O'Donnell, Hilary Williams, and veterans such as Alastair MacLennan, Brian Connolly, and Boris Nieslony. The international connections made through platforms like *Unit 1* have in turn lead to many Irish artists travelling abroad and presenting at international festivals and exhibitions. These opportunities have been invaluable to artists wishing to further their experience and skills in performance, as opportunities in Ireland are scarce.

In Galway, *Live@8* had been running since 2008, initially a monthly and then a bi-monthly event presenting new contemporary art performance, video, film, sound, and music in the social context of a bar on the docks of the city. Organised by Vivienne Dick, Maeve Mulrennan, and Áine Phillips, *Live@8* presented the work of hundreds of national and international live artists, film makers, musicians, and creatives, with each event guest curated by notable Irish and international curators and artists. *Live@8* was an important platform for work in a city with scant visual art infrastructure. Galway's art scene has also benefited from an increased appetite for performance and interdisciplinary live work developed through *Tulca Live* and increased teaching of performance in Galway's Centre for Creative Arts and Media[17] by artists such as Aideen Barry and Amanda Coogan, and the migration of artists from the Burren College of Art in Clare where Áine Phillips is head of sculpture. Maeve Mulrennan had also facilitated many performance events in her role as visual art curator at the Galway Arts Centre (GAC). Victoria McCormack curated a number of performance events in GAC including, in 2012, The Performance Collective (Alex Conway, Pauline Cummins, Frances Mezzetti, Dominic Thorpe, and myself). We presented 14 days of live improvised performance as part of the Galway Arts Festival.

Fergus Byrne with dance practitioner Deirdre Murphy, curated *Transversal* between 2010 and 2012, in which they explored body-based practices and the intersection between dance and performance art. Byrne has been an active member of the performance community since he left college in the mid 1990s and his distinctive practice was influenced by Butoh, body weather training, and martial arts. Byrne studied at National College of Art and Design (NCAD), Dublin, and went on to study Theatre and Contemporary Practice in Scarborough in 2002. His study of Butoh and martial arts are key to his understanding of the workings of the body and he sees these practices as enabling an extension of the limits of his body. Stylistically they inform a focus on slow precise movements. His emphasis on physical activity is drawn out in his performance *Punishment for Galileo* performed at *Livestock* in 2012.

Here Byrne hula-hooped continuously for approximately two hours. Byrne sites Alastair MacLennan's 'actuations' (a term MacLennan uses to refer to his performance works) as an influence on his use of objects and the sense of animating these objects through his body.[18]

For *Punishment of Galileo* he built a wooden hula-hoop through which he hammered small nails. His waist was embellished with gold leafing, and his body was naked save for a pair of shorts. The performance began with cleaning the hoop and applying a last piece of gold leaf to the body. He then put one more nail in the hoop and continued to hula-hoop for the duration of the performance. Over time the nails began to leave a red raw mark around his midriff. Throughout the performance he held a mirror in one hand and a piece of wax in the other, molding and manipulating the wax in his right hand while looking into the mirror in his left hand. We are aware of his act of observation and simultaneous rendering of the 3D wax form. All the time the body is in motion, as with the discovery of Galileo's heliocentric universe. Towards the end of the performance he stops and lays a length of paper on the floor, rolls over it once to reveal the mark of his blood on the paper ground. He then carefully folded this paper, bookending it with the wax and mirrors. This performance, while exploring physical endurance and the limits of the body, also points to the process of representation and mark-making bound up in drawing.

Much like Alastair MacLennan, Byrne's work develops from an active drawing practice. He also teaches life drawing and works as a life model. His work *May I Draw Your Eye*, presented at *Live@8* in 2011, *Unit 1* in 2012 and as part of a performance art series for IETM[19] Dublin in 2013, examines the intimacy of the act of drawing, the relationship of the viewer to the subject, and asks the question who is the viewer and who is the subject being looked at. The viewer is invited to take a seat opposite Byrne at a very narrow table, where the performer grasps the viewer's arm and gazes deeply into their eyes, all the time scratching the likeness of their eye into a copper plate without looking down. This highly choreographed and intimate situation is further heightened through the recorded voice of the performer recounting a narrative about drawing and looking. At a certain point he describes sticking his finger right into his eye and pulling it back out again. The viewer is unsettled by this description, as the delicacy of the eye is emphasised and the sharp scribe cuts deeper into the copper. One is reminded of the famous scene in Sergei Eisenstein's film *Battleship Potemkin* (1925) and the use of innovative

Opposite top: Áine Phillips, *Sex Birth & Death*, Dublin, 2003. Photo: Nigel Rolfe.
Opposite bottom: Fergus Byrne, *Punishment for Galileo*. Photo: Ciara McKeon.

'This out-of-control feeling or certain awkwardness pervades much of his performance. In Thorpe's practice it is not merely incidental, but is a finely tuned examination of this state of uncertainty.'

techniques in editing to achieve discomfort in the viewer. We are also reminded of Francis Bacon's interest in Eisenstein's film. Fergus Byrne has long been influenced by the works of Bacon and in 2010 gave a performative lecture on the role of figuration and physicality in his work at the Hugh Lane Gallery where the Bacon Studio is housed. *May I Draw Your Eye* constantly makes reference to the life drawing construct, and that of representation, all the time making the viewer aware that they too are being viewed. During the performance Byrne recounts how:

> All bodies are the quarries of pursuit. Freud commented, a doctor is looking at the person to make the person better, weller, whereas the painter is looking at the person to get something from that person to strengthen the picture however near he steers to the person. [...] He's still looking at the person for the sake of the painting and not for the person.[20]

Dominic Thorpe also makes his viewers acutely aware of their sensory role and presence in very different ways. He often makes them active participants in the viewing process, by giving them torches as in *Redress State – Questions Imagined* at 126 Gallery in Galway in 2010, or by removing the sense of sight altogether by working in the dark in his performance for *Remnant*[21] at Ballina Civic Offices Gallery, Co. Mayo in 2012, so they are searching or seeking out the work in an active way. As Amanda Coogan notes 'Thorpe's removal of one of our senses refocused our experience of his work into a physical, embodied one'.[22] While Byrne's work often involves continuous actions, Thorpe allows for an enormous amount of empty space and inactivity in his performances. He allows time and space for the actions to develop, creating a sense of hesitancy and uncertainty in the viewer and placing the audience in a position of vulnerability. Thorpe's performances ask the audience to question themselves and their position in relation to the work, and in the context of these issues. This out-of-control feeling or certain awkwardness pervades much of his performance. In Thorpe's practice it is not merely incidental, but is a finely tuned examination of this state of uncertainty. He often steps as if to move with purpose through a space only to hesitate, to reevaluate his move. These slight actions create an unease in the performances. Thorpe developed this approach as a result of working outside of Ireland where he has less control over the environment or material he can use in his performances, quite often pushing him to work with just 'the body and behaviour through the body.'[23]

One such performance, *Redress State – Questions Imagined,* took place for five hours a day over nine days at the artist-run gallery 126 in Galway. Over this period Thorpe worked with a loose framework often improvising with his chosen materials: raw sheep's wool, a bell, charcoal. The space was filled with the warm animal smells emanating from the wool. In the darkness, the piercing sound of a hand-held school bell ringing or making grating noises as it is scraped along the walls. From out of the darkness came the sound of the scratching of charcoal on the wall, like chalk on a board, the sound of footsteps and breathing, of a man pacing through the space. All the time little glimmers of light illuminate tiny fragments of the whole, the word 'silence' is repeatedly scrawled across the walls. Thorpe also wrote adversarial questions, interrogations he imagined the victims of abuse were asked at the Institutional Redress Boards legal hearings.[24]

The cumulative effect of uncertainty and unease in this performance, draws the viewer into an empathetic experience with those who have endured the redress system in Ireland. He ultimately questions the audience, what is their relationship to this situation? What is their responsibility? The redress board was set up to make 'fair and reasonable awards to persons who, as children, were abused while resident in industrial schools, reformatories and other institutions subject to state regulation or inspection'.[25] Thorpe's research found that many people were traumatised following their hearing, some committing suicide. However, in order to receive financial compensation they had to sign a confidentiality agreement stating they would not speak publicly of their experience of the redress board or the compensation received. If they did not comply they would face a large fine and/or a prison sentence. Thorpe's wall writings in the performance space, were informed by meetings with redress board claimants who are prevented from telling their own stories due to this order. Thorpe's work moves away from representation of his outrage at this experience, to a situation that offers understanding of the uncertainty and vulnerability of these people at a wholly visceral level, while also challenging the viewer to question their own complicity in these abuses. It is the enforced silence that requires us to be complicit.

In *Very Very Narrow Mouth* presented as part of *Tulca* in 2011, Thorpe continued to work directly with the reports published following a number

'Anne Seagrave said that her great love of performance is that "you do feel so close to this bare human presence".'

of state enquiries into clerical child abuse. The Ryan, Cloynes, Murphy, and Ferns reports,[26] all chronicled the wide extent of the abuse of children, not just by the religious orders working in these institutions but also by 'teachers, lay workers, charity workers, members of the healthcare and legal professions, social workers, foster carers, police, politicians and civil servants who were found to have either perpetrated, covered up or chosen to remain silent about serious abuses that had happened.'[27] The space, Columban Hall in Galway (a sports hall in a converted church), was lined at eye level with extracts of text from these reports. The performer sat at an oversized table sharpening a spoon and gradually digging a hole with it into the surface of the table. The destruction of this domestic yet officious object draws relationships between public and private complicity and the exposure of our fractured identity as a state and society. We were confronted again with these issues in situations where he urinated abjectly through his trousers or spoke with open mouth, but the words unable to come out. We constantly saw a body that was awkward and pushing against its limits, limits not of physical strength but the boundary of the body and the stuff that wants to come out of it. We were confronted with a litany of evidence that betrayed a systemic cover up of the truth and the continued forced silencing of vulnerable members of society today.

A marked concern with the revelations of the inquiries into abuse in state and church institutions was visible in this period, with artists such as Áine Phillips, Pauline Cummins, and I, all developing works that dealt with these significant events in the history of the state. Cummins and I developed a number of performances around this issue as part of the exhibition *Subject to Ongoing Change* in 2012.[28] During one performance both performers swung a large skipping rope in the central room of the upstairs gallery of The Galway Arts Centre over the course of one and a half hours. The floor was covered in the ashes of burnt paper including pages of the above mentioned reports. The skipping rope, encompassing the entire space as it flew through the air in an almost menacing manner, unsettled the remains of this past.

Opposite top: Alan Delmar, Dublin Live Art Festival, 2013. Photo: FionaKilleen.
Opposite bottom: Frances Mezzetti, Dublin Live Art Festival, 2012. Photo: Joseph Carr.

The innocence of the childhood game of skipping was lost as the violence of the rope lashing the floor caused the dust to rise and unearth the one buried history. The task became gradually more difficult over time as the two bodies continuously kept the rope in motion. The difference in age between the two performers, one clearly of a different generation than the other, is significant. It creates a lineage over time of what remains, a sense of the continued impact on the victims of this state abuse into later life, and down through the generations; a form of collective memory over time. It emphasises that this is not just an experience that affects the victim but continues to impact wider society. Similarly many of the works presented in *LABOUR* looked specifically at the experience of women in Magdalen Laundries in the twentieth century (see Helena Walsh's essay in this book for a comprehensive survey of this exhibition) drawing out this past and its relationship to women in contemporary Ireland.

During the new millennium there has been a sense of urgency in the need to deal wit these monumental moments in our nation's history. Moira Roth notes, there are cycles and recurrences of events, those that are:

> "obdurate" (meaning both stubborn and insistent), resurfacings of certain histories [...] until in some way they are put to rest, perhaps better phrased, redressed. [...] Obviously these redressions of obdurate public history – if this is possible – can, should and indeed must, take place out in the world of economics and politics, but the 'redressing' can (should? Must?) also happen in artists' choices of significant metaphors and healing ritualistic acts.[29]

Ireland in this period has been characterised by vast changes in society, with the economic collapse leading to a reevaluation of where we are as a society. Many artists have chosen to explore these changes but also to explore new possibilities for performance practice despite the reduced funding to the arts since the collapse of the economy. It is outside the scope of this essay to survey the current production of the innovative and ground breaking work happening today. There is no doubt that these younger artists will forge new paths for performance into the future. Performance in Ireland has always and continues to rely on the dedication and tenacity of individual artists and collectives who are determined to continue their practice. Anne Seagrave said that her great love of performance is that 'you do feel so close to this bare human presence'[30] and it is this colliding of human presences in space and time that will continue to feed the practices and interests of performance artists and audiences alike into the future.

Research assistance by Dominic Thorpe and Maeve Mulrennan.

1. Robert Ayers, *Anne Seagrave* (Bonington Gallery, Nottingham Trent University, 2000).

2. Peggy Phelan, *Unmarked: The Politics of Performance* (London: Routledge, 1993), p. 148-9.

3. Amelia Jones, 'Survey', *The Artist's Body*, ed. by Tracey Warr (London and New York: Phaidon, 2000) pp. 16-47, (p. 19).

4. Moira Roth, 'Over and Out Writing from Berkeley to Dublin', in *Appearances Part 1* Catalogue (Dublin: Arthouse, 2001), pp. 12-9.

5. Michel de Certeau, *The Practice of Everyday Life* (Berkeley and Los Angeles: University of California Press, 1984), p. 96.

6. Referenda on abortion in Ireland were held in 1992 and 2002.

7. Mary Russo, *The Female Grotesque: Risk, Excess and Modernity* (New York: Routledge, 1994), p. 8.

8. Ibid.

9. Robert Ayers published a review of the event in the *Scupture Society of Ireland Newsletter*: 'Among [its] shortcomings, apparently, was the fact that typical of projects planned under McGonagle's leadeship, the focus was almost entirely non-Irish [...] what you have is the perception of an institution that has failed to nurture the local roots of new creativity, or an art form that is locally perceived to be particularly healthy and pertinent'. Robert Ayers, 'Performance and The Virtual', *Sculpture Society of Ireland Newsletter*, (Jan/Feb 2002), p. 5.

10. The Allied Irish Bank Arts Awards, a major Irish art prize was awarded from 2001-10.

11. *Amanda Coogan*, artist's website <www.amandacoogan.com/about.html>.

12. Alastair MacLennan, cited by Aidan Dunne, 'Alastair MacLennan', *Irish Times*, 4 February 2003, p. 7.

13. Reference from the Symposium held in conjunction with *Marina Abramović Presents* at the Whitworth Gallery in Manchester, 12 July 2009.

14. Helen Carey, 'Performing, Performance, Re-performing, Re-performance', 24 September 2010, *Amanda Coogan* <http://www.amandacoogan.com/helencarey.html>.

15. Simon Keogh, witness writer notes as part of *Yellow-reperformed*, exhibited in *Out on the sea was a boat full of people singing and other stories* at the Lab, Dublin City Council Arts Office's exhibition space, which I curated in 2011.

16. Writer Simon Keogh was also visible in the space writing his response in real time to the performances each night.

17. The visual art department of Galway-Mayo Institute of Technology.

18. Alastair MacLennan, unpublished interview with Michelle Browne, 4 April 2014.

19. IETM is the International Network for Contemporary Performing Arts, which held its 2013 Spring plenary meeting in Dublin at Project Arts Centre. Michelle Browne curated a series of performances called *Between You Me and The Four Walls* for the artistic programme which included work by Áine Phillips, Fergus Byrne, and a collaboration between Dominic Thorpe and Michelle Browne.

20. From the text of *May I Draw Your Eye*, courtesy of the artist.

21. Remnant was a programme of performance curated by Mayo County Council arts officer Seville Gaynor and Sean Walsh director of Ballina Arts Centre, presenting live performance and an exhibition of documentation alongside a symposium with contributions form Nigel Rolfe, Amanda Coogan, and Dominic Thorpe.

22. Amanda Coogan, 'What is Performance Art?', *Irish Museum of Modern Art*, 2011 <http://www.imma.ie/en/page_212496.htm> [accessed 5 December 2014].

23. Dominic Thorpe, unpublished interview with Michelle Browne, 4 April 2014.

24. The Redress Board was set up under the Residential Institutions Redress Act, 2002 to make fair and reasonable awards to persons who, as children, were abused while resident in industrial schools, reformatories and other institutions subject to state regulation or inspection.

25. 'Welcome', *Residential Institutions Redress Board*, <http://www.rirb.ie/> [accessed 14 October 2014].

26. The Ryan Report (otherwise known as the Commission to inquire into Child Abuse) report was published in 2009. The Cloynes Report was published in 2011 and The Ferns Report was published in 2005. All were official Irish government inquiry into the allegations of physical and sexual abuse of children in state institutions (Ryan Report) and catholic diocese in Ireland.

27. 'Performed during the Tulca Festival of Visual Art at Columban Hall Sea Road Galway16 Nov 2011', *Dominic Thorpe* <http://www.dominicthorpe.net/projects/very-very-narrow-mouth/>.

28. The Performance Collective, *Subject to Ongoing Change* July 2012, Galway Arts Centre.

29. Moira Roth, 'Over and Out Writing form Berkeley to Dublin', *Appearances Part 1*, Catalogue, (Dublin: Arthouse 2001), pp. 12-9 (p. 13).

30. Ayers, *Anne Seagrave*, p. 16.

RIGHT HERE RIGHT NOW

IRISH PERFORMANCE ART

KILMAINHAM GAOL
Thurs 4th November 6pm - 10pm

20 PERFORMANCES SIMULTANEOUSLY OVER FOUR HOURS

Alastair MacLennan
Aine Phillips
Brian Connolly
Dominic Thorpe
Declan Rooney
Francis Mezzetti
Brian Patterson
Sinead McCann
Ann Maria Healy
Catherine Barragry
Helena Walsh

Pauline Cummins
Amanda Coogan
Michelle Browne
Francis Fay
Fergus Byrne
Alex Conway
Niamh Murphy
Meabh Redmond
Sandra Johnston
Victoria Mc Cormack

Part of RIGHT HERE RIGHT NOW Performance Art Festival 4th - 5th November
Curated by AMANDA COOGAN, DOMINIC THORPE and NIAMH MURPHY

CLIODHNA SHAFFREY

RIGHT HERE RIGHT NOW

In Dublin on the 4 November 2010 an unusual event took place in Kilmainham Gaol, a former prison that is now a museum, where 20 artists from around Ireland came together to perform in a live durational performance lasting four hours. The artists occupied the ground floor of this prison building; a site so closely associated with the founding of the nation state and ideas of identity that its resonant histories could only become part of the spirit of the event and a necessary part of the experience of the performance.

Opposite: *Right Here Right Now*, Dublin, 2010. Clockwise from top left: Alaistair MacLennan. Photo: Sebastian Dooris; *Right Here Right Now* poster, 2010; Dominic Thorpe. Photo: Joseph Carr; Ann Maria Healy. Photo: Tracy O'Brien.

265

'At any moment some thing or body might fall or break or crack under the pressure of continual durational strain. The potential for rupture hung in the air.'

The Gaol's interior is an oval void of concrete and steel, with three-stories of prison cells circulating off catwalks and an imposing iron staircase running up its central spine. The architecture projects an uncanny aura into the site where the heroes of the 1916 Rising were executed. Architecture and memory intertwine perfectly in the prison's 1980s transformation into a museum of empty spaces, enabling visitors an imaginary contact with the raw material of the many tragic events that have happened here. Over the years Kilmainham Gaol has been used from time to time as a striking context for exhibiting and siting art, and, its choice for *Right Here, Right Now* would again prove powerful.[1]

On arrival at the Gaol, a crowd had gathered and was already moving amongst the performers, who seemed at first like remnants from hidden histories trapped here. They seemed physically present, yet as if out of another time. Their movements slowed down in constant repetitive action, lost in their presentness. Unlike many other theatre or performance events there was no entrance or exit by the performers and we came into a scenario already live. Some of the artists were confined within cells, others located at fixed points within the ground floor, while a few moved restlessly throughout the space. Each performance was a unique thing – a work in itself, ephemeral and most likely never to be repeated. And yet, the co-existence of 20 live performances, in this charged panoptical site, created something unexpected – a sort of bizarre spectacle on one level, and on the other, a group installation of living sculptures, choreographing a rhythm between each other and between the audience whose direct encounter and physical closeness to the presence of the artists, in real time, enabled a very different type of viewing experience to unfold.

We who came were audience, spectators, voyeurs, and witnesses, but also part and parcel of the collective event, our presence binding the idiosyncratic performances into a discordant ensemble. If performance art claims to have a special relationship with the viewer – the audience's live immediate responses considered essential to the completion of the work – *Right Here, Right Now* can live up to such claims. As the evening moved on, the place was filled with more and more people. We had long queues to witness specific performances in the cells, and as only one or two people were allowed in sequentially, the experience became at times uncomfortably intimate. We could come and go if we pleased, but many stayed the full duration and over these four hours as the intensity heightened. The artists who at first appeared almost spectral, became increasingly real, as we became physically and consciously alert to the actuality we were in. It was John Cage who aspired to the idea that people might realise that they themselves are doing their experience and that it's not being done to them.[2] Over time, as Amanda Coogan writes of live durational art, 'clarity becomes more apparent and the work starts to soar'.[3]

Staged in a very different way to the conventional performance art festival where one performance will follow another, the smörgåsbord form of multiple simultaneous performances had the power of something whole – a *Gesamtkunstwerk* (total work of art) – comprising action, noise, the softer sounds of sweeping, skipping, shuffling feet, objects, props, colour, smell, live tableaux, and the body in space. Sited in Kilmainham Gaol at a time of deep political and economic crisis in Ireland, the performances carried an additional critical edge. The sustained tension that became increasingly palpable throughout the evening began to unhinge any sense of harmonious conciliation, of feelings of immersion or being embedded within a scenario or film scene where the Gaol's chilling histories might perform as a mere backdrop to the event. The vulnerabilities made present; the strange and visceral images conjured; the futile repetitions; the cold crowded space didn't always leave scope for identification and togetherness, but conversely enabled disrupted feelings of friction, awkwardness, exclusion, and discomfort. At any moment some thing or body might fall or break or crack under the pressure of continual durational strain. The potential for rupture hung in the air. The juxtaposing of spatially constructed performances with those which were more rigidly controlled, altered the very structure of seeing so that moments of intense concentration were punctured and broken and lighter, wittier energies released. It was precisely in these contradictions between something that could seem so perfectly complete and contained and then have the suggestion of something totally precarious or unsafe that gave *Right Here, Right Now* an urgent immediacy, or, the kind of conflicting energy that Chantal Mouffe describes as an antagonistic dimension always present in social space.[4] While conceived primarily as a showcase of distinct and individual Irish artists' practices – where performance is a central element – it was possible to read the event as an expression of the continuing fragility of human life in the frame of world politics.

Right Here, Right Now had all the feeling of a landmark event; 'an occasion', as one commentator put it 'which the public had been waiting for'[5]. The event was political, aesthetic, absurd, and with an artistic autonomy that did not try to collapse art into life, but rather opened up possibilities to think critically through art about the world we are in. Conceived of as a site-specific event by its curators (Amanda Coogan, Dominic Thorpe, and Niamh Murphy) that would bring live durational performance art out of its marginalised zone and celebrate its meaning and growing significance within the mainstream contemporary art in Ireland, this event also seized the moment to hold a mirror to ourselves and to direct the gaze of the performance inwards. The choice of Kilmainham Gaol as its venue – which had gone through its own transformation from a place crystallizing ideologies of nationhood and nationality to one that presented a new sense of place, embracing the spirit of questioning, uncertainty and exploration offered that critical moment to converge context with art.[6] That it would be through the promotion of live durational art practices, critically associated with freedom of expression and with its emphasis on immediacy and spontaneity, happening in the here (Kilmainham Gaol, with all the signifying referents as former prison – internship, control, discipline, punishment, containment, authoritarian, institution) and the now (politically unstable and economically broken Ireland) gave the experience a vital, more tangible edge. And this tangible edge must be aligned to the presence in time and space of the artist, and the special relationship that exists between artist and audience that seeks, as French philosopher Jean-François Lyotard writes, to unite in some way the audience with the artist into a group, collectively experiencing the event's destablising effects.[7]

This is not to suggest that *Right Here Right Now* presented some sort of audience-artist coherence and easy identification with the works. Many people who came were experiencing live performance art for the first time, and even perhaps for those more experienced arts audience, this event came 'out of blue', completely unexpected in its presentation of co-existent performances. How to behave, how to react were all part of the interaction and all part of the challenges of this event. It did not create a space of conviviality à la Bourriaud's relational aesthetics, but rather created a sort of hybrid composed of the possibility for hushed concentrated contemplation where the potential for distraction was everywhere present and where the sensations of discomfort jostling with absurdity sustained

> 'The choice of Kilmainham Gaol as its venue [...] presented a new sense of place, embracing the spirit of questioning, uncertainty and exploration offered that critical moment to converge context with art.'

the tension. The creative strategy for staging *Right Here, Right Now* supported the condition for multiple viewing experiences. You could experience some of the works from many perspectives and then walk away when finished viewing, and perhaps come back again to note something had changed or shifted in your absence.

Think, for example, of the extraordinary installation that Sinéad McCann had created at the entrance to the large hall where a necklace of lemons placed on the floor defined her space. Inside this space she had placed a table (whose glass top came from a social welfare office), a stepladder, neon lighting, and an electric counting machine, such as you see in social welfare, passport and immigration offices, and in banks, controlling your progress from queue to counter. McCann, who was dressed in black and wearing a large white wig made of tea bags, sat at the table, drank tea, and climbed the ladder, ate the lemons. Her strange performance creating a fictionalised scenario that seemed more like a dream sequence or, as James Merrigan insightfully suggests, drew on surreal filmic images such as those of David Lynch or Stanley Kubrick to create its effect.[8] The tragic-comic performance, with its narrative undertow and collection of signifying props, might read as the unveiling of authority as a construct, where in times of recession the system's power increases over vulnerable individuals' lives. In other performances we were only given a restricted view. To see Alex Conway's cowboy we had to look through a tiny spy hole in the prison door where watching him felt like looking through the lens of a camera, or down the barrel of a gun. Inside the cell Conway, dressed in blue jeans with red t-shirt, cowboy boots, and hat, paced and whistled like a wild animal (to a backing track of a Johnny Cash song) and every so often, he'd stop to stare straight at you, his glass eye coolly piercing the on-looker's gaze. Conway's performance cleverly orchestrated to double as an iconic image from the American West, might also, in its light-hearted, tongue in cheek resonance, have brought attention to the current debates within contemporary performance and its problematic relationship to documentation as work of art.[9] The surreal beauty of Alastair

Right Here Right Now, Dublin, 2010.
Top: Catherine Barragry. Photo: Joseph Carr.
Bottom: Sinéad McCann Photo Tracy O'Brien.

Right Here Right Now, Dublin, 2010.
Top: Victoria McCormack. Photo: Sebastian Dooris.
Bottom: Francis Fay. Photo: Sebastian Dooris.

MacLennan's live tableau as still life also suggested the idea of an image. Rather than the filmic however MacLennan, who sat immobile for the full four hours, balancing on his head a plate of fish and potatoes, was more human sculpture or 3D painting, skillfully paired down to its visceral essence to capture the melancholic presence of a lonely man looking into the abyss, or, perhaps, this 'portrait' was more the embodiment of the serene dignity of a still and silent being who remains undisturbed by a world in flux.

This ability to take on the human condition and represent the Other has been at the centre of performance practices from the 1960s and 1970s onwards, bringing audiences into direct contact with The Body, often through durational performances which can be painful or difficult to endure. These works raise questions about established norms – sexual and social – and increasingly today draw attention to the processes of identification as a social construct. In Sandra Johnston's performance, where only a few people were permitted into her cell at a time, she circled the room slowly, leaning sometimes for support against the prison wall, breathing in and out of an empty water glass and dragging a chair and a pair of old boots loosely caught around her ankle. Her frail and delicate presence embodied the notion of captivity, demonstrating Johnston's incredible ability to tread the precarious ground of representing the Other (the prisoner). Being brought so close to witness her, we became complicit in the construction of this identity. And so it was with each of the 20 performances, giving scope for different interpretations and meanings to issue forth, while all around the energies and sounds that filled the space appeared to take their cue from Fergus Byrne's relentless skipping, like a lone drum beat in a looped ritual, there to keep time.

Such divergent set ups focused attention on the primacy of personal perception, the structures of seeing and the sensations in experiencing. And with a mix of established and acclaimed artists performing alongside a whole generation of younger emerging practitioners, the event demonstrated the exceptional range evident in performance art in Ireland today. But *Right Here, Right Now*, was more than a showcase; the focus on individual practice through a collective ethos had the feeling of a major site-specific temporary artwork composed of multiple and fragmented parts where the context resonated through the artists' works, the architecture providing spatial bearings and the first-hand encounter with the artist's body demonstrating the potency of Live Art to create illusion as much as to present an embodiment of reality.

In this way *Right Here, Right Now* – with its urgent title – was full of surprises, obscure references, symbolic metaphors, oblique signifiers, and visual magic. It neither fell into the didactic territories of some politically motivated art (though all the work had a critical edge) and nor was the art overwhelmed by its potent site (though the site resonated fully in the work). The focus was on the here and now – the present moment where the suspension of time was concentrated by slowed down movements, repetitive actions, ritualistic looping, and stillness creating a space for Time. 'Performance's only life is the present' writes American feminist scholar Peggy Phelan,[10] and when there is substantial time, as in live durational art, the 'extension' of the present has a transformative power over the work and our perception of it, as viewers. Robert Wilson, the theatre director, whose long durational pieces have lasted up to seven hours, speaks of the 'battery of energy', 'the complexity in things' that are revealed through very slowed-down movements, concentrated actions, and complete stillness.[11] Live durational performance provides a means of breaking with the familiar and habitual to bring greater awareness through the body to our experiences of being in the world. What became apparent over the four hours, and what proved so memorable about *Right Here, Right Now*, was that this inward view to looking outwards to understand the world and being in the world could co-exist with performances such as Brian Connolly's, Sinéad McCann's, Michelle Browne's, Ann Marie Healy's, or Dominic Thorpe's, which might read as staged metaphors drawing on a range of sources from film, literature, politics, and everyday life to critique and analyse structures of society, contest dominant hegemonies, and to comment on injustices that prevail. In the introductory text to the event, Alastair MacLennan, the renowned and leading Irish practitioner, expresses this so well in his remarks about the artists he most admires: 'who overcome the most, within and without themselves, 'take on' the human condition, and who (in effective art) comment on political and social corruption.'[12]

Today performance art is receiving greater focus than ever within the mainstream curatorial programmes of galleries, museums, and biennials. Amanda Coogan celebrates what she terms 'the second wave of performance art', suggesting that performance art is 'coming in from the cold' and is being increasingly acknowledged as offering possibilities for a unique engagement of an audience that is exciting for the viewing public.[13] She lists the first appointment of a Curator in Chief for Performance at the Museum of Modern Art, New York (MOMA), as one amongst a number of significant indicators of this trend. We might also note how performance has become an element in the work of many leading contemporary artists, such as: Francis Alÿs, Rirkrit Tiravanija, Patty Chang, Maurizio Cattelan, Sophie Calle or, in the performative lectures of Walid Raad/The Atlas Group, who uses fictionalised documentation to explore the realities of violence in the Lebanon. In relational aesthetics or participatory practices, with their emphasis on immediacy of face-to-face encounters, and interactions, performance has also become a central strategy in much of the work. Here though, borders between art-life dichotomies sometimes merge to create a space of conviviality or literal engagement, suggesting perhaps a different emphasis to the consciousness-raising or contemplation sought in live performance. The Polish artist Wladyslaw Kazmierczak suggests that performance art 'doesn't follow after art, it has a more open terrain,' and he speaks of the freedom performance gives 'to do what he wants to do in the context of art, or beyond art [...] where he can use everything in his art and present it by himself'.[14] Performance art is constantly evolving as a practice, where definitions vary greatly on what it is, where new forms embrace the use of technology, permit pre-recorded material and the internet as a legitimate form of experience and where artists are constantly challenging and critiquing the practice from within. What *Right Here, Right Now* demonstrated, as a major event introducing the public to live durational art, was the vitality of performance art in Ireland today. It is central to a growing number of artists' practice and as a medium it has the capacity to incorporate the political within the aesthetic. In this way, performance art is by and large, a critical form of art making – embracing elements of shock, discomfort, absurdity, eccentricity, humour and real pleasure, prompting audiences to observe the meaning-making processes that govern our lives.

Artists performing at *Right Here, Right Now* were; Áine Phillips, Amanda Coogan, Brian Connolly, Dominic Thorpe, Frances Mezzetti, Brian Patterson, Sinéad McCann, Catherine Barragry, Fergus Byrne, Michelle Browne, Ann Maria Healy, Helena Walsh, Francis Fay, Pauline Cummins, Victoria McCormack, Alex Conway, Sandra Johnston, Meabh Redmond, Niamh Murphy, and Alastair MacLennan.

1. Kilmainham Gaol has become a site for unprogrammed artistic happenings ranging from a staging of Shakespeare's *Tempest* and Handel's opera *Tancred*, to acting as venue for the annual Sculpture in Context show (1998) and Beckett's play *Catastrophe* (1999); in 1998 the artist Brian Hand undertook a residency in the Gaol and the exhibitions *In a State*, (1991) was followed by an exhibition commemorating the bi-centenary of Robert Emmet's death (2003). See also in Pat Cooke, 'Kilmainham Gaol, Interpreting Irish nationalism and Republicanism', *Open Museum Journal*, 2 (2000) pp. 1-11.

2. Roselee Goldberg, *Performance: Live Art since the 60s* (London: Thames and Hudson, 2004), p. 63.

3. Amanda Coogan, *Acumulator* <http://www.amandacoogan.com/accumulator-essay.html>.

4. Chantal Mouffe, 'Artistic Activism and Agnostic Spaces', *Art and Research, a journal of ideas, contexts and methods*. 1.2 (Summer 2007), <http://www.artandresearch.org.uk/v1n2/mouffe.html> [accessed 10 December 2014].

5. Cliodhna Shaffrey, unpublished interview with Dominic Thorpe, 10 December 2010.

6. Cooke, 'Kilmainham Gaol'.

7. Jean François Lyotard writes on eventhood and the sublime and the destablising of boundaries of meaning resulting from experiencing the event. Lyotard, Jean François, *The Post Modern Condition: A Report on Knowledge* (Minneapolis: University of Minneapolis Press, 1984).

8. James Merrigan's unpublished essay on works by Sinéad McCann and Alex Conway as part of *Right Here, Right Now*, 2010.

9. The problematic relationship between performance art and its documentation are under review as Douglas Davis questions in his article, 'Performance Photography', is the picture of an art event also art? Such debates push defined parameters beyond interpretations that might emphasise the authenticity of our first hand encounter with the artists' body. See also Peter Richards, 'The Current State of Performance Art in Northern Ireland', *Circa*, 111 (2005), pp. 64-67.

10. Peggy Phelan, *Unmarked: The Politics of Performance*, (London and New York: Routledge, 1993), p. 146.

11. Katherine Waugh and Fergus Daly's film essay, *The Art of Time*, (In association with Harvest Films, 2009). In the film Daly and Waugh's interview with Richard Wilson, focuses on his 1976 work *Einstein on the Beach*, which was created in collaboration with the composer Philip Glass.

12. *Right Here, Right Now* Press Release, 29 October 2010.

13. Ibid.

14. Wladyslaw Kazmierczak in conversation with Brian Connolly, *Performance Art Northern Ireland* (Belfast: Bbeyond, 2010), pp. 66-8.

FERGUS BYRNE

FRAGMENTS ON THE PERFORMANCE COLLECTIVE:
Subject to Ongoing Change at The Galway Arts Centre, Dublin, Ireland

The text is a commentary on the work of The Performance Collective, *Subject to Ongoing Change*. The group; Dominic Thorpe, Pauline Cummins, Frances Mezzetti, Michelle Browne, and Alex Conway improvised an ensemble for four hours without pause every day, for two weeks in the galleries of the Galway Arts Centre.[1] The collective formed four years previously in mutual support of each other's art practice. Their sessions evolved into a collective performance practice, working with space, time, materials, movement, gesture, traces, sound, voice, provocation, silence, duration, and immersion.

This text is my reading of actions as they happened and my internal thought processes as I watched. I don't seek to resolve the various questions that arise for me. Rather I see these as part of the effect of the work and aim to make this live questioning clear in the text.

Opposite top left: Dominic Thorpe and Frances Mezzetti, The Performance Collective – *Subject to On Going Change*, Galway Arts Centre, 2012. Photo: Joseph Carr; Top right: Pauline Cummins, Alex Conway, and Michelle Browne. Photo: Joseph Carr; Bottom left: Photo: Joseph Carr; Bottom left: Dominic Thorpe, *untitled*, The Performance Collective, Broadcast Gallery Dublin 2011. Photo: Joseph Carr.

Granted, it is a text extensively developed after the event. The focus is on conveying the improvisatory quality of the work and how certain mechanisms operate within it. These mechanisms are principally the way performers engage each other and the way I make sense, even prior to writing, of what I see. Text in italics is directly from my live notes. Their inclusion and the occasionally abbreviated phrasing of the overall text are intended to increase its immediacy. At certain points in the text pronouns are used to describe actions by performers without specifying names. It is a deliberate device to occasionally separate their everyday persona from the person that they become in performance.

***

MEANING

So many objects take on transferred meaning.[2] A hotel bell becomes a puck pushed by a broom handle. This is already a displacement, by associative thinking, of what I actually saw. Or perhaps a puck became a hotel bell for the want of a nail; for the want of meaning. The kingdom was not lost but was formed within my mind on the basis of actions wrought with objects out there on the gallery floor.

She pushes a hotel bell along the floor with a broom stick. But I could never read the broom as a hockey stick so readily. Few objects are pushed as a puck but the broom had not strayed so far from its standard use.

Action occurs until it finds its meaning in dialectical relation to something else. A shallow tray becomes a water vessel. Michelle walked the length of the gallery dribbling water from a kettle on floor until she found that tray and now the action seems quite appropriate. She carries the tray, slopping meniscus and stands below Dominic who dips his ties in the water. And he wrings one out over her head. Her shoulders rise in response. He showers her with water from the tray. And then, fierce sentiment as he walks her paternally through the space to the front gallery. I recall that in the pub they laughed about how he takes this caring attitude toward her in practice.

The concrete actions become poetic in the simple recording of many of these unforeseen incongruous juxtapositions. I note down what occurs and their collective trace takes on unexpected resonance. Out of the same window at which Alex knelt sentry, Dominic holds a white shirt on a brush handle.

> 'A strong trust exists between them that they can and will work without direction whilst maintaining a commitment to the immediate moment.'

Here the dialectic is between things I have seen but the performers have not. Their actions interrelate through the additional layer of my experience. The white shirt of surrender held out the same window in which a mock sentry knelt earlier. But Dominic did not know of Alex's action. The individual's commitment to his/her task works best when simultaneous encounters and those between past and present are entirely accidental within the improvisation. 'Accidental' may be the wrong word as it does not account for the strong working practice the collective developed over much time together.[3] The shared pool of material means narrative links inevitably occur. A strong trust exists between them that they can and will work without direction whilst maintaining a commitment to the immediate moment.

The consistency of this approach makes it all the more apparent when a performer requests or suggests something of another, by gesture or by mouthed word. Such communication betrays desire on the part of the artist to create an image rather than accepting that circumstance may not engender the image forming. I think of Alex arriving beside Michelle with a line of silver cake cups balanced along both arms. 'Coal', he voiced faintly knowing that the verbal was forbidden. The cups were then filled with pieces of the coal that lay about the floor. The image was achieved but was less magical for having occurred in this way. Black Market International's phrase 'The Art of Encounter' is worth recalling in this regard.[4] What occurs in an encounter without any coercion? The Performance Collective work very much in this vein in their interactions. There were scant few such moments of direction in the six days I saw. On the day I participated as a guest I experienced that sense of all encounters being equal and their consequences of the moment.

DUSK TILL DAWN - MIDWAY POINT

God, a smile is allowed as the crack that lets the light in like a strange amusement park. At nightfall, most rides are closed. But the ghosts linger and unusual beings are active. 'He' wanders from one end of room to another seeing what's on offer. This audience member has to navigate his own journey through the space. 'She' bathes her feet in his torch light but he is not amused. What is at stake here is an inner experience and those who come for the surface bubble leave quickly with little to say. But she returns each day to observe herself in their actions. To the point of needing to leave and wanting to stay. What does one do when performance affects one so emotionally? [5]

Dominic scrapes the wall. Pitch of sound screeches through to front space where I stand.

Amp is turned off. We're in netherworld.

Silence.

Red balloon mouth crawls on all fours from back room to front.

Holding that space

After great moment.

No sense to move on

At this point I was furious. A stunning piece of performance had riveted the entire audience. He crawled on all fours through the space holding an inflated balloon in his mouth illuminated by a red light within. In unlit rooms it was a beacon for all eyes. We watched as he crawled. She followed him placing a chair on his back. Yet alongside the audience, two performers also stood agape. It had reached an end and I wanted to see the attention diverted from him, given his focus that took us to this point. He crawled back and some shadow play followed with the use of torchlight shone on him by a performer. There followed a lull in which my energy wanted to bounce off walls, driven mad at how performers could be paralysed by one of their own and fail to take ownership of the space. Everybody, audience and performers hovered not knowing where or whether it would go.

Anthony Howell's analogy of homeostasis is relevant.[6] The energy of the room collapsed at a point because the balance was not maintained. Two states of homeostasis:

'the maintenance of metabolic equilibrium within an animism by a tendency to compensate for disrupting changes'

or a

'universal tendency in all living matter to maintain constancy in the face of internal and external pressures'.

Was the lull described above a collapse of homeostasis? Or perhaps I should accept it as distinguishing the collective's working method from theatre. No devices are used to redirect the performance. It finds its own way as naturally and undramatically as time itself.

My own response was to move about the room, to be active within the lull. In these points of inactivity shared by audience and performers the situation became more like a happening, to use a well-worn term. Perhaps more precisely a non-Happening, as in that space I felt I could act and do what the situation called for; audience interaction of a real kind wherein I had complete agency in my action, starting with the very choice to act. Can the group strategise so as to inculcate such moments?

2.34 am. After the wonderful solo where from here?

Retire. Crockery., broken mirror.......

God, it's so quiet. Marie Celeste

At 4am I wonder can they sustain. What drives it?

Is this the way of night-time?

At 3am what would anyone perform in sobriety whilst maintaining this relationship of audience to performers?

We are all seen and seldom quiet at such times so here we stand in a sort of waking dream where nobody will pretend it is day. Because the pretence would not last long and that would be acting.

Exit, with feathers in her mouth.

Still.

'It's kinda like Newgrange'.

That thought came to me at one point, so manifest. I can hardly explain why, bar reminding you, dear reader, of the circumstances; early morning in an unlit space with familiars and strangers sharing a wordless environment. It emptied my mind of so much else that sensitivity to the distant past surfaced. At the window Pauline draws her fingers through the condensation. Its squeaking sound pervades the night.

***

> 'Debris of feathers, pooled ink, charcoal, paper, fag ends, rawl plugs, dairy milk wrapper, pen, lollipop stick, screw and plasters littered the floor.'

Each day 'He' gets up and advises himself to do less than the day before. At the end of each day the audience are ushered out and the doors closed upon the space. We have taken to giving a round of applause from outside the closed door, a bit like support for trapped miners remote from public life. As they unwind from their four hours each runs through the things they did. He is amazed by the contents of their stories, how full and diverse they are while he might have spent an age rubbing his head against a wall or persisting in some similar activity that would threaten to yield less than sustenance would require.

He is not alone. On their long night Alex had sat at the window. Prior to the moment when he captivated the audience with the red-lit balloon mouth crawl on all fours, he had done little. This occurred at around 2am. Precision is elusive at such hours of the night. Up to that point he sat mostly by the window shutters looking as much like an audience member as many who came curious to see a performance from dusk until dawn.

Anything at such an hour has unique quality. The choice by the collective to extend their grueling daily four-hour schedule to include a seven-hour night session is evidence of their desire to truly test their limits. The day following this session began in a perfectly natural way; clean-up. Unlike previous days, when all trace was removed, there was no clean up at 6am. The audience walked into the space later that afternoon to see performers cleaning the room in silence. Debris of feathers, pooled ink, charcoal, paper, fag ends, rawl plugs, dairy milk wrapper, pen, lollipop stick, screws, and plasters littered the floor. Cleaning actions began to yield unusual behaviours beyond the standard methods of the job.

Alex places rubbish behind the door, then places himself behind the door and closes it over on himself. Fran clears floor with a fork and spoon. An upturned plinth is a container for feathers. She makes the most surreal device in counterpoint to Pauline hoovering; Fran blows feathers out of a shoe with a cardboard tube. Her resolve is intense. Inhalation and exhalation has a persistent rhythm that ultimately leads her to tears. When I return to watch her, she is knelt on the floor, crying. 'Where do you go?' I wonder at her ability to sound her emotion. She later explains that blowing the feathers led to this. It is a rare witnessing of private emotion. The performance space allows for this but that capacity first exists in the person. After the crying she laughs. Dominic exchanges a look and smile with her for the laughter which doesn't stop.

Progressive
movement
through
images.
Each
instigator
of the
next

Efficiency is achieved in a task at the exclusion of mental/physical faculties not directly related to the task. Holistic activity will engage the whole being and time may be longer but richer.

I wrote that thought while watching Michelle clean the ink from the floor. She used her clothing while crawling on the floor, her arms and torso extending in wide arcs, mopping and scrubbing. The complete immersion in the potential of the action, allowing the body to stretch itself while at work is perhaps what allowed her to persist; an extension that in retraction feeds its motion. Somebody later remarked that it was like a dance. But I wrote at one point 'cleaning machine', a contradiction to my holistic notion. Within these four hours everything else passed around her, interactions occurred at moments while with this repetitive action the floor was finally polished.

The work occurs entirely in the moment and does not attempt to represent anything. Little is forced or demanded by any performer of another. So the reasons for everything occurring are of an evolutionary character and constitute their own narrative. At its most intense the audience witnesses events crafted entirely in real time from moments that will never repeat. While it can seem internal or self-absorbed such a reading is probably more related to a viewer seeking instant gratification. A performer can rapidly move psychically from inside to outside should it be required.[7] Frances displayed this capacity during the night-time. A fight was developing outside on the street and on seeing its escalation from the window she emitted a huge scream, like a siren. The fighters moved on. Who knows to what end but the sensitivity to her environment, our environment, prompted this urgent reaction. It did not break performance state and makes me wonder what performance state, as opposed to any other, is?

Throughout their time the street was never remote from the performers' minds. The windows issued forth various arrangements of objects – a falling lemon, chain of shirts, free turf, a guillotined head. The window, an organ of communication, was crucial in facilitating engagement with the public. And so those who fought violently on a Saturday night registered quickly on Frances's sensory radar.

The action and all I saw was characterised by real time. It was rare that somebody did something to move toward some intention, at least overtly. There was little haste. In this state there was little instant reaction bar the urgency of the siren. Consequences evolved. Faces did not punctuate time with expression. Time made its impression as the performers made theirs. The time accumulated in their bodies and informed each following day.

The collective used no clocks to check time passed or remaining. I had that liberty of knowing the passing of time. My notes register time checks and consider the rise and fall of energy. Had I chosen equally not to observe time my writing might be different.

It is now over. If you'd like to leave now we'll be shutting the doors.

1. Programmed as part of The Galway Arts Festival 2012. Maeve Mulrennan, visual art curator, made the bold step of dedicating two weeks of the gallery's programme to Performance Art.

2. Anthony Howell, *The Analysis of Performance Art: A Guide To Its Theory And Practice* (Amsterdam: Harwood Academic Publishers 1999). I am using the psychiatric term, 'transference' as Howell does in his analysis of performance art.

3. The Performance Collective is a group of five leading artists in Irish performance art. The group initially was set up in 2007 by Michelle Browne, Alex Conway, Pauline Cummins, Frances Mezzetti, Dominic Thorpe, and Amanda Coogan to support each others work through peer critique and workshops. We have since made work with numerous contexts and worked alongside many performance artists, including members of Belfast based Bbeyond. See *The Performance Collective*, artists website <http://www.theperformancecollective.com/>.

4. Black Market International (BMI) was founded in 1985. Boris Nieslony, Jurgen Fritz, Norbert Klassen, Jacques Van Poppel, Zygmunt Piotrowski, Nigel Rolfe, and Thomas Ruller were working with BMI in the early years. For over 25 years the group has presented its unique, durational performances throughout the world […]. BMI has always avoided the definition of an organised group. Its main aim is to promote, just like in a 'black market' the free exchange of ideas, emotions, and energies, and to achieve through the principle of contamination, the ideal of Art of Begegnung (the Art of Encounter).

See *Black Market International*, artists website <http://www.myriamlaplante.net/_/bmi/bmi.html>.

Taken from Black Market International's website: 'The Art of Encounter is the expression of an active awareness of the effects of human acts in the context of an unavoidable relational nature in the world. Aware of this, performance artists find a laboratory of encounter, creativity, observation and reflection in human interlinks'. 'The Art of Encounter', *Black Market International* <http://theartofencounter.tumblr.com/> [accessed 2 December 2014].

5. One regular visitor, Nicola Williams, whom I interviewed, found herself projecting her reality into the actions of the performers, 'so that they were all representing me'. When this became emotionally overpowering she would look at Pauline Cummins, the one performer through whom she could observe things with more distance.

6. Howell, *The Analysis of Performance Art,* pp. 135-48. Howell applies the psychoanalytical term 'transference' in a discussion of the use of objects.

7. Fergus Byrne in conversation with James King, he mentioned an exchange he had with a dancer while on a workshop with Alastair MacLennan. They discussed how all activities were performed without any warm-up. The work operated from inside to outside; working with what is already inside and drawing from this reservoir rather than the energy of a warm up. The skill seems to be in being able to bring the inner out at the required moment to maximum effectiveness.

OUT OF IRELAND:
Irish performance art internationally

Emigration has always been a valid, active choice for Irish artists. The geographical boundaries of the island have tempted us to breach them; the scale of the island has given us realisation of wider possibilities, opportunities, and audiences elsewhere. This is especially true of experimental and radical artistic practices in Ireland. During the twentieth century, a conservative and traditionally focused culture compelled many avant-garde artists to leave this country along with tides of economic migrants. The 1980s in Ireland was a period of severe economic recession and, coupled with the violent civil and military conflict in Northern Ireland, large numbers emigrated to the United Kingdom, Europe, the United States of America, and other places.

Opposite: Alastair MacLennan and Manuel Vason,
Collaboration #3, Belfast, 2006.

Alongside the economic or cultural imperatives to leave the island, artists were increasingly aware, since the 1960s, of the vibrant international performance art scene thriving on internationalism and mobility as live artists must exist, interact and be present in the context of the showing of their work. Festivals and group exhibitions or events are also most appropriate to the presentation of performance art due to the enrichment of works when shown simultaneously, in sequence or in proximity. In these contexts works can communicate in simultaneity, feeding off and interpenetrating conceptually, formally, and in practical ways. For audiences, the experience of viewing diverse performances concurrently is dynamic and engaging. This is true especially of durational work as the experience of viewing very long extended performances side-by-side often becomes resonant with interesting coincidence and strange juxtapositions.

Since the first art performances of Dada in the early 1920s, based in Zurich but magnetising artists from all over Europe, performance artists have drawn together from around the world and dispersed again to disseminate and spread ideas, processes and networks. The small scale of local performance communities has made this expansion important and necessary for artistic cross-fertilization and creative exchange to take place. Due to our remote location and size, Irish performance artists in particular have relied on complex international networks to support practice by building world wide communities in the 1980s and 1990s. Before the internet, modes of communication such as phone calls, postal correspondences, and a trusting expectation that artists would turn up to festivals, exhibitions, and events typified the lives of performance curators, programmers, and organisers. The development of the World Wide Web enabled these communities to expand along with the arrival of low cost airline travel in the 1990s.

Due to our proximity to the UK and our shared history, most international exchange has taken place between these two islands. One of the largest and longest running festivals of performance and Live Art was the National Review of Live Art in the UK, based in Glasgow and directed by Nikki Millican from the late 1970s to 2010. The Live Art Development Agency in London, directed by Lois Keidan, has also been a major supporter and advocate for Irish performance. As an artists agency it provides resources and assistance for UK and Irish artists in all areas of creative and professional development as well as curating projects and publishing internationally to promote and disseminate artists work. The agency has been key in the evolution of dozens of Irish performance artists in the last ten years, myself included.

'There is a sense that Irish artists abroad engage with systems of belief - commenting on and critiquing, often satirizing the indelible belief systems of their Irish culture with the distance of exile.'

In this chapter I introduce a number of Irish artists who have developed their performance careers abroad. All of them have returned to Ireland to present work over the years, as a result generating vigorous cultural exchanges internationally. These artists have contributed their Irish artistic sensibilities to global cultural production, acting as emissaries to communicate and express ideas about Irish cultural identity and experience through their live practices. They have also brought international influences and references, trends and innovations back to Ireland, enriching the culture of live work here. The artists I write about are Brian O'Doherty/Patrick Ireland and Gearoid Dolan aka screaMachine both based in New York, John Carson who lives in Pittsburg, Anne Tallentire, Denis Buckley, and Kira O'Reilly who all live in London. Also in England are Frances Hegarty and Maurice O'Connell, while André Stitt is based in Wales. Other significant Irish artists living in London who are not covered in this chapter but whose work is presented elsewhere in this book are Helena Walsh and Áine O'Dwyer.

BRIAN O'DOHERTY

The first public performance in Ireland at the Project Arts Centre in Dublin was by the New York-based Irish visual artist Brian O'Doherty in 1972. According to Brenda Moore-McCann, author of the monograph *Brian O'Docherty/Parick Ireland: Between Categories* (2009), *Name Change* was 'arguably the most important gesture within the artist's oeuvre. *Name Change* was also the earliest performance art in Ireland.'[1] In this work O'Doherty assumed the alter ego Patrick Ireland, an artistic alias adopted in protest against the Bloody Sunday massacre in Derry in 1972. This persona defined a unified Irish national identity that was invented to highlight the politically divided condition of the island. The action was intended as a protest at the British military presence in Northern Ireland and the failure of the authorities to ensure civil rights for all. This second self prevailed until an official burial of Patrick Ireland's effigy in 2008 in the grounds of the Irish Museum of Modern Art in Dublin. Amid short speeches and a keening vocal performance by artist Alanna O'Kelly, the formal cessation of Patrick Ireland as an entity recognised the progress towards peace in the country. Brian O'Doherty resumed his existence with the words 'we are burying hate'.[2]

A serial identity swapper, O'Doherty assumed other personae throughout his career but his role-play as Patrick Ireland captured the imagination of audiences in Ireland and internationally. To embody a divided nation was a provocative act not without humour, particularly as O'Doherty/Ireland maintained the alter ego for decades. Brenda Moore McCann believes the essence of his work lies in 'a transformation of thinking, looking beyond material objects to underlying systems of belief.'[3] There is a sense that Irish artists abroad engage with systems of belief – commenting on and critiquing, often satirizing the indelible belief systems of their Irish culture with the distance of exile.

ANDRÉ STITT

The conflicted political situation in Ireland, particularly in the 1980's, provoked artists both to leave and to reflect on their experience after leaving. The objectivity of expatriation enabled clarity of perspective and a focus of description, representation, and enactment. André Stitt left Northern Ireland for London in 1980 at the height of the Troubles, travelling and making work internationally until 1999 when he moved to Cardiff to work at Cardiff School of Art and Design (Cardiff Metropolitan University). Responding to the traumatic experiences of growing up in a place saturated by hostility and warfare, he created provocative and politically challenging work. A predominant theme in his performance is that of communities and their dissolution often relating to trauma, conflict and art as a redemptive proposition. In his chapter earlier in this book, 'Performing Political Acts: Performance Art in Northern Ireland: Ritual, Catharsis, and Transformation', he describes how he developed 'akshuns' that were rituals to heal the psychological wounds of a war-torn city (the Belfast of his childhood) and explored ritual as a means of empowerment and for reclaiming or transforming identity.

As a young artist in London, Stitt could gaze back at Belfast and begin to understand how the rituals of both divided communities were played out in public presentations and declarations of identity. He was then able to invent his own developed rituals or akshuns that posited new forms of identity enactment, redressing the social structures and creating transformational performances that provided examples of liberating ways

> **'The separation between art and life was dissolved in Stitt's espousal of the communal 'squatting' culture in London and the realisation of urgent political problems (similar to those in Belfast) that exist all over the world.'**

of being. His works, being activist and inserted within the flow of life, provided cathartic release. He assigned to his live artwork the aesthetic of punk and ideologies of anarchism. In the words of Terry Hooley, a prominent figure in the Belfast punk scene of the late 1970s, 'New York has the hair cuts, London has the trousers but Belfast has the reason.'[4]

Many Irish performance artists, like Stitt, emigrated to London and other UK cities during the 1980s; infiltrating the performance scene there with these deep seated motives for activist art and transformative performance. I believe the power and prominence of Live Art in the UK in the last decades was seeded and nourished by the impact of Irish artists who were both escaping from and creatively enflamed by the problematics of the society they left. Irish artists had the 'reason' to engage in an integrated life/art paradigm and to use intense and embattled life experiences to speak of freedom, transformation, trauma, and healing and to insert art into life to try to change it. These certainties gave authority and conviction to their performance work and the works functioned as forms of social indictment and catharsis.

When Stitt arrived in London in the 1980s he began doing covert guerrilla actions 'developed through [his] experience of the construction of Belfast during the Troubles [...] and performed art that could encapsulate political and cultural issues in an everyday situation.'[5] Through making experimental art in Belfast he learned discipline of observation and interrogation that was now applied to his new living environment of London. This discipline was honed into the creation of performance art during those years as a device for drawing attention to issues of repression, marginalisation, disenfranchisement, power, and control. The separation between art and life was dissolved in Stitt's espousal of the communal 'squatting' culture in London and the realisation of urgent political problems (similar to those in Belfast) that exist all over the world. Stitt acknowledges that his life strategies and 'methods [he] employed in a warzone like Northern Ireland became a tactical expression of art making.'[6]

Top: Gearoid Dolan aka ScreaMachine and Áine Phillips, *Madonna*, National College of Art and Design, Dublin,1985.

Top right: Maurice O'Connell, *Sign of the Times*.

Bottom right: Gearoid Dolan aka ScreaMachine, *Separate* (Detail), Tulca Live, 2005.

Photos courtesy of the artists.

Top: André Stitt, *Conviction*, 2000.

Top left: André Stitt, *Scars*, Belfast, 1979.

Above: *Have U Met Nosti* (poster),
International Performance Festival, Dublin,
curated by Sascha Perfect, 2007.

Photos courtesy of the artists.

In 1984 Stitt created a performance for the Young Tory Party in London which began with him riding a mechanical Rodeo horse dressed as Ronald Regan (the then President of the US). 'Regan' then proceeded to enact sex with a blow-up doll representing the British Prime Minister, Margaret Thatcher. Stitt remembers the audience of young Tory politicians as debauched and degenerate:

> very 1980s, very end of empire, champagne and puking up everywhere with young Tory 'dolly' birds with skirts up their arses being fucked against walls in the back of the room ... they all seemed to enjoy the performance egging me on to stick more mayo, ketchup, and hot dog sausages up Thatcher's arse.[7]

Stitt held up a mirror to the Tory audience and in his own words 'Art is not a mirror, it's a fucking hammer'[8] he offered his spectators a satire of their own contaminated values and lives. During the 1980s he produced much work for London galleries and alternative spaces and toured the USA.

From the 1990's to the present Stitt has travelled throughout Eastern Europe, China, Australia, and South America with performances exploring the abuse of human rights, the human condition, the search for understanding, love, and compassion.

In his recent work engaging with Northern Ireland through performance, *Triple AAA* in 2013,[9] Stitt bears witness to his history and that of the divided island of Ireland. The fact of declaring a final work (before his active career comes to a natural end) shows a definitive resolution of personal and public conflict, and perhaps a provisional sign that a catharsis has been performed through his work on this subject.

JOHN CARSON

John Carson left Belfast to study for an MFA in California Institute of the Arts, in 1981, and returned to the UK for 23 years before moving to Pittsburgh as Head of the School of Art, Carnegie Mellon University in 2006. A colleague of Stitt's, Carson created an emotionally intense, often humorous series of performances responding to his fractured experience of Irish identity. His singularity is 'an imagination played out in the enormous shadow of memory' as described by Mic Moroney in *0044 Irish Artists in Britain*.[10] Carson's early work examined Irish identity, as Andre Stitt outlines in his chapter earlier in this book. At CalArts Carson examined the influence of the USA on the Irish psyche

'Ask yourself why are you doing a live performance. Remember that there is an audience. Do you really need an audience - what's in it for them? Don't be nervous, it can only go wrong.'

in his work *American Medley* where he travelled to 50 iconic American locations made famous in song, sending postcards back home as documentation. He subsequently turned this process-based project into a staged performance where he sang his way across the States in 11 minutes. In 1983 he presented *American Medley* at the Institute of Contemporary Arts in London where his Belfast art colleague and fellow artist Declan McGonagle was then director. Much of Carson's performance based work uses singing where he pits his amateur voice, untrained but expressive and passionate, alongside trained musicians; using interpretations of well known pop and rock and folk songs as propellers to examine cultural preconceptions about the Irishman abroad.

In *Off Pat* made in 1985-87, Carson merged his disconnected collections of stories and images into a live performance using a newscaster format. He juxtaposed sometimes grim and tragic stories with ridiculous images, which were projected in slide format behind his formally seated presence. He explains:

> the images and stories contradict each other, overturning expectations and cultural prejudices. For example I tell one story where the Irishman seems to be the butt of the joke then flip it so the Englishman is the fall guy.[11]

This performance toured the UK, USA, and Australia.

In the 1990s he found that his storytelling performances lent themselves to video and his work was commissioned by the Arts Council of England and BBC 2 for television, consequently reaching wide audiences. He continues to acknowledge the influence of CalArts as being crucial to his development as an artist by opening up his world into a wide network of artists and venues and by providing rigorous critical context. At CalArts he 'was challenged to retain a sense of proportion, but Belfast was always [his] reality gauge.'[12] His formative years in Belfast located his practice firmly in issues of identity, while working and living abroad secured that rooted interest and broadened it into the examination of cultural complexity, cultural mix, and displacement.

John Carson's Performance Art Tips

Ask yourself why are you doing a live performance.

Remember that there is an audience.

Do you really need an audience – what's in it for them?

Don't be nervous, it can only go wrong.

Don't worry if you make a mistake, you are the only one who knows the script.

Don't be afraid of silence, use it.

You have the floor.

Understand the special contract between you and the audience.

Know whether you are after truth or effect.

Use any device to achieve the effect you want.

Don't disregard the lessons and techniques of theatre.

Recognize the place of laughter.

Be prepared but be prepared to improvise.

If you want to be sure it's going to work and happen on time, try it out beforehand.

Allow for the unpredictable.

People do not always do what you want or what you expect.

If you are going to be cruel, make sure it's on purpose.[13]

FRANCES HEGARTY

Frances Hegarty moved from Donegal to Britain as a teenager, studying fine art at Leeds Polytechnic during the late 1960s. Influenced by a prevailing anti-modernist philosophy she made a number of live performances as an undergraduate. Documentation of this early work is not available, but by the 1970s she began to record her live work using video and photography, regularly exhibiting the documentation as artworks in their own right. She has latterly made performance only to camera; concentrating on the mediated image of the self, using autobiographical experiences to speak of emigration and cultural dislocation.

'Hegarty has explored the realities of emigration via the limits of language and the chasm between two languages. She enacts the tensions between looking back at a rich cultural heritage without nostalgia and anxieties about the future.'

Growing up speaking Gaelic before living in both Britain and Ireland entailed a degree of cultural displacement. Subsequently, Hegarty has explored the realities of emigration via the limits of language and the chasm between two languages. She enacts the tensions between looking back at a rich cultural heritage without nostalgia and anxieties about the future.

Hegarty's work interrogates the tradition of the self-portrait in art through performance, film, and video. This work invokes the self-viewing self, the self viewed by others, and the self as mediated via the lens and various imaging and recording apparatus. An early performance *Ablative, Genitive, Dative* (1984) presented in the Art and Research Exchange, Belfast, addressed the construction of self images using the camera. As part of her performance Hegarty photographed the photographer documenting the work as well as the audience; confronting passivity and triggering the performativity of the viewer.

In the 1980s Hegarty was influenced by the women's movement and the politics of the Greenham Common Women's Peace Camp.[14] *Groundswell* (1987), presented in London's Chisenhale Gallery, consisted of a huge mound of soil and pigment surrounded by a ring of 20 television sets on which a pair of hands clench and strike at the screen. A live performance lasting an hour involved Hegarty walking around the mound, responding to the images on the screens and their associated sounds. *Groundswell* was a discursive response to the ideologies of the Peace Camp, in which the experience of the individual is imbricated with the directives of politics and popular culture as asserted through the news media.

In Hegarty's work, notions of cultural partition are paralleled with gendered and political divisions. Feminist theory has animated much of the work, especially where it is concerned with female self-projection along with the manifestation and demonstration of subjectivity. Feminists such as Shoshana Felman discuss the impossibility of writing female autobiography within patriarchal culture.[15] In response to such challenges, Hegarty has found ways of generating autobiography using performance and new media. In *Auto Portrait #2* (2000) she performs directly to camera, breathlessly speaking summarised narratives of her lived experience. Although edited, this work began as a video-recorded performance, acknowledging the presence of an audience for the mediated self.

Since 1997 Hegarty has also worked collaboratively with British artist Andrew Stones. In their video work *Orienteer (A to Z, Dawn to Dusk)* (2000) a lone runner (Hegarty) seems to cross the city of Birmingham from east to west along a series of streets arranged in alphabetical order, starting on Alexandria just before dawn, ending on Zion in darkness. The epic traverse is contrived in post-production from 25 separate runs undertaken by Hegarty along each of the streets shown. Beginning in miniature, almost invisible in a dark suburban street, the female figure becomes the agent of a time-compressed gazette of a modern British city, with its various zones: suburb, city centre, post-industrial wasteland, etc.

Monica Ross writes of this work:

> The default of the physical is again compensated for by the digital special effect. The orienteer becomes a technologised figure, marked out only by the flashing stripes of her synthetic suit. As the runner reaches her destination she closes on the camera's viewpoint, only to disappear from it. We hear the animal sound of her pressurized breathing, a gasping for breath. Sound again recuperates the physical reality of a body under stress which is beyond the frame.[16]

Hegarty's work, even when mediated by the camera remains connected to physical experience and real bodily engagement with place.

She now travels back and forth regularly to Donegal and feels closer to Ireland, working here more often and enjoying a stronger support structure with other Irish artists. 'I have let go of cultural alienation', she now affirms.[17]

Opposite: Frances Hegarty and Andrew Stones, *Orienteer (A to Z, Dawn to Dusk)*, 2000. Video stills courtesy of the artists.

ANNE TALLENTIRE

Anne Tallentire arrived in London in 1983 to pursue a post-graduate degree in Fine Art Media at the Slade School of Art. Her work employs a wide range of media and her live work is more frequently performed to camera and is incorporated with other media into installation. Performance is central to her thinking and approach to making art, in what might be considered an expanded mode of production that relates to constituencies of time and place.

In London her work evolved to engage issues concerning the politics of location and identity. The first performance she made in the UK, *Forbidden Heroines,* was in collaboration with Alanna O'Kelly at the *Live London Filmmaker's Co-op (Channel 6)* curated by Tina Keane in 1987.

Another work *Altered Tracks*, was made for *Off The Map,* presented at Chisenhale Gallery London in 1989; an exhibition that included work by six Irish women including performances by Alanna O Kelly and Frances Hegarty.[18] The performance *Altered Tracks* consisted of lines drawn in charcoal on the concrete floor representing the lines on Tallentire's hand. A recorded voice read palmistry interpretations of these lines, one voice in an English intonation and one Irish accented. A series of photographs functioned as a back-drop installation, these images depicting stones on a map of her homeland in Armagh. The performance involved the artist walking barefoot and placing stones along the lines as she listened to the readings. She created a poetic and geo-political space resonant with the experience of diasporas. Typical of Tallentire's working methods, the performance residue remains as an installation in the gallery for the duration of the exhibition.

The Gap of Two Birds was presented at the Showroom London in 1989 and *Live at The Project*, Dublin in 1990. This performance and installation comprised of a Super 8 film transferred to video, looped and screened on a monitor and four glass panels inscribed with the words 'north' and 'south' from which rubbings in charcoal were made onto sheets of white paper. These documents were then offered to members of the audience who were invited to discuss the reasons for their selection in an interactive, dialogic exchange between the artist/participants. This audience intervention was considered part of the performance element of the work and the piece continued for five hours.

In the mid-nineties, Tallentire returned to Ireland to create *Inscribe I,* presented between London and Derry, and *Inscribe II*, both presented

'[...] their works embrace a minimal aesthetic to speak about marginality and 'a dismantling, re-figuring and re-ordering of materials and systems, primarily in relation to conditions of social and political life.'

between London and Dublin.[19] These works involved the use of new communication technologies to stream live footage performed to camera between the cities. Addressing issues of bodily presence and absence, *Inscribe I* and *II* emphasised the process based performance Tallentire pioneered where the experiences of the artist, audience, and the self in relation to site or location of action is problematised. *Inscribe I* was co-located at the Walls of Derry and London Wall Buildings in the City, with Tallentire present at one of these walls, methodically scrubbing an area of stone. The viewer watches a pre-recorded video image of her scrubbing cloth in hand making a palimpsest, a space to inscribe. But lines and marks under and from the surface appear inexplicably as the hand wipes. These vestigal marks suggest an ambivalence of language and communication that belie the sophistication of the digital exchange via ISDN technology at the time. *Inscribe I* and *II* also involved conversations transmitted between audiences simultaneously in Dublin, London, and Derry. The live actions were mundane: emptying and lining up a box of old pen nibs, reading a passage from a book on managing institutions and improvising actions on the street and in the studio.

Since 1993 Tallentire has worked collaboratively with artist John Seth, who she met at The Slade. Their collaborative practice was formed under the name 'work-seth/tallentire' in 1997. Producing various performative installations actively over a ten-year period, work-seth/tallentire deconstructs myths and expectations of the experience of viewing art and the process of creating the artwork. Both artists share interests in post-colonial histories and are concerned with political and historical issues of lived experience. Keen to avoid over-determinism however, their works embrace a minimal aesthetic to speak about marginality and 'a dismantling, re-figuring and re-ordering of materials and systems, primarily in relation to conditions of social and political life.'[20] Their work regularly involved simple repetitive actions over long durations as part of gallery installations and exhibitions. In *Trailer* 1998 made in Dublin for Project Arts Center's *Off Site*, they adhered for ten days to a strict schedule of everyday actions, working with found objects or locations and documenting their chosen object or site on video. The video screening would subsequently happen at random locations which changed daily, the audience informed by telephone shortly in advance of the event. The work thus traversed the city and incorporated the experience of the city into its frame.

In 1998, Tallentire was the sole representative for Ireland at the Venice Biennale and showed *Instances*, a three-part work including a 53 minute video performance. In this work she performs a series of actions to John Seth's camera which focus on the gestures and manipulations of her hands and body in relation to objects such as a diminutive table, a pair of dainty kid gloves, and the unsealing of ancient floorboards to reveal buried articles as a series of improvised moments. Irish artist Jaki Irvine writes in *Instances* catalogue that Tallentire is 'deliberately bringing to the surface, by way of a series of task-like gestures, the question of unseen work as unseen attention and unheard knowledge.'[21] These ideas of the unseen are reflected in the absent or oblique performance strategies often used by Tallentire in her practice. In the Slade School of Art in 1988 she performed a vigorous and durational act of cleaning in advance of the installation *Bound Words – Stolen Honey* that addressed the complex interpenetration of Irish with British law.[22] The performance was seen by those incidentally passing through the space. The trace of her meticulous action is visible in the subsequent installation. In other work her performance is viewed both to camera and people passing by during the recording. She explains 'I have in various ways exploited the idea of what could be termed 'absent performance' in works such as *Inscribe I* and *II, Trailer* and *Dispersal*.'[23]

Tallentire's use of performance regularly centered on interactive dialogues with the audience and the employment of common actions, work-a-day processes within installations that demythologized the artist's act of creation. Michel De Certeau's analysis of city living and the performativity of everyday life informs much of her live work.[24] As seen in *Drift 2002-2012* Anne Tallentire continues to respond in her work to performance as a subject, and writes 'I increasingly work with recordings of actions made by others to extend the parameters of performance beyond the actions of the self to that of others.'[25] Tallentire has produced a body of work that created new innovative models of performance that have become standard modes for much Live Art and contemporary art practice today.

DENIS BUCKLEY

In 1985 Denis Buckley left Limerick School of Art and Design (LSAD) for London and became involved with *The People Show*, an experimental performance art company based in the East End. He considers his art school education to have been apolitical but the new experience of living in a politically engaged community during the immediate aftermath of the UK miners strike and the closure of the Greater London Council[26] changed his views on the responsibility of the artist to society. His involvement with *The People Show* also awakened an interest in performance and direct connection with the general public as the audience for art. Since the 2000s Buckley has created solo performances for festivals and gallery events in the UK, Ireland, Australia, and the USA. His work has explored cultural identity, particularly from the viewpoint of the exiled. Since 2001 he has appeared only in the persona of 'The Irishman' to explore perceptions of Irish identity and better understand the unforeseen losses inherent in long-term emigration. *Searching For The Unimagined Conscience Of My Race,* a piece Buckley made in 2011, encapsulates in its title alone, the purpose and goal of much of his oeuvre.

Buckley writes:

> My nationality or identity was not to the fore in terms of my practice until I passed the marker of a longer time in England than I had spent growing up in Ireland. Conditions of displacement emerged then when I understood I had lost certain aspects that I wasn't even aware I had.[27]

His considers an 'Orientalism' was at play during his education at LSAD whereby Irish cultural heritage was diminished in a comparable way to the general patronizing attitude of Western towards Eastern, Asian, and African societies that Edward Said theorised.[28] According to Said these societies have been essentialised as static and underdeveloped, their heritage and contribution to world culture dismissed. When Denis Buckley arrived in London he realised the broader, heterogeneous context for his own specific cultural background in relationship to the multiplicity of cultures around him.

> Being among communities and artists from many differing cultures, collaborating with some and watching others striving to posit their own visual identity from among the ingredients of their background was formative in my determination to make my performance work figure in a European super culture but with the nuances of my (Irish) language rich past.[29]

Issues of language play an important role in his work and he often uses scripted live utterances and recorded voice and image in his performances.

A Rose for Jack Doyle is a moving image work made in 2004 which incorporates live performance, exploring displacement among Irishmen in London, a well documented group who have suffered both physical dislocation from their native culture and the colonizing imposition of the culture they then inhabit. For Irish men who emigrated to London from the 1950s onwards, their experience was often lonely and alienated with many suffering homelessness and addiction. The expressions and struggles of masculine identity in relation to cultural identity is addressed in Buckley's performance work. In *You I Love You*, 2002 (presented at the National Review of Live Art in the UK) the artist meditates on masculine self esteem and *Why Are Men Angry* in 2004 invited participation from men with a history of violence.

Buckley has returned regularly to Ireland to perform and exhibit work, most recently presenting a mid-career retrospective at Siamse Tíre, Tralee County Kerry titled *The Irishman: End Of Exile* in 2013. At this exhibition, Buckley signaled the end for the artist, of the persona 'The Irishman'. Another recent work presented at Dublin's Absolute Fringe Festival in 2011 was *What Are Poets For (In Destitute Times)* in which Buckley used live narration, video projection with visual imagery of a burning shovel in a verdant garden. Buckley sits squarely behind a commanding desk and delivers a monologue extrapolating on themes of poetic acts of creation, disillusionment with religion and society before concluding that words themselves hold power and confer meaning.

MAURICE O'CONNELL

On 4 October 1999, Maurice O'Connell packed a few bags, took the cat and flew to Cornwall where he continues to reside and make performance and experimental theatre in Britain and internationally. Originally from Dublin, he developed unique forms of interactive performance during his art education at National College of Art and Design (NCAD), Dublin, and subsequently focused on the structures and eccentricities of human behaviour, communication, and social exchange. He developed a practice centered on stand-alone, one-person performances using story telling, conversation, and exchange while characterising himself within various multiple identity constructs.

Opposite top: Anne Tallentire, *The Gap of Two Birds*, The Showroom London,1990. Photo: Yael Goldberg.
Opposite bottom: Denis Buckley, *Snake*. Photo: James Emmett.

'[...] the museum staff found the work challenging as everyone who worked at the museum were daily aware that his life depended on them, his welfare their duty, and that this situation was the expressed manifestation of the usually unspoken contract between artists and institution.'

In 1995, he created a one month long interactive performance at the Irish Museum of Modern Art in Dublin entitled *Role, Response, Research Unit 1*. In this work he handed himself over to the care and responsibility of the museum staff, 24 hours a day for 30 days. Inhabiting a sealed space containing a bed, bucket, and closed circuit television camera, his actions were visible to the remote audience in the foyer of the museum. Viewers could speak to him via the CCTV apparatus, but he could only communicate through gesture, written word, or actions. Though O'Connell was locked into this room, he held the key and could leave at night to empty the contents of his waste bucket. He also opened the door three times a day to museum staff who provided meals.

Through this work, O'Connell wanted to make explicit the fundamental nature of the relationship between the art institution, its curators, the artist, and his audience. In this three way relationship, the duty of care lies with the institution and its agents, acts of communication engage the artists and audience and the artist is dependent on both for reaction, response, creative, artistic, social, and economic survival. O'Connell found the experience uplifting, emerging after his 30 days tired but mentally refreshed and physically fit (from fitness exercises he practiced daily). He admits the museum staff found the work challenging as everyone who worked at the museum were daily aware that his life depended on them, his welfare their duty, and that this situation was the expressed manifestation of the usually unspoken contract between artists and institution. The audience responded energetically to the work: many people returned often to speak to the inmate, to read him books and sometimes to commune with him in silence in front of his camera. O'Connell explains 'I wanted the museum to witness the deep engagement of the audience and the revelation that they are up for a lot more than passive reception of an art work.' He energised the relationship between the museum and its audience while generating relationships of intimacy and depth between himself and his visitors.

Before O'Connell left Ireland, he realised that becoming international was necessary for the evolution of his practice. He speaks about internationalism and mobility as being key to success in the type of work he makes and admits that he often represents other countries as their envoy at global events.[30] He has returned to Ireland occasionally for projects, recently conducting a one-on-one performance with the Irish Taoiseach (Prime Minister) Enda Kenny, taking him on a four-hour mountain hike to talk about dialogue. Currently, O'Connell's work addresses the limits and potential of language and acts of communication dependent on context such as the particular communications that happen between security guards, health care workers or authority figures and their service users in controlled spaces. He wants to expose the subtle power relations at work in our everyday lives, the links and bonds that cause us to act or behave in prescribed ways, sometimes contrary to our natures. 'Empathy, sympathy, pathos and ethos' are his current themes.

For ten years he has worked with a theatre company November Club based in Northumberland creating promenade ensemble performances in public site specific spaces with communities and other artists. The company's productions often use historical events to create real time fictional incidents connected to the places and communities where the work is staged. The themes of their performances take cues from the historical and contemporary context of the site.

KIRA O'REILLY

'I feel so of Ireland and not of Ireland'[31]

Kira O'Reilly left Ireland permanently at the age of 19 for Britain. She had spent formative years living between London and the rural Listowel, County Kerry. Influenced by the post punk movement, bands such as The Virgin Prunes and writers William Burroughs and J.G. Ballard, she studied visual art at the University of Wales Institute Cardiff, graduating in 1998. Her work began with intense body based performances and developed in recent years into biotechnical practices and writing that considers speculative reconfigurations around The Body (the discursive body) and her own body, addressing a flickering between the two.

Travelling widely, performing and teaching throughout Europe, Australia, China, Mexico, and the USA, her work has been at the forefront of Live Art practices that use duration; pushing the limits of the body, opening or wounding the body and using blood as a primary material.

In her early work she considered her body as a site in which narratives of personal, sexual, social, and political threads could be woven into acts of communication and shifting permutations of meaning. She has written:

> action exceeds language. I make these works because words fail me – I can't put 'it' into words, I just have to do it, or be it. Representation fails me because I desire to make work about things that are, perhaps, unrepresentable. A trauma occurs as a wounding, a temporal/spatial relationship in which possibilities can be explored.[32]

In 2000 O'Reilly was invited to exhibit a video of her performance *Wet Cup* at the Infusion festival in Limerick. The live performance has been presented in London, Denmark, and Croatia. In this astonishing work O'Reilly's body is inscribed with small superficial cuts by her assistant Ernst Fischer who then applies 22 heated glass 'cups' onto her flesh causing a vacuum suction on the skin, pulling tiny rivulets of blood to the surface and filling the cups. The cups are carefully removed. The entire piece has a sacred ceremonial quality, unsettling and elegantly beautiful in its execution. The use of old medical blood letting techniques in her work (she also worked with leeches to draw blood in previous performances) invokes notions of trauma and stigma towards a 'spoiling' and opening of the body that suggests an alterity or otherness. These works question the exclusivity of medical discourse that has long dominated theorising of the body within Western society, especially the bodies of women.

In O'Reilly's performances a complicated intimacy is established alongside an exposure of the dynamics of looking, where the audience struggles to simultaneously confirm and deny what they are seeing or doing. In *Untitled Action for the Arches* in 2005, at the National Review of Live Art in the UK, she invited audience members to share deeply charged time and space with her intimately in a one-on-one encounter. She invited her audience to hold her naked body in their arms before choosing whether or not to cut her with a scalpel.

The performance revealed the complexity of power relations in intimate encounters, uncovered the vulnerability of one to another with resonances of trauma and abuse but playing with interchanges of power; the artist relinquishing it, the participant receiving it or visa versa depending on inclination or enthusiasm.

By asking the audience to take a risk with me a sense of intimacy is established, creating a direct and immediate dialogue. They become collaborators; complicit from the moment they make the decision to be there. Each performance feels like some kind of contract between myself and the audience, clearly negotiated by each party.[33]

In 2004 O'Reilly completed a residency and research fellowship at SymbioticA, art science collaborative research lab of the School of Anatomy and Human Biology, University of Western Australia, where she was concerned with exploring convergence between contemporary biotechnical tissue culturing and traditional lace making crafts, using skin at its cellular level as material and metaphor. In following work she explored cell cultures, pigs, chick embryos, spiders, webs, and other microbes as materials for various actions and performances.

For *Biopolitics, Society and Performance* Conference, Trinity College Dublin in 2012 she conducted a three-day performance work *Untitled (techné)* in the Pearse Centre where the republican and historical Ireland Institute is housed. O'Reilly used 12 fertile chicken eggs at early stages of incubation and development. Over the three days she engaged in a relationship of touch and scrutiny of the eggs, on day one wearing a red lab coat but transforming by day three into a glittery green clad showgirl. On the second day O'Reilly began dissection, exposing the beating precursor hearts and tapping out their rhythms on the hands and wrists of viewers who were invited singly to her vivisection table.

In Irish law the status of the human embryo is accorded the same right to life as the mother, and the embryos O'Reilly uses are similar in appearance to human ones. She explains: 'It is a quiet and soft work. Its materials are particular in their potentials as materials and signifiers and take on special relevancy in an Irish context, but spectacle is thwarted by its deferral, nothing is 'seen', everything is 'felt''[34] In an apt mirroring, often the complex cultural attitudes and political issues exposed by this performance are felt, not seen in Irish society. In my view, much of O'Reilly's work addresses issues that are simmering but urgent, especially in relation to women's histories and bodies. She confronts social taboos to expose their contradictions and through her work reveals cultural and political limitations on The Body, with an elegant and penetrating intent.

ANNE SEAGRAVE

> My work is often autobiographical (as is the work of Frida Kahlo). It sometimes relates to a social or political episode (as does the work of Ana Mendieta) and it may also explore issues of the inner psychological self (as does the work of Francesca Woodman). Occasionally I inhabit another identity (as does Cindy Sherman) or I may simply orchestrate or manipulate a scene (such as Eulalia Valldosera).[35]

One of Ireland's most celebrated performance artists living in Europe is Anne Seagrave. Originally born in Nottingham, England she moved to Ireland as a young artist in 1987. Although often in Barcelona from 2000, she was mostly based in Ireland until 2008 when she moved permanently to Krakow. Her work is movement-based with a strong visual emphasis and her performances are often accompanied by original video-installations and audio recordings. Developing her own distinctive style over the years, her work has evolved into a uniquely beautiful and unsettling innovative mode of performance. She has performed for more than 30 years mainly in Europe, the USA, Canada, and South America. In 1985 she was invited by the Richard Demarco Gallery in Edinburgh to go to Poland and present performances in five major Polish cities. In the audience for her Krakow performance was the artist and curator Wladyslaw Kazmierczak. This was the beginning of a fruitful creative relationship which brought Seagrave back to Poland many times during her career, most often creating site-specific performances for the BWA Galeria in Ustka.[36] In turn, she invited Kazmierczak to Dublin to present his work along with other Polish artists Ewa Rybska and Pawel Kwasniewski. During the period she resided in Ireland she was instrumental in organising many Live Art events, supporting the work of younger emerging performance artists and inviting international artists to perform here.

Anne Seagrave devised a site-specific exhibition for the Temple Bar Gallery in 1999 entitled *Falling Into People's Mouths*. It contained three video elements, two singing hand driers, and a singing drinking fountain. Every day she presented a one-hour performance interacting with the visual and sculptural elements of the installation and the architecture of the space. The video works were produced in collaboration with Fred Benoist, who she continued to work with on projects in 2002 and 2004.

Opposite top: Maurice O'Connell, *Olympian*. Photo courtesy of the artist.
Opposite bottom: John Carson, *Off Pat*, 1985-87. Photo courtesy of the artist.

'In my opinion a self portrait is not a piece by
the artist, but a piece of the artist [...] I believe
that art is not a product, it is a process.'
Anne Seagrave

From 1984 to 2010 she created many works for the National Review
of Live Art in the UK where she was recognised by the festival as an
Honorary Associate Artist. Director Nikki Millican acclaims Seagrave's
contribution to the festival: 'Ever since Anne Seagrave's memorable
Platform performance in 1984 her generosity of spirit was always present,
even if she was presenting her own work during a festival she made herself
available to support other artists.'[37] In 2007 she was nominated resident
artist and presented *Jamais Vu*,[38] a staged self portrait publicly erased by
the artist over five consecutive days. In this performance Seagrave was
naked, her slender muscular body covered in a dusty white paint, and she
constructed a repetitive series of actions and movements, sometimes wild
and frenzied as she spun with a fresh egg balanced in her eye socket, at
other intervals hypnotic and uncanny as she proceeded with a kitchen sink
faucet between her legs, a narrow rectangular mirror attached to her chest.
The performance took place within an installation of video projections
and objects which she used as props in the live performance. Her video
work uses images of her own body in movement and in relationship with
objects, often furniture such as chairs or tables or architectural structures.
These images sometimes distort or duplicate her body using a refined
monochrome aesthetic with sound compositions to create a haunting,
evocative deep space or space of infinity.

In 2008 she completed an Arts and Humanities Research Council
Fellowship at the University of Ulster in Belfast focusing upon the theme
of artistic use of self image in performance, Live Art, and within other
forms of visual art practice.[39] Through this work she aims to highlight
the complexity of an artist's use of self-portraiture, auto depiction, or
self-representation. She proposes that an artist's use of self-image is a form
of self-portraiture. By interrogating these issues, especially in her own
performances, Seagrave also suggests an alternative currency of ideas and
a re-evaluation of the art object. Her work can be understood within
the traditions of self-portraiture but she never clings to an illusion of a

perfect self. She explores herself as subject and subjected in opposition to the objectification preferred by commodity culture. Through her live presentations Seagrave aims to widen the public definition of art away from the production of objects for sale, and toward recognition dialogue.[40]

Seagrave retired from frequently touring performance in 2008 but is currently making and showing a small amount of multi media performances, video and painted self-portraits in galleries in Poland. She writes: 'In my opinion a self portrait is not a piece by the artist, but a piece of the artist [...] I believe that art is not a product, it is a process.'[41] It is this process based orientation emerging from Seagrave's development of movement performance and the creation of visual elements within it that allows her to state her work is now a piece of herself. In her work the distinction between self, image, object, and subject is fused.

GEAROID DOLAN AKA SCREAMACHINE

Gearoid Dolan attended the National College of Art and Design in Dublin during the early 1980s, performing publicly[42] while still a student. His body based performances, influenced by punk aesthetics incorporated film, analogue video, and audio technologies to create animated projections, slide shows, and sound art to accompany his live actions. He emigrated to New York City in 1987 and started branding his works with the name 'screaMachine'. Since then he has been performing in the underground performance scene in New York, dipping in and out of the established art world of galleries and institutions, doing street interventions and developing new media techniques. In 1989 Franklin Furnace featured his *Survival... Against All Odds* series. In 1990 at PS1 Contemporary Art Center Dolan presented a month long installation and performance series. Through the 1990s Dolan further developed and refined the A/V components to his work, moving into digital media and video projection. For ten years he presented new works in his storefront studio in Manhattan, in nightclubs and underground spaces and developed video works for web streaming in its infancy and was an early pioneer of the medium. In 1999 he presented his first *Drive-By* video performance at DUMBO Arts Festival, the start of a 13 year run presenting new works at this event.

Dolan acknowledges that one of the main reasons he moved to New York was to work in a wider political arena with a more global perspective. He writes:

Sascha Perfect, *Intimacy*, 2007. Photo courtesy of the artist.

Anne Seagrave, *Girl With the Falling Down Stockings*, in *Self-made* a Unit 1 event at Crawford Gallery, Cork, 2014. Photo: Ciara McKeon, courtesy of the artist.

I immediately got involved in more universal themes, reflected partly by 1980's US politics and by their global implications. I continued to address issues that were more Irish in nature, but this became more generalized over time. Working in this multicultural world gives one a wider perspective and a less culturally esoteric iconography. Often in this situation, artists tend to 'stick to their own', making work about their specific ethnicity or culture, like Irish artists doing Irish related works only. I found the opposite for myself: I enjoyed being less ethnocentric, being concerned with the bigger picture and not being cubby-holed into an Irish identity.[43]

Political content pervades Dolan's work and his themes range from issues of masculine identity to global capitalism and colonization. His live performances are characterised by a sense of emphatic aggressiveness delivered with emotional tenderness within a complex technological structure. His use of projected imagery and soundscape enhances and elaborates the action he presents, adding a dense profusion of data, noise, and images. Immersive performative installation is a preferred format for Dolan. At DUMBO Arts Festival in 2008, he created *Torture*. It featured the naked performer, covered head to toe in small photo stickers depicting images of torture from Abu Ghraib Prison. He was spread eagled against a corrugated iron fence, as though ready to be body searched. A huge animated undulating modified US flag was projected onto the performer and fence, dominating the street. In front of his body another animated video played. In this video, surgical tongs grab the Abu Ghraib images and drag them around in coordinated sequences, dancing on the sidewalk. Next to this is a table with real surgical tools sitting on stainless steel trays. Audience members and passers-by were encouraged to take a tool of their choice and step into the active area and use it to remove a single sticker from Dolan's flesh and return both to a waiting steel tray. Accompanying this was an audio track featuring sampled audio clips of the then US president George W. Bush making statements denying torture practices. The piece created a tension between the actions of audience and performer as participants interacted directly with the performer's skin, pulling on it with menacing tools, all the while taking symbolic responsibility for the actions of their country. The performance ended when the body was picked clean some hours later, the audience slowly engaging with this ominous scene in the cold light rain.

Dolan returns to Ireland to perform regularly (2005 Tulca Galway, Darklight Festival Dublin among others) but remains a resident of NYC where he has received awards and support to enable him to continue his work. He writes 'being Irish is what gave me my perspective, my values and these are clearly evident in my work' while not addressing his Irishness explicitly, his work engages more universal issues 'I feel I have more important things to discuss, more pressing, more fundamental issues.'[44]

INTERNATIONAL EVENTS AND FESTIVALS

As global mobility increased, especially during the 1990s and subsequently, Irish performance artists continued presenting live work all over the world and inviting international artists and curators back to Ireland. World styles, aesthetics, and subject matter have naturally infected the work of Irish artists, often putting world politics, environmentalism, and global activism at the center of contemporary practice.

Irish performance artists based in Ireland have greatly benefited from the support of international events and festivals, galleries and museums since the 1980s. One of the most prominent Live Art and performance art festivals in Europe, running for over 30 years (1979-2010) and directed by Nikki Millican was the National Review of Live Art in the UK (NRLA), based for most of its life in Glasgow at the Arches and Tramway venues. This festival platformed and commissioned many Irish artists, myself included, during its history and functioned as a valuable stepping stone for artists to present their work further afield in Europe, Asia, and America. The scale of the NRLA was such that curators, programmers, and festival directors came from across the world to view new work and select artists for their events. For three years, from 2007 to 2009 I functioned as Irish selector for platform artists (emerging performance practitioners) and before me, Lois Keidan and NRLA director Nikki Millican implemented a policy to disregard the political border and include southern Irish artists as well as northern in this annual survey festival. The NRLA had affiliations (and formed a network called *A Space For Live Art*) with European festivals in Belgium, France, the UK, Slovenia, Finland, Germany, Poland, and Spain, and many Irish artists benefited from these links. The importance of these festivals for a generation of Irish artists cannot be underestimated. These events brought the attention of the performance art world to Irish artists and visa versa. In my own experience, the encounter with exciting and provocative new global work deeply influenced my practice and the opportunities afforded by my NRLA exposure provided a confidence, profile, and network for the creation and presentation of new work in my ensuing career. Often one of the features of living and working as an artist on this small island at Europe's edge is the local impact an international reputation can produce. 'If you can make it abroad, you can make it at home', an adage that resonates with many artists who have enjoyed international recognition in advance of local success.

Another significant performance festival that supported the early work of Irish performance artists was The Castle of Imagination in the north of Poland, directed by Wladyslaw Kazmierczak. In 1993 he inaugurated *Irish Days*, inviting Alastair MacLennan to bring a number of Irish performance artists to participate in an event at the Galeria BWA in Ustka. The purpose of the project (and subsequently *Irish Days II* in 1994) according to Alastair MacLennan was to facilitate the intermix of Irish artists from the north and south, to foster exchange and dialogue between international artists with the hope of further exchanges and collaborations, meetings and exhibitions in the future. Anne Tallentire, one of the invited artists in 1994 writes 'there is a commitment to experimental, predominately speculative, temporary, performative practices; residues, action, actuations, interventions.'[45] Anne Seagrave notes that:

> Poland has a long history of artist's run initiatives which is called here 'the pitch-in culture', where everyone pitches in, helps, organizes, participates and discusses, with the aim to present an alternative to established state supported or commercial art practices. The Irish artists too were invited to 'pitch in' and in my opinion we responded very well to this invitation and philosophy.[46]

Further festivals and events took place throughout the 1990's and 2000's in Poland as strong creative relationships developed between Irish and Polish artists and curators.

INTERNATIONAL ARTISTS IN IRELAND

International artists have also travelled to Ireland, to present work and curate festivals and events that helped influence and shape new directions in Irish performance practice. In 1972 the English artist Stuart Brisley came to Belfast to present *Chairs* in Anti-festival at Queens University and *Between the Wall and the Floor* in *Darkspace* at the Project Arts Centre in Dublin in 1979. His political and social engagement along with an abject, corporeal 'body in struggle' aesthetic influenced the earliest generation of performance artists in Ireland. Another prominent international artist to work here is Marina Abramović, who with her collaborator and partner

> 'Our complex social, political and cultural context and troubled history has deeply influenced the performance and Live Art produced here, or produced by our artists abroad.'

Ulay performed *Rest Energy* at ROSC 1980. In this piece a bow and arrow is held taut by the performers' body weight, Ulay holding the bow with an arrow pointed directly at Abramović. One slip or break in concentration between the two performers and the arrow could pierce Abramović's heart. She later returned for a retrospective exhibition at IMMA in 1995 and again in 2001 to curate the performance event *Marking the Territory* at the Museum of Modern Art in Dublin. Over a three-day period 23 artists from 16 countries performed at the museum, including Irish artist Amanda Coogan.[47] This event marked a significant turning point in that performance and Live Art practice was recognised as part of mainstream art practice by a major Irish art institution.

Since the mid 2000s there have been countless international opportunities for Irish performance artists as world networks become more permeable and receptive with instant flows of communication and a global culture of artists self-organising to lead their own professional and creative initiatives. Artists have become nomadic, often listing a number of locations where they are 'based' or 'based between'. Specific local cultural issues affecting artists become less important as the experience of being a world citizen prevails and we realise how implicated we are in larger global narratives. Our unique perspectives as located human beings still affect our contribution to this global story however, as each artist brings attention to what she or he recognises as being locally urgent and critical.

Looking at the biographies and oeuvres of Irish performance artists since the 1980s it is apparent how politicized the work coming from Ireland has been, and still continues to be. Our complex social, political, and cultural context and troubled history has deeply influenced the performance and Live Art produced here, or produced by our artists abroad. In Anthony Sheehan's article 'Survey Ireland: South of the Border 1984', published in *High Performance* magazine (reprinted in this book) he makes reference to the observation by American audiences that 'politics was read everywhere' in the work. Performances by both Northern and Southern Irish artists

over the last 40 years have acutely interrogated the political divisions and tragedies of war on this Island. Performances by feminist artists since the 1980s have exposed the power structures of patriarchy; dissecting its anatomy to reveal the blatant gender inequities, the strategies of sexual power and confinements of sexual identity we have suffered in Ireland. Our recent economic boom and subsequent collapse have produced a new generation of artists who are using live action and image to reflect this society back to itself and the world. We have had the reason and the motivation to be political in our art, to make activist Live Art and the legacy of our work confirms this.

We live in exciting times where artists influence each other across the world and across their individual life-worlds; absorbing each other's techniques and approach, adding to them and inventing new way to exchange ideas and processes. We are engaged in a live global conversation on subjects that really matter to us all.

Opposite: Kira O'Reilly, *Stair Falling*, Manchester International Festival, 2009. Photo: Marco Anelli.

1. Brenda Moore McCann, *Brian O'Doherty/Patrick Ireland Between Categories* (United Kingdom: Lund Humphries 2009), p. 24.

2. *The Burial of Patrick Ireland* (1972 - 2008) The Irish Museum of Modern Art on the 17, 18 and 20 May 2008, <http://www.imma.ie/en/page_170640.htm> [accessed 10 December 2014].

3. Moore McCann, *Brian O'Doherty/Patrick Ireland*, p. 185.

4. Spoken by the character of Terry Hooley in *Good Vibrations*, biopic of the 1970s Belfast Punk scene, written by Colin Carberry and Glenn Patterson and directed by Lisa Barros D' Sa and Glenn Leyburn (United Kingdom/Ireland, The Works, 2013).

5. Roddy Hunter, 'André Stitt Re-Mapping a Psyche', in *0044 Irish Artists in Britain* (United Kingdom: Eblana Editions 1999), ed. by Peter Murray, pp. 144-51, (p. 148).

6. Unpublished email correspondence with Áine Phillips, 22 February 2014.

7. Ibid.

8. Andre Stitt *Announcement*, 1978 (photocopy paper, marker and tape) 27 x 21cm.

9. Stitt discusses this performance in detail in his text 'Performing Political Acts. Performance Art in Northern Ireland: Ritual, Catharsis, and Transformation' earlier in this publication.

10. Mic Moroney, 'John Carson, Laughter in the White Cube', in *0044 Irish Artists in Britain* ed. by Peter Murray (United Kingdom: Eblana Editions 1999), pp. 32-7, (p. 37).

11. John Carson, unpublished interview with Áine Phillips, 9 March 2014.

12. Ibid.

13. John Carson, Performance Art Tips, *Circa* 111 (Spring 2005), p. 49.

14. Greenham Common Women's Peace Camp was a women-only peace camp established to protest at nuclear weapons being sited at RAF Greenham Common in Berkshire, England. The camp survived from 1981–1991.

15. Shoshana Felman, *What Does a Woman Want, Reading and Sexual Difference* (London, Johns Hopkins Press, 1993), p. 14.

16. Monica Ross, *Frances Hegarty Selected Works* 1970–2004 (Cork: Gandon Editions 2004), p. 30.

17. Frances Hegarty, unpublished interview with Áine Phillips, 24 March 2014.

18. Other artists in the show were Rose Ann McGreevy, Carol Key, and Rosie McGoldrick. The exhibition developed from projects by the Irish women Artist's Group set up by Anne Tallentire. The group consisted of Irish women artists living and working in Britain.

19. The London performance work was commissioned by Strike projects with Siraj Izhar and in Dublin, commisioned by Living Art Projects.

20. From *Artists at Work: Anne Tallentire* in conversation with Lisa Panting. Lisa Panting, 'Artists at Work: Anne Tallentire', *Afterall*, 10 May 2011 <http://www.afterall.org/online/artists-at-work-anne-tallentire> [accessed 2 December 2014].

21. Jacki Irvine, *Instances* exh. catalogue, (Irish commissioner of the Venice Biennale 1998).

22. In *Bound Words – Stolen Honey* Tallentire locates the politics of the work in Ireland's laws and British colonial administrations. The work addressed the Brehon Laws, a system of jurisprudence in Ireland up to the seventeenth century that was suppressed by British rule for its communitarian values. An open book was placed in the performance space, detailing one branch of the Brehon law specific to beekeeping. The egalitarian nature of these statutes was revealed in the logic of the regulation proclaiming that where the bee dances, the honey shall be shared. A video played an account of Maurice Maeterlinck's 1901 text *The Life of the Bee*. This description is revised from Sabina Sharkey in *Anne Tallentire* (Dublin: Project Press, 1999).

23. Anne Tallentire, unpublished email correspondence with Áine Phillips, 2 April 2014.

24. Michel de Certeau, *The Practice of Everyday Life*, trans. Steven Rendall (Oakland CA, University of California Press 1984).

25. Tallentire, unpublished email correspondence with Phillips, 2 April 2014.

26. The UK miners strike 1984-85 was a major industrial action affecting the British coal industry. The Greater London Council (GLC) was the top-tier local government administrative body for Greater London from 1965 to 1986. The politics of the GLC was far left and sought to promote co-operatives and economic democracy.

27. Tallentire, unpublished email correspondence with Phillips, 2 April 2014.

28. Edward Said, *Orientalism* (London: Penguin, 1978).

29. Denis Buckley, unpublished email correspondence with Áine Phillips, 24 March 2014.

30. Unpublished interview with Áine Phillips, 14 March 2014.

31. Kira O'Reilly, unpublished email correspondence with Áine Phillips, 19 March 2014.

32. Kira O'Reilly, 'Artists Talking, Exposing contemporary visual artists' practice', *a-n Magazine* (April 2001) originally published as 'One Hundred wound sites or more' <http://www.a-n.co.uk/artists_talking/artists_stories/single/59800> [accessed 31 October 2014].

33. Ibid.

34. O'Reilly, unpublished email correspondence with Phillips, 19 March 2014.

35. Quotation taken from an artist statement by Anne Seagrave, unpublished email correspondence with Áine Phillips, 31 March 2014.

36. Now called the Baltic Gallery of Contemporary Art in Ustka, Poland.

37. Nikki Millican, unpublished email correspondence with Áine Phillips, 6 April 2014.

38. *Jamais Vu* was premiered at The Granary Theatre's Bodily Functions programme (Cork) in 2005.

39. For more information and a database Seagrave created on artists use of self-image see: <http://www.imma.ie/en/page_168765.htm> [accessed 4 December 2014].

40. Irish Museum of Modern Art, 'Anne Seagrave: Why Me? Artist's Use of Self Image', *IMMA Irish Museum of Modern Art* <http://www.imma.ie/en/page_212621.htm> [accessed 10 December 2014].

41. From an artists statement published on: <http://www.artsfoundation.co.uk/Artist-Name/all/156/Seagrave-Anne> [accessed 4 December 2014].

42. He performed at the Irish Exhibition of living Art, Dublin in 1985 and at Temple Bar Gallery in 1987.

43. Gearoid Dolan, unpublished email correspondence with Áine Phillips, 12 March 2014.

44. Ibid.

45. Anne Tallentire, 'Irish Days, Irish artists report from Irish Days II in Poland', ed. by Sandra Johnston and Brian Connelly, *Circa* 70 (1994).

46. Seagrave, unpublished email correspondence with Phillips, 31 March 2014.

47. Amanda Coogan, 'What is performance art', *IMMA's Education & Community Essay Series* 3 (Dublin: Irish Museum of Modern Art, 2011). Available to download at: <http://www.imma.ie/en/page_212496.htm> [accessed 10 December 2014].

INDEX

The letter 'n.' followed by a number indicates a footnote.
Numbers in **bold** indicate images of performances and/or performers.

Opposite: James King, *untitled*, Unit 1, Dublin, 2013. Photo: Ciara McKeon.

Kate Antosik-Parsons is a contemporary art historian and visual artist from the San Francisco Bay Area. She is a research associate of the University College Dublin (UCD) Humanities Institute. In 2012 she was awarded her PhD for her doctoral thesis entitled, 'Remembering and Forgetting: Memory and Gender in Irish Time-Based Art' (School of Art History and Cultural Policy, UCD). Kate was the primary researcher for the Guerrilla Girls *Project Ireland*, commissioned by the Millennium Courts Art Centre (2009, Portadown, NI). She has published essays on feminism and Irish performance art; the transformative potential of performance art; video art, masculinity, and gendered memory; and visualizing Irish migration. Kate has lectured in Art History, Irish Studies and Women's Studies at UCD. Her research interests include art, gender, performance, and memory studies and body politics. www.kateap.com

Michelle Browne is an artist and curator based in Dublin. She has exhibited and performed her work nationally and internationally since 2006. She has an honors degree in Sculpture from the National College of Art and Design (NCAD), Dublin, and also holds a degree in English Literature and Italian from National University of Ireland Galway. Michelle has published articles and reviews in Ireland on performance and collaborative practice in *Circa* Art Magazine, *Visual Artists Ireland News Sheet*, and *Create News*. She has curated a number of exhibitions including *Out of Site* (2006-08), *Between You and Me and the Four Walls* for IETM (2013), at Project Arts Centre in Dublin, Tulca Season of Visual Art (2010) and *These Immovable Walls: Performing Power* at Dublin Castle (2014). www.michellebrowne.net

Fergus Byrne is a member of the Visual Arts Centre based in Dublin, Ireland. His practice is multidisciplinary. He holds a BA in Fine Art from NCAD and an MA in Theatre and Contemporary Practice from Hull University. He performs mostly solo work and occasionally in group projects. Interests are in drawing, writing, movement improvisation, and sculpture. Recent projects include: *Weave*, Improvisation and community, Brussels; *Headin' Out* with Tallaght Community Arts; *No Less than the Trees and The Stars* choreographed by Becky Reilly; and *Generation* at The Dock, Carrick on Shannon. His writing can be found in *Pallas Heights 2003 – 2006* (Pallas Publishing), *Self as Selves* (IMMA publication) and *Hello Sam, Brian O'Doherty & Joe Stanley* (IMMA Publication) as well as occasional articles in the *Visual Artists Ireland News Sheet*. www.fergusbyrne.ie

Amanda Coogan was awarded the Allied Irish Bank's Art prize in 2004. She has performed and exhibited her work extensively including; The Venice Biennale, Liverpool Biennial, PS1, New York, Galeria Safia, Barcelona, The Irish Museum of Modern Art, Limerick City Gallery of Art, The Whitworth Gallery, Manchester, Royal Hibernian Academy, Dublin, Van Gogh Museum, Amsterdam, The Museum of Fine Arts, Boston, Centre Culturel Irlandais, Paris, and the Hugh Lane Gallery, Dublin. Coogan completed her doctoral thesis on live durational performance art in 2013 at the University of Ulster. Her works encompass a multitude of media; objects, text, moving and still image but all circulate around her live performances. Her expertise lies in her ability to condense an idea to its very essence and communicate it through her body. The long durational aspect of her live presentations invites elements of chaos with the unknown and unpredicted erupting dynamically through her live artworks. Her work often begins with her own body presenting both solo works and group performances. www.amandacoogan.com

Danny McCarthy studied at the National College of Art and Design, Dublin. He currently lectures in Sound Art in the School Of Music and Drama, University College Cork (UCC) as well as visiting lecturer and workshop facilitator in various institutions. He has pioneered both performance art and sound art in Ireland and he continues to be a leading exponent exhibiting and performing both in Ireland and abroad including SPAN2 in London and at 'Hearing Place' in Melbourne, Australia. His work is in the collections of the Arts Council Of Ireland, Crawford Municipal Gallery, and Limerick City Gallery and numerous other public and private collections in Ireland and abroad. He is a founding director of Triskel Arts Centre and of the National Sculpture Factory and is a director the Sirius Arts Centre Cobh. He is the recipient of numerous awards and bursaries from both the Irish Arts Council and Dept of Foreign Affairs, Culture Ireland, and has represented Ireland abroad at various exhibitions. www.dannymccarthy.ie

Megs Morley is an artist, writer, filmmaker, and independent curator. Her practice explores the representation of social and political situations in art, cinema, and archives, and strategies of artistic resistance that include intervention, self-organisation, and collectivism. The recipient of numerous awards and commissions including the Arts Council of Ireland, Morley has worked with many public and independent institutions, including the Arts Council of Ireland, the Model Sligo, 126 Gallery, Galway City and County Councils, the National University of Galway, Tulca Contemporary Art Festival, Eva International, and the National Irish Visual Arts Library. Recent films made in collaboration with Tom Flanagan have been shown in the Centre du Pompidou, Paris, the Model, Sligo (2012), The Good Children Gallery New Orleans (2012) and CCA Derry. www.theartistledarchive.com

Áine Phillips is based in the west of Ireland and has been exhibiting multi-media performance works internationally since the late 1980s. She has created work for diverse contexts; public art commissions, the street, club events and gallery exhibitions including City of Women Ljubljana, Kyoto Art Centre Japan, Stanley Picker Gallery London, Judith Wright Centre for Art Brisbane Australia, Tanzquartier Vienna, National Review of Live Art in the UK Glasgow, Bunkier Sztuki Krakow, Museum of Contemporary Art Cleveland, USA, and Galway Arts Centre. She is involved with artist led projects and curates Live Art events in Ireland. She writes 'subjective criticism' on visual art and performance, is published internationally and is head of sculpture at Burren College of Art in Ireland. *Live Autobiography* is the title of her practice based PhD awarded in 2009 at the National College of Art and Design in Dublin. www.ainephillips.com

EL (Emily Lauren) Putnam is a scholar and interdisciplinary, conceptual artist working predominately in photography, video, and performance art. Just as she utilizes a variety of media in her artistic practice, her work draws from multiple themes and sources, including travel and tourism, materialism, and explorations of gender and sexuality. These ideas become intertwined through notions of personal and cultural circumspection. Dr. Putnam has presented artworks and performances in the United States and Europe, and has been a member of the Mobius Alternative Artists Group since 2009. She has recently concluded her PhD at the Institute for Doctoral Studies in the Visual Arts. Her writing and research examines art making through the lenses of critical theory, visual studies, and performance studies in order to examine the material relations and the structuring of power in the contemporary, transnational art world. She is particularly interested in exploring the interactions of aesthetics, politics, and economics at art festivals, like the Venice Biennale. She has published articles in *Big Red & Shiny, Seismopolite: Journal of Art and Politics, Sage Reference*, and other arts and philosophy publications available in print and on-line. www.elputnam.com

Clíodhna Shaffrey is a curator whose practice includes exhibitions, public art commissions, writing, and the development of longer-term projects in contexts including *House Warming* (2009) co-curated with Ruairi O Cuiv as the inaugural exhibition for Rua Red, Tallaght, *Eigse Carlow* (2006), *Peripheral Visions* (2005) a year long programme of video art for Cork City of Culture, co-curated with Nigel Rolfe. Clíodhna is on the Board of Directors with Temple Bar Galery and Studios and she is on the Artists' Panel Advisory Group with the Irish Museum of Modern Art (IMMA).

Anthony Sheehan is the Artistic Director of the Triskel Christchurch, Cork's principle arts centre. He was previously the Director of the Fire Station Artists Studios in Dublin, and a practicing performance artist.

André Stitt was born in Belfast, Northern Ireland in 1958. He studied at Ulster Polytechnic and Belfast College of Art and Design, Ulster University 1976-80. From 1980-99 he lived and worked in London, increasingly travelling and making work internationally throughout the eighties. In 1999 he moved to Wales to take up position as Subject Leader and Senior lecturer of Time Based Art at Cardiff School of Art and Design, Cardiff Metropolitan University (UWIC). He is currently Professor of Fine Art at Cardiff School of Art and Design, Cardiff at UWIC, and a Fellow of the Royal Society of Art.

Working almost exclusively as a performance and interdisciplinary artist from 1976-2008, Stitt gained an international reputation for cutting edge, provocative, and politically challenging work. His 'live' performance and installation works have been presented at major museums, galleries and sites specific throughout the world.

His work has been included in group exhibitions at PS1, New York (2000), Venice Biennale (2005), Baltic Contemporary Art Centre, England (2005), Bangkok Art and Culture Centre, (2008), Galerie Lehtinen, Berlin (2011), John Moores (2012), Walker Art Gallery, Liverpool. www.andrestitt.com

Karine Talec is originally from France and has been living in Northern Ireland since 1999. She holds a Degree in Political Sciences and graduated in 2013 with a first class honours BA Fine Art at the University of Ulster (UU) and is currently undertaking a PhD on Northern Ireland performance art at UU. She works with a wide variety of media and materials such as made or found objects, drawing, video and light as material, either as part of installations or performances. She strives to create work that reflects her political, philosophical, or spiritual concerns, in particular the ideas of collective consciousness and empathy. She is interested in the authentic, human aspect of performance art and how the aesthetics can hold a connective, transformative, and poetical potential. www.karinetalec.com

Helena Walsh is a live artist from Co. Kilkenny Ireland. Based in London since 2003, and completed her Masters in Fine Art at Chelsea College of Art and Design in 2004. Helena has showcased her work at many established venues such as Bodily Functions, Cork, The National Review of Live Art, Glasgow, The Zaz Festival, Israel, and Art Radionica Lazereti, Croatia. In November 2010, she performed at *Right Here, Right Now*, a showcase of Ireland's prominent live artists in Kilmainham Gaol, Dublin. In 2012 Helena co-curated *LABOUR*; a live touring exhibition of 11 female live artists resident within or native to Northern and Southern Ireland. Helena received a Doctorate Award from the Arts and Humanities Research Council in 2009 to undertake her practice-based PhD in the Drama Department of Queen Mary University of London. Her Doctorate was completed in 2013 and explores Live Art, femininity, and Irish national identity. www.helenawalsh.com

ACKNOWLEDGEMENTS

Absolute thanks to my editorial committee Pauline Cummins, Michelle Browne, Ceile Varley, Brian Connolly, and Dominic Thorpe for steady support and frequent help with the complex decisions. More thanks to Dominic Thorpe who encouraged me do this book and Ceile Varley for her editing expertise and advice, as well as to Máiréad Delaney and Harriet Curtis for proofreading and copyediting. Aesthetic thanks to David Caines for the design and layout.

Perfect thanks to the authors for writing the texts, the artists and photographers for the images and the hundreds of practitioners who contributed to the timeline of performance art in Ireland. Enthusiastic thanks to academic colleagues and friends in many third level institutions in Ireland (across departments and colleges of fine art, theatre, dance, and music) for sharing information and interest in this project. Extra thanks to the Burren College of Art where I teach, for many visible and invisible supports. The National College of Art and Design provided access to informational resources and the Irish launch of this book while director Declan McGonagle offered generous assistance. The National Irish Visual Artists Library (NIVAL) at NCAD facilitated and enabled the research and development of this publication.

Complete thanks to the publishers Intellect Books and the Live Art Development Agency for believing in the future as well as the history of performance art in Ireland and its international relevance. LADA directors Lois Keidan and CJ Mitchell helped and encouraged me at every step. Funding thanks to the Arts Council of Ireland.

Áine Phillips
November 2014

CREDITS

First published in the UK in 2015 by

Live Art Development Agency
The White Building, Unit 7, Queen's Yard
White Post Lane, London, E9 5EN, UK
www.thisisLiveArt.co.uk

and

Intellect, The Mill, Parnall Road,
Fishponds, Bristol, BS16 3JG, UK
www.intellectbooks.com

First published in the USA in 2015 by

Intellect, The University of Chicago Press,
1427 E. 60th Street, Chicago, IL 60637, USA

Edited by Áine Phillips, 2015

Cover images: Sandra Johnson and Dominic Thorpe, *Due Process 2*;
Third Space Gallery, Belfast, 2011. Photograph by Jordan Hutchings.

Designed by David Caines Unlimited
www.davidcaines.co.uk

Printed and bound by Gomer Press, UK

ISBN 978-1-78320-428-1

Published with the support of the Arts Council of Ireland and Arts Council England.